Stamatia Devetzi,
Hans-Joachim Reinhard (Eds.)

PROVISION FOR SURVIVING DEPENDANTS IN SOCIAL SECURITY

A NEW ARCHITECTURE FOR THE 21ST CENTURY?

AN INTERDISCIPLINARY SERIES
OF THE CENTRE FOR INTERCULTURAL AND EUROPEAN STUDIES

INTERDISZIPLINÄRE SCHRIFTENREIHE
DES CENTRUMS FÜR INTERKULTURELLE UND EUROPÄISCHE STUDIEN

CINTEUS · Fulda University of Applied Sciences · Hochschule Fulda

ISSN 1865-2255

19   *Juliana Damm, Maren Mlynek*
     Die AfD und Geflüchtete
     Was rechte Ideologie gesellschaftlich bewirkt
     ISBN 978-3-8382-1448-1

20   *Julian Wessendorf*
     Euroskeptizismus auf dem Vormarsch
     Positionen der politischen Rechten im
     Europaparlament
     ISBN 978-3-8382-1557-0

21   *Kirsten Nazarkiewicz, Norbert Schröer (Hrsg.)*
     Verständigung in pluralen Welten
     ISBN 978-3-8382-1345-3

22   *Stamatia Devetzi (Ed.)*
     Practical issues of European Social Security Law: A Dialogue
     between Academia and Practitioners
     ISBN 978-3-8382-1706-2

23   *Jasmin Berger, Geronimo Groh, Simone Lettner (Hrsg.)*
     Sprache(n) und Grenze(n) – Sprachgrenzen: Übersetzen,
     Dialekt und Literatur, Literarische Mehrsprachigkeit
     Frontières linguistiques – langue(s) et frontière(s) : L'art de la
     traduction, dialecte et littérature, plurilinguisme littéraire
     ISBN 978-3-8382-1910-9

24   *Stamatia Devetzi, Hans-Joachim Reinhard (Eds.)*
     Provision for Surviving Dependants in Social Security: A New
     Architecture for the 21st Century?
     ISBN 978-3-8382-2036-9

Series Editors

Stamatia Devetzi
Volker Hinnenkamp
Gudrun Hentges
Anne Honer †
Matthias Klemm
Hans-Wolfgang Platzer

Stamatia Devetzi,
Hans-Joachim Reinhard (Eds.)

PROVISION FOR SURVIVING DEPENDANTS IN SOCIAL SECURITY

A NEW ARCHITECTURE FOR THE 21ST CENTURY?

Bibliografische Information der Deutschen Nationalbibliothek
Die Deutsche Nationalbibliothek verzeichnet diese Publikation in der Deutschen Nationalbibliografie; detaillierte bibliografische Daten sind im Internet über http://dnb.d-nb.de abrufbar.

Bibliographic information published by the Deutsche Nationalbibliothek
Die Deutsche Nationalbibliothek lists this publication in the Deutsche Nationalbibliografie; detailed bibliographic data are available in the Internet at http://dnb.d-nb.de.

ISBN (Print): 978-3-8382-2036-9
ISBN (E-Book [PDF]): 978-3-8382-8036-3
© *ibidem*-Verlag, Hannover • Stuttgart 2025

Leuschnerstraße 40
30457 Hannover
Germany / Deutschland
info@ibidem.eu

Alle Rechte vorbehalten

Das Werk einschließlich aller seiner Teile ist urheberrechtlich geschützt. Jede Verwertung außerhalb der engen Grenzen des Urheberrechtsgesetzes ist ohne Zustimmung des Verlages unzulässig und strafbar. Dies gilt insbesondere für Vervielfältigungen, Übersetzungen, Mikroverfilmungen und elektronische Speicherformen sowie die Einspeicherung und Verarbeitung in elektronischen Systemen.

All rights reserved. No part of this publication may be reproduced, stored in or introduced into a retrieval system, or transmitted, in any form, or by any means (electronic, mechanical, photocopying, recording or otherwise) without the prior written permission of the publisher. Any person who does any unauthorized act in relation to this publication may be liable to criminal prosecution and civil claims for damages.

Printed in the EU

Acknowledgements

The present book is the outcome of a scientific congress which took place in September 2023 at the University of Applied Sciences, Fulda in cooperation with the European Institute of Social Security, Leuven. Both institutions granted valuable support with financial and personal resources and contributed significantly to the success of the event. Special thanks to all authors and organisers for their efforts and patience. We appreciate very much that CINTEUS included the work in its book series.

A special acknowledgment goes to our language editor, Niki Rodousakis, for her quick, thorough and careful editing of our chapters – thank you very much!

Fulda, March 2025

Stamatia Devetzi
Hans-Joachim Reinhard

Contents

1 *Stamatia Devetzi and Hans-Joachim Reinhard*
   Introduction: Provision for Surviving Dependants in Social Security 9

2 *Ulrich Becker*
   Survivors' Benefits: A Systematic Introduction 19

3 *Eberhard Eichenhofer*
   Navigating Survivors' Benefits: Legal Perspectives and Considerations 39

4 *Guido Van Limberghen*
   Minimum International and European Standards for Survivors' Benefits 53

5 *Verena Zwinger and Christoph Freudenberg*
   How to Design Survivors' Benefits in the 21st Century? 87

6 *Hans-Joachim Reinhard*
   Survivors' Benefits and Divorce 105

7 *Thomas Gächter*
   Survivors' Benefits in Switzerland 121

8 *Martina Axmin and Jenny Julén Votinius*
   Survivors' Benefits in Sweden: Social Security Developments, Collective Agreements and Gender Aspects 135

9 *Suvi Ritola*
   Modernising Survivors' Pension: The 2022 Reform in Finland .. 153

10 *María Salas Porras*
    Survivors' Benefits and the New Concept of Family: Challenges for the Spanish Social Security System 185

List of Contributors 207

1 Introduction: Provision for Surviving Dependants in Social Security

Stamatia Devetzi and Hans-Joachim Reinhard

This book explores survivors' benefits, a key pillar of social security systems in many countries around the globe. Traditionally based on the breadwinner model, these benefits aim to protect dependents from financial hardship following the death of a primary income earner. While their design and implementation varies significantly across nations, this book focuses on recent developments in selected countries, analysing the legal, social and policy dimensions of survivors' benefits. It also sheds light on how international and European legal instruments address survivors' benefits and assesses reforms of these benefits in the 21st century, highlighting their evolving role in social security systems.

Pensions for surviving dependents are a distinctive feature of a social security system. Pension payments are typically personal benefits granted to those who have paid contributions. This principle has applied since the introduction of the first social insurance scheme under Bismarck in 1889 and has been adopted by all subsequent social security systems with old-age or disability insurance. In most cases, however, social security pension payments not only support the individual contributor but also provide financial assistance to their family.

As long as the principal beneficiary is alive, the family, and particularly his or her spouse, continues to be insured. However, the personal relationship between the contributor and the dependant may lead to a security gap if the (primary) earner dies. Without an alternative source of income, the surviving partner faces a heightened risk of poverty, especially in old age. This is also the case if the surviving partner is no longer able to work.

This situation has historically affected women disproportionately and continues to do so for two reasons: first, women generally have a significantly higher life expectancy than men. Secondly, many women either do not participate in the labour force or only work for a limited period due to caregiving responsibilities for children or other relatives. As a result, they often contribute less or not at all to social security systems.

However, it was not until 1911, 25 years after the introduction of the first social insurance system, that the first regulations for the protection of surviving dependants were introduced. In line with the male breadwinner model, these early provisions initially covered women only. Many social security systems in different countries adopted this model, gradually introducing benefits for survivors in the event of the primary breadwinner's death. Yet not all women qualified for these benefits, as eligibility was often limited to those deemed in need due to disability, old age or low income.

Survivors' pensions continue to be viewed as compensation for the loss of financial support from the primary income earner. They are not considered an independent pension entitlement but are derived from the deceased's old-age pension. In some cases, eligibility requires a minimum duration of marriage and, as a rule, entitlement to the benefit ceases in the event of remarriage. If the deceased's old-age pension was low, the survivor's benefit will also remain low. In other words, although the provision of a survivors' pension is a positive first step, the surviving spouse may still face financial insecurity.

This applies not only to entirely contribution-based social security systems but also – albeit to a lesser extent – to tax-financed systems where (old-age) benefits are nor directly tied to previous earnings. These tax-financed systems typically provide a basic amount designed to ensure a minimum level of financial security. While this amount exceeds the minimum subsistence level, it may still fall short of providing adequate financial stability in old age. To address these gaps, all tax-financed systems have since been supplemented with contribution-based supplementary and/or occupational pension schemes, which may also introduce similar disparities.

Initially, survivors' benefits were restricted to legally registered marriages, a limitation that remains in place in many countries today. However, societal norms have changed. Long-term partnerships without formal marriage are increasingly common. In response, some countries have adapted to this trend and have extended survivors' benefits to unmarried partners, provided they can demonstrate the stability and permanence of their relationship.

A more recent trend is the recognition of same-sex marriages and partnerships. Several countries have taken steps to recognise such relationships as equivalent for the provision of survivors' benefits.

When survivors' benefits were first introduced, eligibility was conditional on the partner's death in view of the low life expectancy and high rate of (work-related) accidents at the time. With advances in medical care and improved safety standards, many marriages today do not end with the death of a partner: a large number of partnerships end in separation or divorce. Initially, most countries, excluded divorced spouses from receiving survivors' benefits. This changed in the 1970s, when many social security systems introduced eligibility for survivors' benefits after divorce.

This publication focuses on survivors' pensions for spouses. Surviving dependants also include the deceased's children. However, orphans' pensions as benefits for surviving dependants are only dealt with in passing, as their provision is generally straightforward and uncontested.

Subject matter experts from different European countries have contributed to this book, sharing their national experiences, highlighting key issues, examining international and European frameworks on survivors' benefits and analysing recent reforms.

Ulrich Becker explores the purpose, structure and reforms of survivors' benefits across various countries, focusing on their role in providing financial support to surviving dependants following the death of a breadwinner. He highlights the disparities in survivors' benefits schemes across European countries, questioning whether such benefits are at risk of becoming obsolete. Drawing on international legal frameworks such as ILO Conventions and the European Code of Social Security, Becker examines the objectives of these benefits, which are designed to address the loss of subsistence caused by death, focusing on maintenance guarantees rather than on direct legal obligations. The chapter analyses regulatory instruments, categorising them by conditions related to surviving dependants (e.g. remarriage, income or age thresholds) and the relationship between the insured person and the survivors. Reform trends in Scandinavia, the UK, and France have pursued differing approaches, often reflecting shifts in social policies, gender roles and labour market objectives. Scandinavian countries have transitioned from traditional widows pensions to short-term transitional benefits, the UK has introduced lump-sum payments and capped monthly allowances to encourage workforce re-entry, while France, by contrast, maintains a hybrid, complex model based on marriage entitlements.

Becker's analysis highlights the tension between supporting dependants and promoting self-reliance, emphasising the need to adapt survivors' benefits to modern and evolving family structures and societal change. He concludes that while survivors' benefits are not universally diminishing, their evolution is influenced by national priorities and broader socio-political contexts.

The next chapter by *Eberhard Eichenhofer* explores survivors' benefits within social security frameworks, focusing on their historical foundations, current challenges and potential future reforms. Traditionally based on the male breadwinner model, these benefits were designed to alleviate financial hardship for widows and children following the primary wage earner's death. However, in light of changing family structures, gender roles and economic conditions, survivors' benefits are increasingly subject to scrutiny.

Eichenhofer identifies five key dimensions of survivors' benefits: their derivative nature, that they arise from the death of the principal beneficiary, their foundation in family obligations, the evolving principles of gender equality, and the potential for alternatives such as pension splitting. He argues that while survivors' benefits are framed as rights that reflect familial interdependence, they also place a significant financial burden on social security systems. Rooted in traditional family structures, these benefits are facing growing scrutiny in terms of their relevance in contemporary contexts, where dual-income households and gender equality are becoming the norm. The question is whether these benefits, initially designed as long-term entitlements, should instead serve as transitional financial support.

Legal debates increasingly focus on expanding eligibility to domestic partners and divorced spouses, reflecting the growing recognition of diverse family structures. The chapter also raises questions about the fairness of universal survivors' benefits, noting that while orphans benefits are considered essential for alleviating economic hardship following the loss of a parent, spousal benefits may inadvertently reinforce outdated dependency models. The discussion calls for reforms that would align survivors' benefits with contemporary socio-economic realities, emphasizing the need for transitional support and greater equity. Alternatives such as pension splitting and strengthened individual rights within family law are proposed as a path forward.

Guido Van Limberghen examines how international and European legal instruments address survivors' benefits amidst evolving socioeconomic realities, such as increased female labour force participation, diverse partnership models, and rising divorce rates. His analysis explores the implications of these trends for survivors' benefit schemes and evaluates the adequacy of existing standards established by the International Labour Organization (ILO), the Council of Europe (CoE), and the European Union (EU). These instruments, spanning three generational frameworks, set minimum standards for survivors' benefits. While earlier frameworks (e.g. ILO C039) reflect traditional male breadwinner models, more recent instruments advocate for gender-neutral provisions and expand eligibility to encompass atypical workers and self-employed persons. Beneficiaries typically include spouses and children, with eligibility criteria based on dependency, marriage or residency. These benefits are designed to replace income, offering flexibility for national legislation to adjust schemes, though inconsistencies and outdated definitions remain a challenge.

The chapter underscores the need for reforms to address gaps in coverage and outdated dependency models, advocating for a more inclusive and flexible approach. It calls for aligning survivors' benefits with evolving social realities while adhering to international and regional standards. Policymakers should leverage the flexibility of these frameworks to ensure comprehensive and equitable social protection systems.

Freudenberg and Zwinger examine the development, design and reform of survivors' benefits in the 21st century, addressing the challenges socio-economic trends pose, including gender equality, evolving family structures, and increased labour force participation. Survivors' benefits, initially created to protect widows from falling into poverty under the traditional male breadwinner model, have since evolved to serve broader goals such as maintaining widows and widowers' standard of living. The chapter compares survivors' benefit schemes across 47 countries, focusing on eligibility, replacement rates and socio-economic impacts.

The chapter's findings reveal that although women continue to make up the majority of benefit recipients, the share of male beneficiaries is rising due to narrowing gender gaps in life expectancy and increased female labour force participation. Replacement rates vary widely, influencing the ability to maintain pre-death living standards. The analysis highlights that survivors' benefits can help reduce gender pension gaps but may also disincentivize labour market participation, particularly among younger recipients.

Reform trends include raising the eligibility age, introducing transitional benefits, implementing income testing, pension splitting and expanding coverage to include registered and same-sex partnerships. The analysis highlights the need for reforms that align survivors' benefits with modern socio-economic realities, such as dual-income households and increased female workforce participation, while ensuring compliance with international social security standards and human rights frameworks.

Focussing on the complex relationship between survivors' benefits and divorce within social security systems, *Hans-Joachim Reinhard* discusses the challenges divorced spouses, particularly women, face in acquiring financial security. While survivors' benefits have traditionally been designed to support the financial needs of widowed spouses, they often fail to accommodate the realities of divorce, leaving gaps in the protection for divorced partners with lower incomes due to caregiving roles or other disparities.

Historically, survivors' benefits were tied to traditional family models and legal marriages, excluding divorced spouses. Divorce laws used to incorporate the "fault principle", denying benefits to individuals deemed at fault for the divorce, which disproportionately disadvantaged women. While fault-based systems have largely been phased out, the rise in divorce rates and the growth of non-traditional family structures necessitates a re-evaluation of survivors' benefits. Divorce often leaves lower-earning spouses reliant on maintenance payments, which cease upon the principal beneficiary's death, thus exacerbating financial vulnerability. Various approaches to survivors' benefits for divorced spouses are analysed in this chapter: the "inheritance law solution", the "maintenance solution", the "surviving spouse solution" and the "divorced spouse solution".

Pension-sharing mechanisms in countries such as Canada, Switzerland and Germany, where pension entitlements accrued during marriage are divided between the partners, are also discussed. While equitable, these systems face challenges such as legal complexities and gaps for migrant spouses due to limitations in cross-border contexts.

Reinhard argues that current frameworks often inadequately address the needs of divorced spouses, leaving many of them financially vulnerable. He advocates for reforms to integrate family and social security law, thereby ensuring fair and inclusive solutions that reflect contemporary family dynamics.

The following chapters examine developments and reforms of survivors' benefits in four European countries: Switzerland, Sweden, Finland and Spain.

Thomas Gaechter provides an in-depth analysis of Switzerland's survivors' benefits scheme, emphasising its distinctive characteristics and ongoing reforms. Switzerland's three-pillar social security system integrates universal, occupational and voluntary insurance, aiming to ensure that basic needs are fulfilled, living standards are maintained, and individual needs are addressed. Survivors' benefits replace family law obligations when a breadwinner dies, ensuring financial support for dependants. However, the system reflects the traditional family model, favouring widows over widowers and full-time over part-time employees, many of whom are women. The first pillar provides basic coverage but often falls short in meeting the needs of beneficiaries due to high living costs, necessitating supplementary benefits. The second pillar offers occupational insurance which ensures equal legal treatment for all genders, but exclusions for low-income earners create disparities.

Despite reforms, gender disparities persist. Widows continue to enjoy broader entitlements compared to widowers, who face stricter eligibility criteria.

A landmark European Court of Human Rights ruling highlighted these systemic inequalities. The case of Max Beeler, a widower who was denied pension payments, resulted in a decision against Switzerland, leading to reforms aimed at aligning widowers' entitlements with those of widows. Nonetheless, the Swiss government's approach largely focuses on limiting overall costs, which may result in reduced benefits rather than expanded eligibility. Proposed changes include limiting survivors' pensions to parents with dependent children and offering transitional support to widows and widowers under the age of 55 who do not have children.

While progress towards gender equality continues, adjustments often prioritise cost-saving measures over expanding benefits. The system's conservative design lags behind evolving family structures and labour market realities, highlighting the need for modernisation of survivors' benefits to meet contemporary needs.

Martina Axmin and *Jenny Julén Votinius* examine Sweden's survivors' benefits scheme, positioning it within the nation's welfare framework, which emphasizes individual self-reliance and gender equality. Sweden's welfare model is characterised by universal benefits, equitable income redistribution, and robust occupational insurance schemes negotiated through collective agreements.

Sweden's survivors' benefits scheme has undergone significant changes, reflecting societal shifts such as increased female workforce participation. The abolition of widows pensions in 1999 marked a shift towards gender-neutral adjustment allowances. These are temporary benefits intended to support surviving spouses transition to a single-income household, with eligibility extending beyond 12 months only for those with young children. Benefits include survivors' protection within the public pension scheme, and occupational pensions that offer additional safeguards, such as group life insurance, repayment coverage, and family protection plans.

Survivors' benefits play a limited role in Sweden, as the welfare system prioritises individual income over family-based entitlements. This approach aligns with Sweden's high rate of female employment and emphasis on gender equality. However, the relationship between public and occupational insurance schemes may perpetuate some inequalities, particularly along gender lines.

The authors highlight the importance of addressing inequities within the survivors' benefits framework, advocating for reforms that align with Sweden's broader goals of gender equality and comprehensive social security.

In the following chapter, *Suvi Ritola* explores the modernisation of Finland's survivors' pension scheme following the 2022 reform, which aimed to align the system with contemporary family structures and economic realities. Significant changes were made to address existing inequities and better reflect shifts in societal norms, including increased gender equality and the recognition of diverse family structures.

The Finnish pension system consists of earnings-related and residence-based pensions, providing both income maintenance and basic security. Traditionally, survivors' pensions were lifelong for spouses and included orphans pensions for children under 18. The 2022 reform introduced a fixed-term payment of ten years for surviving spouses, or until the youngest child turns 18, shifting from lifelong support to more targeted, short-term assistance. It also expanded eligibility to cohabiting partners with dependent children, recognizing the growing diversity of family structures. Additionally, the age limit for orphans pensions was raised from 18 to 20, improving financial support for young adults.

The reform aimed to address gender disparities, as women, who have historically been the primary recipients of survivors' pensions, now participate more equally in the workforce. Measures such as the fixed-term spouse benefit and extended orphan support promote inclusivity while ensuring financial sustainability. The reform, however, has limitations. It continues to exclude common-law partners without children and includes a lengthy transition period, meaning older generations still receive lifelong benefits.

The changes reduce long-term expenditure on survivors' pensions, aligning with broader goals of balancing costs and ensuring fairness. The chapter emphasises the need for continuous adaptation of social security systems to keep pace with evolving societal and demographic trends, while maintaining their protective role.

In the final chapter, *María Salas Porras* explores the development of survivors' benefits within Spain's social security system, highlighting the challenges arising from evolving family structures and societal dynamics. Spain's framework integrates elements of both the Bismarckian and Beveridge models, aiming to mitigate financial hardships for dependants following a breadwinner's death. However, the benefits have limitations, particularly in addressing contemporary family realities.

Its key components include the death grant, widowhood benefits, orphans benefits, family member pensions, and lump-sum compensation for work-related deaths. The death grant, at EUR 46.50, is insufficient to cover funeral costs which often range between EUR 3,000 and EUR 6,000. Widowhood benefits are granted to legally recognised spouses and de facto partners, with varying conditions based on relationship status, duration and past contributions. Divorced or separated spouses may also qualify if they were dependent on the deceased's pension income, reflecting a progressive legal approach.

Orphans benefits are provided to children under the age of 21 or even up to 25 in specific circumstances, with extensions available for children with disabilities or in cases of gender-based violence. These benefits cover up to 70 per cent of the deceased's regulatory base, though they often fail to prevent beneficiaries from falling into poverty. Family pensions target economically dependent relatives such as grandparents or siblings, while lump-sum compensation supports survivors of work-related fatalities.

Spanish legislation has adapted to include diverse relationships, including same-sex and de facto unions, but does not sufficiently address gaps in financial adequacy. Survivors' benefits are designed to offset income loss rather than meet financial need, encouraging employment among beneficiaries. Despite progressive measures, *Salas Porras* argues that the system requires further reforms to better align with contemporary family structures and economic realities.

2 Survivors' Benefits: A Systematic Introduction[1]

Ulrich Becker

1. Initial Considerations

1. When researching survivors' pensions across Europe, one might encounter a European Union website – marked with a warning sign – which reads: "Not all EU countries pay survivors' pensions"[2] This finding is quite surprising. After all, "survivors' benefits" are typically considered an integral part of a modern welfare state's "standard social security benefits". These benefits, which from a conventional perspective also characterise the welfare state in an international context – at least when measured against ILO Convention No. 102 on minimum standards of social security[3] – serve as a benchmark. The Convention, ratified by 63 countries,[4] outlines the risks social security systems are expected to address,[5] including not only illness, unemployment, old age, occupational accidents and disease, maternity, and disability, but also death.

Accordingly, the provision of survivors' pensions remains, or at least *should* remain, the norm in European states. In this context, the information on the European Union's website raises an important question: do current trends

---

[1] I would like to thank Dr. Christian Günther and Dr. Anika Seemann for providing information on the United Kingdom and Scandinavia.
[2] Available at: https://europa.eu/youreurope/citizens/work/unemployment-and-benefits/death-grants/index_de.htm.
[3] Available at: https://www.ilo.org/dyn/normlex/en/f?p=NORMLEXPUB:12100:0::NO:12100:P12100_INSTRUMENT_ID:312247:NO.
[4] Overview available at: https://www.ilo.org/dyn/normlex/en/f?p=NORMLEXPUB:11300:0::NO:11300:P11300_INSTRUMENT_ID:312247:NO.
[5] Even though the agreement itself allows for flexibility regarding the respective obligations of individual states, i.e. the applicability of its regulations in ratifying countries, in line with Art. 2.

(also) point towards a reduction in survivors' pensions across Europe, and potentially beyond? In other words, are survivors' benefits at risk of becoming obsolete?[6]

2. In this introduction, I will not provide a comprehensive overview of existing survivors' benefits schemes,[7] but will instead focus on their functions and structure, and present some select examples. The aim of this chapter is twofold: first, to shed light on the purpose, or the social policy function, of survivors' benefits and their institutional foundation in the context of international law and, on that basis, to provide a brief, systematic overview of the main regulatory instruments being used to ensure the effectiveness and functionality of survivors' benefits schemes (see Section II). Second, three examples of recent reforms are discussed, which not only reflect emerging trends, but also demonstrate that the role and purpose of survivors' benefits are driven by national priorities and institutional contexts that extend beyond countries' pension schemes themselves (see Section III.).

2. Function and Regulatory Instruments

2.1. Objectives and Institutions

2.1.1. International Agreements and Social Policy

Article 64 of the European Code of Social Security[8] (EOSS), as revised in 1990,[9] describes the purpose of survivors' benefits as follows: "The contingency covered [meaning the risk being covered] is the loss of means of subsistence suffered by the surviving spouse and children as a result of the death of the breadwinner". The original version of 1964, which continues to apply in

---

[6] For Germany, see Frey W, Scheiwe K and Wersig M (2015) 100 Jahre Witwen- und Witwerrenten - (k)ein Auslaufmodell? Baden-Baden: Nomos, p. 69.

[7] For a comprehensive study in terms of both geography and content, see Freudenberg C, Kapuy K, Zwinger V and Technical Commission on Old-age, Invalidity and Survivors' Insurance International Social Security Association (2022) How to design survivor benefits in the 21st century? ISSA (available at: https://www.researchgate.net/publication/364915432_How_to_design_survivor_benefits_in_the_21st_century).

[8] ETS No. 139 of 6.11.1990, text available at: https://www.coe.int/de/web/conventions/full-list?module=treaty-detail&treatynum=139.

[9] ETS No. 48 of 16.4.1964, text available at: https://www.coe.int/de/web/conventions/full-list?module=treaty-detail&treatynum=048.

Germany to this day,[10] corresponds to Art. 60 of ILO Convention No. 102 of 1952, which regionalises the global standard. The focus in both versions is on the loss of the means of subsistence and this loss is the loss of a widow.[11] Similarly, Art. 21 para. 1 of ILO Convention No. 128 on Invalidity and Old-Age Benefits and Survivors' Benefits, which serves as the ILO's Pension Insurance Convention, but has only been ratified by 17 states, uses identical wording.[12] Hence, existing international social law paints a clear picture of the purpose of survivors' benefits.

In light of the discussions that are taking place in several countries, it is important to highlight that the intended purpose of a 'maintenance guarantee' for survivors does not inherently carry direct legal consequences. This is also true for national benefits schemes, which while often inspired by international agreements, also significantly influence and contribute to the formulation of such international regulations. As a rule, the existence of a legal maintenance obligation is not a prerequisite for granting a survivors' pension. The link between family and social security law is primarily socio-political in nature, but can also become established in national law, for instance in the case of pension regulations for divorced persons. In Austria, receiving maintenance payments from a former spouse is a prerequisite for divorced persons to actually qualify for survivors' benefits[13].[14]

In this context, the question whether survivors' pensions should be treated as inherent or derived rights holds more conceptual than practical significance. This question has been raised in France, for example, but mainly with a view

---

[10] Germany has signed but not ratified the revised version (as of January 2023, cf. https://www.coe.int/en/web/conventions/full-list?module=signatures-by-treaty&treatynum=139).

[11] Art. 60(1): "The contingency covered shall include the loss of maintenance of the widow or children as a result of the death of the breadwinner; the widow's entitlement to benefits may be made conditional on her being regarded as incapable of supporting herself under national legislation."

[12] Overview available at: https://www.ilo.org/dyn/normlex/en/f?p=NORMLEXPUB:11300:0::NO:11300:P11300_INSTRUMENT_ID:312273:NO.

[13] § 258(4) ASVG (https://www.ris.bka.gv.at/GeltendeFassung.wxe?Abfrage=Bundesnormen&Gesetzesnummer=10008147).

[14] It represents a reverse scenario where a pensioner is not eligible to receive a pension because he/she served a prison sentence, yet the survivors are still entitled to benefits to ensure their maintenance, cf. on the legal situation in Austria § 89(5) ASVG (fn. 13).

to potential reforms.[15] The special nature of survivors' benefits is not so much the result of a dispute over legal terms than it is over the socio-political ambiguity[16] associated with such benefits. On the one hand, they are meant to cover survivors' living expenses, yet in most countries around the world, survivors' benefits only provide a percentage of the amount the deceased was entitled to – in other words, survivors' benefits only guarantee partial coverage. On the other hand, the benefits must align with the fundamental principle of social law, namely self-reliance.[17] Today, this principle is tied to both labour market policies aimed at boosting workforce participation as well as to equality objectives. Survivors' benefits primarily cover surviving spouses and partners, while children and their needs are (mainly) addressed in other benefits schemes.

This complex and "mixed" socio-political setting often creates challenges for integrating survivors' benefits into a coherent legal framework. For example, in its 2007 report to the French Senate, an expert commission aptly described the French social law on survivors' benefits as "*quelque peu hybride*" (somewhat hybrid). This is particularly obvious with regard to "converted pensions" (*retraite de réversion*), a contributions-based system that is blended with a means-tested provision of social benefits.[18]

2.1.2. Institutional Setting and Social Law

An assessment of survivors' pensions is particularly relevant in legal systems where social insurance continues to play a decisive role. The hybrid nature of

---

[15] See Borgetto M and Lafore R (2019) Droit de la sécurité sociale. 19th ed. Paris: Dalloz, 652.

[16] As well as a number of other social security objectives, for Germany, see Frey, Scheiwe and Wersig (fn. 6), p. 41 et seq.

[17] For this principle, see Becker U (2010) Introduction to the General Principles of Social Security Law in Europe. In: Becker U, Pieters D, Ross F, Schoukens P (Eds.), Security: A General Principle of Social Security Law in Europe, Groningen, Europa Law Publishing, p. 16.

[18] Rapport d'information n° 314 (2006-2007), presented in May 2007, at II: "Le droit français de la réversion apparaît aujourd'hui quelque peu hybride, combinant une approche contributive et patrimoniale avec une logique d'allocation sociale reflétée notamment par l'existence d'une condition de ressources pour les ressortissants du régime général et des régimes alignés." (available at: https://www.senat.fr/rap/r06-314/r06-314_mono.html#toc1).

survivors' benefits is evident in such states because all insurance-based benefits are typically financed through contributions and are thus considered as having been "earned". Their allocation is therefore not contingent on the recipient's income level, and such benefits take precedence over other types of social security benefits. Explaining the unique features of survivors' pensions becomes even more complex within this institutional framework.

Two potential solutions are conceivable. First, in many countries, some benefits provided within the scope of an insurance system are financed through taxes. This is the case for minimum – pensions, for example.[19] If benefits are financed through taxeseven if this applies to the country's entire pension system –, this diminishes the link between provision (by being insured and paying contributions) and the right to this benefit, thus opening up possibilities to deviate from the principles of social security law and to place greater emphasis on personal responsibility.[20] In this vein, also ILO Convention No. 102 distinguishes between the allocation of additional benefits and survivors' pensions based on the level of contributions made.[21] Second, social protection of survivors might completely be transferred to a tax-financed support or assistance scheme. Yet, in this case, the unique nature of survivors' benefits would get lost: survivors would receive benefits just because they are in a specific situation of need, but these benefits could not be calculated in a way which would allow to take the individual standard of living into account, i.e. different amounts of contributions. In most countries, survivors' benefits therefore remain a part of pension schemes – even if the social risk (death) and the specific need following from the realisation of this risk (loss of maintenance) do not relate to one and the same person.[22]

---

[19] Overview in MPISOC (2021), Pension Maps, Visualising the Institutional Structure of Old Age Security in Europe and Beyond, 2nd. ed, Schneider S, Tedora P and Becker U (Eds.) (available at: https://www.mpisoc.mpg.de/sozialrecht/forschung/forschungsprojekte/pension-maps/). See also Devetzi S (Ed.) (2023) Minimum Income in Old Age, a legal comparison of selected European countries, Athens: Sakkoulas Publications.

[20] On the importance of system types and their financing for the design of social security benefits, see Becker U (2022) § 1. In: Ruland F, Becker U and Axer P (Eds.) Sozialrechtshandbuch. Baden-Baden: Nomos, 7th ed., para 14 et seq.

[21] Art. 60 para. 2 ILO Convention No. 102 = Art. 60 para. 2 EOSS.

[22] As would be the case for invalidity or old age as social risks, cf. on the function of old-age security and the role of age limits in this sense only, Becker U (2007) Alterssicherung

In terms of institutional design, social security against death (or rather against the loss of maintenance that arises from death) is in many countries distributed across multiple layers of social benefits schemes, i.e. different tiers of protection. This complicates an analysis of survivors' benefits, which can only be hinted at here.

The significance of the different layers of protection depends on the overall structure of the country's old-age security schemes, especially the role of the secondary tier, namely occupational pensions, which varies greatly from country to country.[23] In this respect, one would have to look at each tier (public pensions, occupational pensions, private insurance) and at how the corresponding benefits are calculated and which conditions they depend on. In fact, these conditions might differ from one tier to the other, as can be learned from the individual supplementary protection in France.[24] Last but not least, to effectively assess the extent and adequacy of social security benefits for surviving dependants, it is important to examine the relationships between all social security schemes and to consider the overall picture. Moreover, an analysis must also take the rules on taxation governing survivors' benefits into account.

2.1.3. Instruments for Achieving the Intended Objectives

Institutional aspects will not be explored further here. Instead, we will examine the instruments used to achieve the social policy objectives of survivors' insurance.

In this context, a distinction can be made that is linked to the unique nature of survivors' benefits. This entails differentiating between requirements relating to the surviving dependant(s) and their circumstances, on the one hand, and those that relate to the relationship between the persons involved, i.e. between the deceased and the survivors, as well as the deceased's own circumstances,

---

im internationalen Vergleich. In: Becker U et al. (Eds.) FS Ruland. Baden-Baden: Nomos, 576 et seq.

[23] See MPISOC, Pension Maps (fn. 19).
[24] Cf. Borgetto M and Lafore R (2019) Droit de la sécurité sociale. 19th edition. Paris: Dalloz.

on the other. In short, the former can also be referred to as the conditions relating to the scope of the claim, while the latter signifies the conditions relating to the grounds for the claim.

2.2. Scope of Entitlement: Regulations Concerning Surviving Dependants

With regard to the first point, regulations relating to three specific circumstances can be identified in an international comparison:

(1) First, defining situations of need: This primarily concerns remarriage, which often terminates entitlements to survivors' pensions in many countries. The rationale behind this is that entering into a new partnership alleviates the need for maintenance that arose from the previous partner's death. This rule can also be linked to the grounds for the claim, as entry into a new partnership severs the connection to the deceased partner.

(2) Secondly, determining the surviving dependants' ability to alleviate their situation of need on their own: Many countries implement age thresholds for receiving survivors' pensions. In Belgium, for example, the threshold in 2024 is 49 years and 6 months for spouses of deceased persons.[25] The rationale behind these regulations is based on the assumption that younger survivors are better equipped to assume personal responsibility for their own maintenance, and they are therefore encouraged to pursue gainful employment, which aligns with labour market policy objectives. Such age thresholds are expressly permitted in two recent international conventions, ILO Convention No. 128[26] and the revised EOSS[27], provided, however, that survivors can work and do not have care responsibilities for minor children.[28]

---

[25] Since 2015, the minimum age has been increased by 6 months every year, starting at 45 years, and reaching at 50 years in 2025, see https://www.sfpd.fgov.be/fr/droit-a-la-pension/pension-de-survie.

[26] Art. 21 para. 2: "A widow's entitlement to a survivor's benefit may be made conditional on reaching a prescribed age. The age may not be higher than the age prescribed for entitlement to old-age benefits."

[27] Art. 64 para. 1.

[28] Art. 21 para. 3 ILO Convention No. 128 and Art. 64 para. 3 EOSS rev.: "However, an age condition shall not be allowed if the spouse: a) is considered incapacitated under prescribed conditions; or b) has at least one dependent child."

(3) Third, identifying the concrete requirements related to need: These range from offsetting other benefits to verifying concrete need. These different levels of requirements offer insights into the classification of survivors' benefits. As previously noted, international agreements distinguish between benefits that are based on contributions and those that or not.[29]

2.3. Grounds for Entitlement: Regulations Relating to Insured Persons and Their Relationship with Surviving Dependants

Two distinct groups of preconditions with regard to eligibility criteria for survivors' benefits can be distinguished.

(1) The first group of preconditions concerns the insurance or other social security law requirements related to the coverage of the deceased person – i.e. with regard to the acquisition of a transferable entitlement. This is also dealt with in various international agreements.[30]

(2) I would like to briefly address the second group of preconditions, which relates to the relationship between the insured person and their surviving dependants. It concerns both a temporal and a relational component. The former refers to the requirement that the relationship between the insured person and the survivor must have existed for a specified period prior to the insured person's death. The relational component is of particular significance as it reflects evolving social dynamics in the regulations governing survivors' benefits. Traditionally, survivors' insurance was directed at children and widows; even ILO Convention No. 128 specifically mentions "wives and children". While the traditional family model has now become obsolete, gender discrimination continues to play a role to this day. As recently as autumn 2022, the Grand Chamber of the European Court of Human Rights (ECtHR) ruled that Switzerland's policy, which terminates widowers' pensions when the youngest child turns 18

---

[29] Art. 60, para. 2, ILO Convention No. 102 and Art. 60, para. 2, EOSS: "Under national legislation, benefits may be suspended if the beneficiary engages in certain prescribed gainful activity, benefits based on contributions may be reduced if the beneficiary's earnings exceed a prescribed amount, and non-contributory benefits may be reduced if the beneficiary's earnings, other resources, or both together exceed a prescribed amount."
[30] Art. 63 ILO Convention No. 102 = Art. 63 EOSS, Art. 24 ILO Convention No. 128 and Art. 66m EOSS rev.

constitutes a violation of Art. 14 in conjunction with Art. 8 European Convention on Human Rights (ECHR).[31]

The key question that has emerged in recent years is whether divorced persons and new(er) forms of cohabitation or partnerships should be included within the scope of survivors' insurance. The answer to this question also determines the extent to which survivors' insurance remains functional in a changing society and at the same time, whether it can still be considered up to date. In this respect, regulations on survivors' pensions reflect the state of social developments. Such regulations can be a consequence of societal change, whereby adjustments to social laws can also have constitutional consequences. In Austria, for example, the introduction of registered partnerships in 2010 resulted in their inclusion in the eligibility criteria for survivors' pension.[32] Following an equality review, the Constitutional Court ruled in 2017 that the distinction between marriage and registered partnerships – particularly of same sex couples – could no longer be maintained "without discriminating against same-sex couples with regard to their sexual orientation."[33] Other EU Member States continue to hold on to traditional concepts. In Romania, apart from children, only spouses are eligible for survivors' pensions. In 2018, Romania defended its refusal to grant a residency right to the same-sex spouse of a Romanian national despite the fact that he was entitled to it as a family member after their marriage in Belgium, citing public order and national identity.[34]

Finally, mention should be made of regulations that address the acquisition of positions under pension law. While these regulations do not exclude survivors' pensions, they might reduce the need for such benefits.

On the one hand, this includes recognition of periods of childcare, which is provided for in many countries. On the other, it involves the splitting of pension entitlements, which may take the form of pension equalisation in the event of

---

[31] ECtHR of 11.10.2022, No. 78630/12 Beeler v. Switzerland (following ECtHR Chamber decision of 20.10.2020).
[32] Insertion of §§ 216 and 259 ASVG by art. 22 of the EPG of 30.12.2009 (BGBl. I No. 135). Further equality in the follow-up of adoption options in Art. 1 No. 22 of the 2nd Social Insurance Amendment Act 2013 (BGBl. I No. 139).
[33] Constitutional Court of 4.12.2017, G 258-259/2017-9, para. 2.4.
[34] ECJ of 5.6.2018, case C-673/16 Coman ECLI:EU:C:2018:385.

divorce. At the same time, however, this introduces special requirements for survivors' pensions. Pension splitting can also occur during marriage. It seems that the splitting of entitlements is less common compared to the inclusion of periods of childcare. This may be attributable to the fact that some countries, such as in Scandinavia, offer adequate minimum social security through their pension systems, reflecting the special value placed on family support.

3. Reforms: Options and Examples

3.1. Human Rights Requirements

Reforms should be undertaken within the framework established by human rights standards. International agreements on the protection of social rights, namely the European Social Charter[35] and the International Covenant on Economic, Social and Cultural Rights[36], remain relatively broad.[37] They assert a right to social protection but lack clarity, even though they are meant to promote continuous improvement.[38] As in other socio-political contexts, the prohibition of discrimination assumes greater significance. This applies not least to special regulations on family relationships, specifically the UN Convention on the

---

[35] Art. 12 ESC of 18.10.1961 (ETS No. 35, available at: https://www.coe.int/en/web/conventions/full-list?module=treaty-detail&treatynum=035) and Art. 12 ESCR of 3.5.1996 (ETS No. 163, available at: https://www.coe.int/en/web/conventions/full-list?module=treaty-detail&treatynum=163).

[36] Art. 9 IPWSKR of 16.12.1966 (available at: https://www.ohchr.org/en/instruments-mechanisms/instruments/international-covenant-economic-social-and-cultural-rights).

[37] General Comment No. 19 on Art. 19 IPWSCR (available at: https://tbinternet.ohchr.org/_layouts/15/treatybodyexternal/TBSearch.aspx?Lang=en&TreatyID=9&DocTypeID=11) contains some general requirements in para. 21 for survivors benefits ("States parties must also ensure the provision of benefits to survivors and orphans on the death of a breadwinner who was covered by social security or had rights to a pension..."), but without specifying the benefits themselves (apart from benefits granted in case of death). The approach of the European Committee of Social Rights in relation to Art. 12 ESC is even more cautious, as death is not mentioned in the list of risks to be covered, see Lukas K (2021) The Revised European Charter. Cheltenham: Edward Elgar Publishing, 177.

[38] Art. 12 para. 3 ESC. The content of the right to social security is left to specific agreements, in this case the aforementioned ILO Conventions nos. 102 and 128; cf. also on the significance of the latter treaty Frey W, Scheiwe K and Wersig M (2015) 100 Jahre Witwen- und Witwerrenten - (k)ein Auslaufmodell? Baden-Baden: Nomos, 19 f.

Rights of Women, i.e. the Convention on the Elimination of All Forms of Discrimination Against Women,[39] whose relevance for survivors' pensions[40] is likely to diminish as gender roles evolve and policies are adjusted accordingly.

The prohibition of discrimination derived from other rights established in the ECHR is more effective. First, this holds true with view to the right to respect for the family life (Art. 8 ECHR). In line with recently consolidated case law, the Court ruled that it is a violation of Art. 14 ECHR in connection with Art. 8 ECHR if a disadvantage becomes a condition for exercising the latter right, in the sense that the requirements for receiving a social benefit necessarily determine the organisation of family life.[41] This may influence the structure of survivors' pensions, as demonstrated by the Beeler case in Switzerland, where legislation was subsequently amended.

The protection of property under the ECHR (Art. 1 ZP No. 1) has a similar effect. It stipulates equal treatment and compliance with the principles of the rule of law. On the one hand, this protection does not, according to the ECHR, depend on contributions. This is a correct interpretation is, at least in the context of the prohibition of discrimination.[42] On the other hand, however, the criteria for protection of legitimate claims remain ambiguous; what is needed are

---

[39] Convention on the Elimination of All Forms of Discrimination Against Women of 18.12.1979 (CEDAW, available at: https://www.ohchr.org/en/instruments-mechanisms/instruments/convention-elimination-all-forms-discrimination-against-women).

[40] On this, see Frey, Scheiwe and Wersig (fn. 6), 18 f.

[41] ECtHR (Grand Chamber) of 11.10.2022, No. 78630/12 Beeler v. Switzerland, para. 72: "Accordingly, for Article 14 of the Convention to be applicable in this specific context, the subject matter of the alleged disadvantage must constitute one of the modalities of exercising the right to respect for family life as guaranteed by Article 8 of the Convention, in the sense that the measures seek to promote family life and necessarily affect the way in which it is organised. The Court considers that a range of factors are relevant for determining the nature of the benefit in question and that they should be examined as a whole. These will include, in particular: the aim of the benefit, as determined by the Court in the light of the legislation concerned; the criteria for awarding, calculating and terminating the benefit as set forth in the relevant statutory provisions; the effects on the way in which family life is organised, as envisaged by the legislation; and the practical repercussions of the benefit, given the applicant's individual circumstances and family life throughout the period during which the benefit is paid."

[42] It is noteworthy that the ECtHR, despite assertions to the contrary (in its decision of 11.10.2022, No. 78630/12 Beeler v. Switzerland, para. 55), refrains from providing specific reasons. The connection with Art. 14 ECHR was dealt with by the ECtHR (Grand Chamber) of 12.4.2006, No. 65731/01 and 65900/01 (Stec and others), para. 51 et seq.

clear provisions.⁴³ In any case, the ECHR does not impose any obligation to provide social benefits as such.⁴⁴ As long as the legitimate claims are protected and proportionality is respected, existing benefits can be cut down or could even be dismantled.

3.2. Case Studies

a) Scandinavia

Fundamental reforms have been introduced in Scandinavia, which is unsurprising for several reasons. Scandinavia has a long tradition of equality policy, a strong institutional background and the universal application of the first layer of security. Sweden abolished the traditional widow's pension and introduced transitional arrangements as early as 1990. This reform sought to reflect the changes in women's employment and in family structures and to eliminate gender-based disparities in the entitlement to survivors' pensions.⁴⁵ A so-called

---

[43] ECtHR (Grand Chamber) of 13.12.2016, No. 53080/13 Béláné Nagy v. Hungary, para. 76: "In cases concerning Article 1 of Protocol No. 1, the issue that needs to be examined is normally whether the circumstances of the case, considered as a whole, conferred on the applicant title to a substantive interest protected by that provision (see Iatridis, cited above, § 54; Beyeler, cited above, § 100; and Parrillo, cited above, § 211). In applications concerning claims other than those relating to existing possessions, the idea behind this requirement has also been formulated in various other ways throughout the Court's case-law. By way of example, in a number of cases the Court examined, respectively, whether the applicants had "a claim which was sufficiently established to be enforceable" (see Gratzinger and Gratzingerova, cited above, § 74); whether they demonstrated the existence of "an assertable right under domestic law to a welfare benefit" (see Stec and Others v. the United Kingdom (dec.) [GC], nos. 65731/01 and 65900/01, § 51, ECHR 2005-X); or whether the persons concerned satisfied the "legal conditions laid down in domestic law for the grant of any particular form of benefits" (see Richardson v. the United Kingdom (dec.), No. 26252/08, § 17, 10 April 2012)."

[44] In summary, ECtHR (Grand Chamber) of 11.10.2022, No. 78630/12 Beeler v. Switzerland, para. 57: "On the basis of all the above considerations, the Court observes that its case-law has now taken on sufficient maturity and stability for it to give a clear definition of the threshold required for the applicability of Article 1 of Protocol No. 1, including in the sphere of social welfare benefits. It should be reiterated in this connection that that Article does not create a right to acquire property or to receive a pension of a particular amount. Its protection applies only to existing possessions and, under certain circumstances, to the 'legitimate expectation' of obtaining an asset; ...".

[45] Thus, the legislative justification, Regeringens proposition 1987/88:171 om reformering av den allmänna försäkringens efterlevandeförmåner m.m.

equalisation pension was introduced, which is provided to spouses and partners who lived in the same household as the deceased for at least five years. Such survivors are entitled to pension payments of 12 months.[46] A pension for widows and widowers was retained within the occupational pension scheme.[47] The situation in Denmark is comparable to Sweden's. A one-off payment of DKK 75,000 is provided to surviving dependants as a transitional benefit.[48] When a pensioner dies, his or her surviving dependants can continue to receive the deceased's pension for three months, provided their own income does not exceed a specified limit.[49]

Norway has followed the examples set by Sweden and Denmark. Surviving dependants previously received a so-called survivors' pension until reaching retirement age, which consisted of the guaranteed pension, plus 55 per cent of the deceased's pension entitlement.[50] However, this pension payment was reduced in accordance with the survivor's income – not only his or her *actual* income, but also his or her *expected* income.[51] However, even this pension, which was based on capitalisation principles, was abolished by a 2020 law, which took effect from 1 January 2024 and was replaced by a transitional pension.[52] This new pension is limited to a term of three years and is treated as secondary to other income, with the expectation that surviving dependants will seek gainful employment. A two-year extension is possible if the survivor is enrolled in an education programme or workforce integration measures. The

---

[46] 80 kap. Omställningspension, SFS 2010:110. Socialförsäkringsbalk (Social Security Code).

[47] Selén J and Ståhlberg A (2001) Survivors' Pension Rights in Occupational and Social Insurance: The Swedish Experience. EJSS: 117 ff.

[48] § 14b, lov om Arbejdsmarkedets Tillægspension.

[49] § 48, lov om social pension.

[50] Provided that a marriage has lasted at least five years or if there are joint children and they are registered in the same household, Chapter 17 folketrygdloven (Social Security Code) (old version).

[51] § 17-8 folketrygdloven (Social Security Code) (old version): "The surviving spouse's pension or transitional allowance shall be reduced in accordance with the income which the surviving spouse has or can be expected to have. In determining the expected income, account is taken, among other things, of age, abilities, education, professional career, work opportunities at home and work opportunities in other places where it is reasonable for the person concerned to take up work. Special emphasis is also placed on the care needs of children."

[52] Lov 18. desember 2020 nr. 139 om endringer i folketrygdloven (nye etterlatteytelser).

fact that Norway had already adopted the Swedish model and introduced a contributory pension scheme did not prevent this latest reform. On the contrary, according to the commission, which was established to prepare the reform, the objective was not only to remove incentives for survivors to reduce or give up their own gainful employment because "social security systems should encourage people as little as possible to decide against income-generating work in favour of social security".[53] Additionally, childcare is now accounted for in the pension system, as amended in 2011, and increases pension benefits. The continuation of survivors' pension is seen as "double compensation" for childcare responsibilities.[54]

b) United Kingdom

In the United Kingdom, a survivors' pension for parents of dependent children (*Widows Pension* and *Widowed Mothers' Allowance*) had already been replaced by other benefits (*Bereavement Payment*, *Bereavement Allowance* and *Widowed Parents' Allowance*) at the beginning of the millennium.[55] The system was further amended with effect from April 2017,[56] with the introduction of *Bereavement Support Payments*. Survivors receive a lump sum payment as well as monthly payments for a period of up to 18 months. The amount depends on whether survivors are entitled to *Child Benefits* or not.[57] In the first year, eligibility is independent of other benefits the survivor is entitled to. The amendment sought to streamline the benefits scheme, making it simpler and faster.[58] One-time, lump sum payments were increased, monthly payments capped, and age

---

[53] Norges offentlige utredninger 2017:3, Folketrygdens ytelser til etterlatte, Forslag til reform (available at: https://www.regjeringen.no/no/dokumenter/nou-2017-3/id2537191/?ch=1), 10.

[54] Norges offentlige utredninger 2017:3, 12.

[55] Welfare Reform and Pensions Act 1999, part 5, section 54-56, in force since 9.4.2001, S.I. 2000/1047, Art. 2(2)(a), Sch. Pt. I (https://www.legislation.gov.uk/ukpga/1999/30/contents).

[56] Part 5, section 30-32 of the Pensions Act 2014, in force since 6.4.2014, S.I. 2017/297, Art. 3(1)(b) and Art. 3(2) (https://www.legislation.gov.uk/ukpga/2014/19/contents).

[57] Single payment of GBP 3,500 and GBP 2,500, respectively, monthly payment of GBP 350 and GBP 100, respectively.

[58] Department for Work and Pensions (DWP) (2011) Bereavement Benefit for the 21st Century, 9, 12 (available at: https://www.gov.uk/government/consultations/bereavement-benefit-for-the-21st-century).

limitations and disqualifications following remarriage were abolished. Initially, the reduction was intended for 12 months, citing concerns that a duration exceeding that period would turn the payments into taxable income replacements.[59] This ultimately was not the deciding factor; instead, socio-political studies tipped the scales in favour of extending the provision of benefits for a slightly longer period.[60]

There were several reasons for the reform. First, it was expected to result in long-term savings.[61] The primary goal, however, was activation. By concentrating benefits to the period immediately following the partner's death, the reform aimed to reduce the long-term risk of creating incentives for prolonged periods of absence from the labour market.[62] The provision of long-term benefits, on the other hand, was assigned to *Universal Credit,* the previously amended scheme of assistance and support benefits. "Death benefits" are thus treated as family benefits for parents – in a country where provisions for orphans had traditionally been minimal. This is a continuation of previous proposals. Beveridge, in his famous report, argued that widows' pensions should only be provided to mothers who are providing care for children,[63] stating: "There is no reason why a childless widow should get a pension for life; if she is able to work, she should work."[64]

c) France

With the final example we return to France, where developments in survivors' pensions have been less clear-cut in one direction only. In 2003,[65] as part of a

---

[59] See counterarguments of the Social Security Advisory Committee (SSAC) (2015) Bereavement benefit reform, Occasional Paper No. 16, 19 ff. (available at: https://assets.publishing.service.gov.uk/media/5a74efa1ed915d502d6cc318/bereavement-benefit-reform-ssac-op16-nov-2015.pdf).
[60] Whereas the SSAC's proposal for an extension referred to parents (op. cit., p. 32).
[61] Replacement of the existing Bereavement Benefits for New Claims from April 2017 - Bereavement Benefits for the 21st Century (in Great Britain), Impact Assessment 2014 / available at: https:/assets.publishiung.services.media.gov.uk/).
[62] DWP (fn. 58), p. 16.
[63] Beveridge W (1942) Social Insurance and Allied Services. London: Parliamentary Archives (BBK/D/495), 11, 64 ff.
[64] Op. cit., p. 64 (para. 153).
[65] Loi n° 2003-775 du 21 août 2003 portant réforme des retraites (available at: https://www.legifrance.gouv.fr/loda/id/JORFTEXT000000781627).

comprehensive pension reform, the conditions for survivors' benefits were eased, with the age limit that had previously applied being abolished. In addition, survivors' pensions were integrated into the general old-age insurance scheme. However, the aforementioned expert commission proposed changes in 2007, essentially to narrow the group of persons eligible for benefits while at the same time improving the terms of those benefits.[66] The minimum age limit of 55 years for eligibility was reintroduced in 2009. Moreover, since these benefits are income-dependent,[67] they are now considered a form of minimum subsistence support.[68] A proposal to implement pension splitting and equalisation, similar to the German model, was rejected.[69]

Macron's second attempt to reform the pension insurance scheme[70] did not include survivors' insurance.[71] It focuses on raising age limits and harmonising schemes that provide some social cushioning. The reform did not revisit an earlier proposal to extend survivors' pensions to partners in a *pacte civil de solidarité* (PACS), i.e. in a registered partnership.[72] It should be noted that partners in a PACS are still not entitled to survivors' pensions. The French *Conseil constitutionnel* – similar to the Austrian Constitutional Court but with the opposite outcome – ruled that French law distinguishes between different forms of cohabitation (*mariage*, PACS and *concubinage*),[73] and that limiting survivors'

---

[66] Cf. Rapport d'information for the Senate (fn. 18) (available at: https://www.senat.fr/rap/r06-314/r06-314_mono.html#toc0).

[67] And at the same time, the general life situation, cf. on this Kessler F (2022) Droit de la protection sociale. 8th ed. Paris: Dalloz, 298f.

[68] Borgetto M and Lafore R (2019) Droit de la sécurité sociale. 19th ed. Paris: Dalloz, 654.

[69] Crit. in so far Kessler F (2022) Droit de la protection sociale. 8th ed. Paris: Dalloz, 297.

[70] Announcement by the Prime Minister Élisabeth Borne of 10.1.2023 (available at: https://www.gouvernement.fr/actualite/projet-pour-lavenir-du-systeme-de-retraites-ce-quil-faut-retenir).

[71] Loi no 2023-270 du 14 avril 2023 de financement rectificative de la sécurité sociale pour 2023 (available at: https://www.legifrance.gouv.fr/jorf/id/JORFTEXT000047445077); see decisions of the Cour constitutionnel: Dec. no 2023-849 DC and no 2023-4 RIP of 14.4.2023, 20 Dec. no 23-5 RIP of 35.2023 (https://www.conseil-constitutionnel.fr/decision/2023/).

[72] Cf. report by Troendle on a corresponding draft law from 2009 (available at: https://www.senat.fr/rap/l09-114/l09-114.html).

[73] Art. 143 ff. and 515-1 ff. Code Civil.

pensions to spouses was compatible with the principle of equality.[74] This approach, on the one hand, aims to preserve the special legal status of marriage. On the other hand, even though the differentiation no longer runs along gender lines, survivors' pensions remain unavailable to a considerable share of the population, given that the number of partnerships is about 200,000 compared to roughly 240,000 marriages.[75]

4. Final Remarks

1. The social risk survivors' pensions cover is not death itself, but the loss of a maintenance relationship due to death. While there is no direct legal relationship between maintenance law and survivors' benefits, there is a socio-political one. Survivors' pensions are family benefits in the form of insurance benefits.

There is some tension between the socio-political goal and the principle of personal responsibility of individuals, which forms the cornerstone of the liberal constitutional order. This is also becoming increasingly difficult to pursue in an era where the expansion of labour market participation and the advancement of gender equality are growing in significance.

2. The international legal framework for survivors' pensions is influenced by national social insurance models and is rooted in the traditional goal of such pensions, which are shaped by the outdated family structure of the single breadwinner. Adapting this framework to reflect changing social roles and modern social policies is associated with the well-known challenges associated with the somewhat cumbersome nature of international agreements.[76]

3. When considering the security objectives of national benefit schemes and whether they effectively provide such security, the complex regulatory landscape must also be considered. First, it is important to recognise that old-age provision is distributed across different tiers of social security in most countries.

---

[74] Thus, on the provision of soldiers, Dec. n° 2011-155 QPC of 29.7.2011 (https://www.conseil-constitutionnel.fr/decision/2011/2011155QPC.htm).
[75] Information from Insee (Institut national de la statistique et des études économiques), available at: https://www.insee.fr/fr/statistiques/2381498#tableau-figure1.
[76] See Becker U, Pennings F (2013) General Introduction. In: Becker, U, Pennings, F and Dijkhoff T (Eds.) Internationals Standard-Setting and Innovations in Social Security, Alpen aan den Rijn: Wolters Kluwer, p. 9.

Second, the structure of the standard pension scheme must be considered, in particular whether it includes a minimum pension or not. Finally, applicable family and tax laws play a role as well.

As regards the conditions for benefit eligibility, a systematic distinction must be made between benefits relating to insured persons and those for surviving dependants. The conditions and evolving changes are, in turn, essential for determining the specific social policy objectives that shape national social security systems.

4. In conclusion, let us return to our initial question: the country cases discussed here do not indicate a trend towards a reduction of survivors' benefits. Instead, we observe different developments across a range of countries. These variations can be explained by the unique institutional design of their social security systems and the social policy agendas each country pursues. And by the nature of survivors' benefits with their strong social policy links to societal role models and activation. In contexts where labour market participation and gender equality are particularly emphasised, efforts to restructure survivors' pensions are also evident. Yet, any reform must consider that pension rights reflect lifelong social positions of the individuals involved.

Bibliography

Becker U (2007) Alterssicherung im internationalen Vergleich. In: Becker U (Ed.) Festschrift für Franz Ruland: Alterssicherung in Deutschland. Baden-Baden: Nomos, 575-610.

Becker U (2010) Introduction to the General Principles of Social Security Law in Europe. In: Becker U, Pieters, D, Ross F, Schoukens P (Eds.) Security: A General Principle of Social Security Law in Europe, Groningen: Europa Law Publishing, 1-20.

Becker U (2022) § 1. In: Ruland F, Becker U and Axer P (Eds.) Sozialrechtshandbuch. Baden-Baden: Nomos, 43-81.

Becker U, Pennings F (2013) General Introduction. In: Becker U, Pennings F and Dijkhoff T, International Standard-Setting and Innovations in Social Security, Alpen aan den Rijn: Wolters Kluwer, 1-9.

Beveridge W (1942) Social Insurance and Allied Services. London: Parliamentary Archives (BBK/D/495).

Borgetto M and Lafore R (2019) Droit de la sécurité sociale. 19th ed. Paris: Dalloz.

Department for Work and Pensions (DWP) (2011) Bereavement Benefit for the 21st Century (available at: https://www.gov.uk/government/consultations/bereavement-benefit-for-the-21st-century).

Devetzi S (Ed.) (2023) Minimum Income in Old Age, a legal comparison of selected European countries. Athens: Sakkoulas Publications.

Freudenberg C, Kapuy K, Zwinger V and Technical Commission on Old-age, Invalidity and Survivors' Insurance International Social Security Association (2022) How to design survivor benefits in the 21st century? ISSA (available at: https://www.researchgate.net/publication/364915432_How_to_design_survivor_benefits_in_the_21st_century).

Frey W, Scheiwe K and Wersig M (2015) 100 Jahre Witwen- und Witwerrenten – (k)ein Auslaufmodell? Baden-Baden: Nomos.

Kessler F (2022) Droit de la protection sociale. 8th ed. Paris: Dalloz.

Lukas K (2021) The Revised European Charter. Cheltenham: Edward Elgar Publishing.

MPISOC (2021) Pension Maps, Visualising the Institutional Structure of Old Age Security in Europe and Beyond, 2nd.ed, ed by Schneider S, Tedora P and Becker U (available at: https://www.mpisoc.mpg.de/sozialrecht/forschung/forschungsprojekte/pension-maps/).

Norges offentlige utredninger (2017) Folketrygdens ytelser til etterlatte, Forslag til reform (available at: https://www.regjeringen.no/no/dokumenter/nou-2017-3/id2537191/?ch=1).

Selén J and Ståhlberg A (2001) Survivors' Pension Rights in Occupational and Social Insurance: The Swedish Experience. EJSS, 117-136.

Social Security Advisory Committee (SSAC) (2015) Bereavement benefit reform, Occasional Paper No. 16 (available at: https://assets.publishing.service.gov.uk/media/5a74efa1ed915d502d6cc318/bereavement-benefit-reform-ssac-op16-nov-2015.pdf).

3 Navigating Survivors' Benefits: Legal Perspectives and Considerations

Eberhard Eichenhofer

1. The Five Legal Dimensions of Survivors' Benefits

Survivors' benefits are an essential component of social security, extending across various dimensions such as pensions, workplace accident insurance, occupational diseases insurance and legislation on social compensation and benefits for victims of war or crime.[1] Survivors' benefits are embedded within the principles of family, inheritance and social security law. Historically, significant distinctions rooted in both legal and societal norms were made between the roles of women and men in paid labour: men as the primary breadwinners were expected to engage in paid labour while women were responsible for household chores and caregiving duties. In the event of the husband's death, survivors' benefits replaced his earnings and provided financial support to his surviving wife and children.

As a category of social rights, survivors' benefits possess distinctive characteristics across five dimensions. First, they are drawn from the principal beneficiary, with entitlement to this benefit extending to additional beneficiaries, namely qualified surviving family members. Second, survivors' benefits only *take effect* upon the (principal) beneficiary's *death* and are thus not applicable during her/his lifetime, thereby precluding simultaneous entitlement of both the

---

[1] Rust U (1990) Familienlastenausgleich in der gesetzlichen Kranken-, Unfall- und Rentenversicherung, Hamburg; Jaenecke P (2011) Gesetzliche Grundlagen der Hinterbliebenensicherung im europäischen Rechtsvergleich, Baden-Baden: Nomos; Scheiwe K (2005) Soziale Sicherungsmodelle zwischen Individualisierung und Abhängigkeiten, Kritische Justiz 38, 127 -151; Scheiwe K (2015) 100 Jahre Witwen- und Witwerrente − (k)ein Auslaufmodell, Baden-Baden: Nomos.

beneficiary and her/his surviving family members to this benefit. Third, survivors' benefits are established within a private law *relationship* between the beneficiary and her/his surviving family member(s). Within this relationship, the latter are financially *dependent* on the former who provided financial support to them during her/his lifetime. Fourth, today, the principle of equal treatment between men and women applies to survivors' benefits, raising the question of its impact on the underlying principle for survivors' benefits. Finally, given that spouses are entitled to equal shares of qualifying pension rights, the question arises whether a division of pension rights between spouses could serve as an alternative to survivors' benefits.

2. Impacts of Derivative Social Rights on Social Security

Survivors' benefits represent a derivative right that is embedded within the framework of social protection. This entitlement is triggered upon the death of an individual whose family members depended financially on her/him. The beneficiary's right to survivors' benefits serves as the foundation for and defines the scope of surviving family members' entitlement to this benefit. Survivors' benefits should *not* be perceived as *individualistic rights*, but should be conceptualised as *communitarian* rights, recognising the beneficiary's familial obligations to support her/his spouse, children or parents as integral members of her/his immediate family. Consequently, the right to survivors' benefits affords individuals protection due to the principal beneficiary's *family commitments*.

This benefit is unique because it establishes a direct correlation between family law obligations and social security. Survivors' benefits hence impose an *extraordinary burden* on social security institutions, given that eligibility is exclusive to individuals who were either married or had children with the principal beneficiary. They establish a tangible *solidarity* that is collectively *provided* by all insured persons *to those with* surviving family members.[2]

Protection following the death of the insured person is selective, as it is only extended to insured persons with a spouse or children, while those without qualified surviving family members are not eligible for such support. Survivors'

---

[2] James E (2009) Rethinking survivor benefits, Social Protection Discussion Papers and Notes from the World Bank No. 52019, Washington D.C. 2009, 36, 40.

benefits represent an additional and costly obligation for social security protection systems, leading to scepticism about their fairness and subjecting them to political scrutiny.

Survivors' benefits are just one category of derivative social rights. These rights, however, extend beyond the risk of death. Family health insurance or long-term care insurance are another type of derivative social rights providing access to benefits in *kind* for the insured person's dependent family members.

Therefore, derivative rights manifest as both consecutive and simultaneous entitlements, offering social security protection in the form of survivors' benefits in old age, in case of disability, work accidents or occupational diseases for the dependent spouse, parents or children of the insured individual. Following the principal beneficiary's death, these derivative rights transform into consecutive benefits, i.e. the qualified surviving family members simultaneously gain access to *medical treatment* and *care* which then become their own rights.[3]

Another component of family protection is embedded in social welfare law, which recognises the family unit as a relevant group entitled to simultaneous benefits.[4]

3. Survivors' Benefits as Rights Acquired by Succession

Survivors' benefits *extend* social rights, *transforming* them into rights for newly eligible persons. As a death-related benefit and *consecutive* right, survivors' benefits become effective upon the beneficiary's death as an inheritable right.[5] Survivors' benefits are thus social rights *inherited* by the *successors* of the insured person, forging a *direct link* between the surviving family members and *the beneficiary's right*, thereby entitling them to the benefit.[6]

---

[3] Rust U (1990) Familienlastenausgleich in der gesetzlichen Kranken-, Unfall- und Rentenversicherung, Hamburg,

[4] BVerfG -27.7.2016 -1 BvR 371/11; ECLI:DE: BVerfG:2016:rs20160727.1bvr037111; Bülow K (2021), Die eheähnliche Lebensgemeinschaft als sozialrechtliche Bedarfsgemeinschaft, NZFamR 2021,400; Dern S / Fuchsloch C (2017) Temporäre Bedarfsgemeinschaft im SGB II – wie soll es weitergehen? SGb 2017, 61.

[5] Alvin F (1947) L'héritage social, salaire et sécurité social, Paris, 12 et sequ.

[6] Fuchs M (2012) Rentenversicherung und Zivilrecht, in Eichenhofer E / Rische H / Schmähl W (Eds.) Handbuch der gesetzlichen Rentenversicherung, SGB VI, 2012, Kap. 31-31.

Survivors' benefits persist beyond the principal beneficiary's lifetime, whose right to the benefit ends upon her/his death and is transferred to her/his surviving family members. The amount of survivors' benefits inherited from the principal beneficiary hinges on various factors related to both the beneficiary and to her/his spouse, children or parents, and include age, income, family status, disability, parental status or insurance periods. These factors dictate the benefit's duration and the applicable conditions, as inherited social security benefits change the parameters of social security protection. Consequently, they are not preserved, but rather redefined.

The life expectancy of surviving family members – not only the spouse's,[7] but the children in particular – often varies significantly from that of the beneficiary. The factors used to calculate the amount of the principal beneficiary's pension change considerably when entitlement to this payment is inherited. The purpose of survivors' benefits is to shield the dependents of the principal beneficiary from financial hardship following her/his death, with social security protection replacing former family law rights.

Upon the death of the household's primary wage earner, a social security entitlement supersedes a legal obligation enshrined in family law. Survivors' benefits for spouses replace between 50% and 70% of the principal beneficiary's pension.[8] This is justified by the fact that the principal beneficiary's pension was drawn from her/his social security payments during his/her lifetime. Those transfers were intended to support the principal beneficiary's core family following her/his retirement and not just the beneficiary alone; therefore, a share of the social security payment continues to be transferred accordingly. Survivors' benefits are directly linked to the principal beneficiary's right to this benefit, which was not received during his/her lifetime. The risk of death is covered in social security independently from other social risks.

---

[7] James E (2009) Rethinking survivor benefits, Social Protection Discussion Papers and Notes from the World Bank No. 52019, Washington D.C., 2009, 39.

[8] James E (2009) Rethinking survivor benefits, Social Protection Discussion Papers and Notes from the World Bank No. 52019, Washington D.C., 2009, 42.

4. Dependence

Marriage and/or parenthood establish familial relationships. Under private law, the household's primary wage earner bears responsibility of financially supporting her/his dependents. If the primary wage earner fails to fulfil this obligation, her/his dependents retain the right to pursue legal recourse against her/him.[9] The relationship between the primary wage earner and her/his family is inherently one of dependence, reflected in the *consumption unit* shared between the principal beneficiary and her/his survivors during the former's lifetime and which ceases upon the beneficiary's death. Moreover, the principal beneficiary's death also terminates her/his *maintenance* obligation. The transfer of the principal beneficiary's entitlement to social security to her/his survivors *compensates* for their *losses* incurred upon the beneficiary's *death*. This transfer of entitlement to protection thus replaces survivors' loss of maintenance.

There is ongoing debate about the formalisation and legal recognition of family status for eligibility to receive survivors' benefits. This debate extends to whether domestic partners or former spouses (i.e. after divorce) should also be entitled to survivors' benefits.[10] The laws governing these issues vary in different countries. They typically distinguish between de facto parent-child and de facto spousal relationships. While the former type of de facto relationships are straightforward, the latter often require formalisation or legal recognition to qualify for survivors' benefits.

The maintenance obligation extends to children of unmarried parents as well. Legislation across states stipulates that children of unmarried parents are entitled to survivors' benefits due to both parents' maintenance obligation for the child. Similarly, support for both the mother and child is also legally provided in case of married parents. In contrast to parent-child relationships, there is no inherent maintenance obligation between unmarried partners. There is therefore no justification for incorporating de facto relationships between domestic partners into the social security system considering that entitlement to private

---

[9] Fuchs M (2012) Rentenversicherung und Zivilrecht, in Eichenhofer E / Rische H / Schmähl W (Eds.) Handbuch der gesetzlichen Rentenversicherung, SGB VI, 2012, Ch. 31-34.
[10] Freudenberg C / Kapuy K / Zwinger V (2022) How to design survivor benefits in the 21st century? ISSA 2022, 4.

law maintenance rights is replaced by entitlement to social rights in the form of survivors' benefits upon the principal beneficiary's death. Social rights are typically only established if a previous maintenance obligation existed.

Only a few countries extend survivors' benefits to de facto domestic partners, treating them as equivalent to formal spouses. If *private law* distinguishes between formal marriage and domestic partnerships, why should social security – which primarily compensates for losses covered by private law protection following the principal beneficiary's death – accept and justify equal treatment of both types of relationships?[11]

Specific arguments are therefore necessary to justify the extension of social rights to domestic partnerships. Survivors' benefits can be extended to a domestic partner who is the parent of a joint child and cares for that child. If the de facto parent-child relationship is recognised due to one parent's maintenance obligation for the other parent, then the entire family is treated as a cohesive unit. If private law recognises such a relationship as a common law marriage – i.e. the domestic partnership holds the same legal status as a formal marriage under civil law, equal treatment in social security is also possible.

5. Equal Treatment between Women and Men and Survivors' Benefts

Survivors' benefits have historically been justified within the context of the *male breadwinner* model,[12] which has profoundly influenced the economic and social status of family members. This model is emblematic of the social division of labour between men and women: women were primarily tasked with unpaid household responsibilities, while men predominantly participated in paid employment on the labour market.

As a result, wives typically relied financially on their husbands, while husbands tended to be financially independent from their wives. Consequently, the

---

[11] Brosius-Gersdorf F (2016) Ehe- und familienverfassungsrechtlicher Reformbedarf bei der Witwen- und Witwerrente in der gesetzlichen Rentenversicherung, SGb 2016, 241, 321.

[12] Shire K / Gottfried H (2021) Convergence and divergence in public gender regimes: Germany and Japan in national and world regional comparison, in Scherger S / Abramowoski R / Dingeldey I / Hokema A / Schäfer A (Eds.) Geschlechterungleichheiten in Arbeit, Wohlfahrtsstaat und Familie, Frankfurt/New York, 85, 87 et. sequ.

death of a spouse impacted men and women differently given their distinct roles within the family: the surviving husband did not suffer an economic loss from his wife's death but lost the individual who provided care and familial support and managed the household. Conversely, the wife lost the primary wage earner upon her husband's death, jeopardising her and the family's livelihood.

In short, traditional survivors' benefits for spouses were designed to alleviate economic hardship upon the primary wage earner's death, usually the husband's. In this traditional economic framework, the widow faced financial uncertainty upon her spouse's death, while the widower's financial circumstances generally remained unchanged following his wife's death and was thus not eligible for survivors' benefits.

Survivors' benefits have been subjected to widespread scepticism because they are based on an *outdated*, traditional family structure. These benefits were initially introduced in the first half of the 20th century, when the *male breadwinner* model prevailed both in practice and normatively.

This family model was characteristic of *traditional industrial societies*, where men were primarily engaged in gainful employment and women assumed the role of caregiver, especially for children. The working husband and father financially supported both the mother and children. With the maintenance obligation resting solely on the husband's shoulders, his wife and children as dependents were entitled to survivors' benefits upon his death. This model explains why survivors' benefits were traditionally provided to wives and children, who both depended on the husband/father as the family's sole breadwinner. Conversely, widowers were not typically perceived as survivors entitled to social security protection. The limitation of social security protection to wives and children as survivors only reflected the traditional family law concept rooted in the male breadwinner model. This private law protection ended upon the primary wage earner's death, leaving the dependents in financial need.[13]

Today, survivors' benefits for spouses must safeguard equal treatment between women and men. The Grand Chamber of the European Court of Human Rights emphasises the importance of gender equality regarding entitlement to survivors' benefits. These benefits, recognised both as a property right and as

---

[13] BVerfG -12.3.1975 -1 BvL 15/71, Rn. 73 et sequ. BVerfGE 39, 169.

a means of supporting family life, are deemed essential from a human rights perspective.[14] According to the Court, if survivors' benefits enable a surviving parent to care for their shared children following the spouse's death, it is imperative to ensure equal treatment for both female and male surviving spouses. Any social security provision for surviving spouses that violates the principle of equal treatment, such as the termination of survivors' benefits for widowers once the youngest child reaches adulthood, while continuing to provide such benefits to widows, is deemed unacceptable.

Adherence to gender equality is firmly embedded in Member States' Constitutions and human rights frameworks. This commitment reflects the evolving roles of men and women in both work and family life in recent decades. These transformative shifts are redefining the traditional foundations of family structures, raising questions about the adequacy and scope of survivors' benefits.

Equal treatment between male and female partners with reference to survivors' benefits highlights a stark contrast between the welfare state's formative phase in the early 20th century and the social reality of the 21st century. The male breadwinner model has become outdated, and the traditional division of labour between genders no longer applies. The active participation of both men and women has become a common feature of contemporary economic and family life. Given these changes, the question arises whether survivors' benefits for spouses are still justified or whether the benefit should be scrapped, especially when both partners are actively engaged in paid employment and contribute to the household income.

If the widower's pension is to be granted under the same conditions as the widow's pension, the determination of survivors' need for and entitlement to the benefit is no longer crucial. Equal treatment for both widows and widowers hinges on their family status, which dictates eligibility for survivors' benefits. Consequently, survivors' benefits are no longer intended to provide security for an individual who was financially dependent on her/his spouse. The transition in marriage from the 'one earner model' to the 'dual earner model' has redefined the dependence of spouses on each other. Survivors' benefits should therefore be adjusted to align with this new concept of dependence.

---

[14] In the judgement of the ECHR of 11 October 2022, No. 78630/12 Beeler v. Switzerland; BVerfG -12.3.1975 -1 BvL 15/71; BVerfGE 39, 169.

Employment fosters self-determination and self-reliance, empowering individuals to develop their abilities in both the economic and social spheres. In today's welfare-oriented economy, there is widespread acknowledgement that active participation of both men and women in the labour market is not only economically beneficial but also socially desirable. Contemporary social policy and social security measures prioritise active participation in the labour force. It is therefore worth exploring to what extent survivors' benefits might hamper women from actively engaging and integrating into the labour market.[15] In other words, the extent to which the economic activity of both spouses influences the determination of a surviving spouse's eligibility for widowers' or widows' pension needs to be considered.[16]

The economic outcome of labour market participation is self-reliance given that workers earn a living wage that sustains a decent livelihood for themselves and their family. If gainful employment allows workers to achieve economic independence, it raises questions about the necessity of providing survivors' benefits in social insurance based on the traditional assumption of continued dependence on the spouse, when both spouses actively participate in the labour market and earn a decent livelihood.

the traditional model of a single male breadwinner has largely given way to a dual income earner model, with both spouses actively engaged in gainful employment. This shift is also reflected in the law on survivors' benefits, which emphasises equality between genders. As dual income earners, both parents jointly bear the responsibility for maintenance of their children. Women's financial dependence on their spouses has diminished, and responsibility for children's well-being is now shared by both parents.

Yet not only families with children, but couples also often rely on their combined income. Even today, the socioeconomic status of many women remains precarious and significantly impacts their social position and level of social protection. Given the persistence of the gender pay gap and the unequal distribution of household and caregiving duties between men and women, it would be

---

[15] Borella M / De Nardi M (2023) Are Marriage-Related Taxes and Social Security Benefits Holding Back Female Labour Supply, Review of Economic Studies 90, 102–131.
[16] Brosius-Gersdorf F (2016) Ehe- und familienverfassungsrechtlicher Reformbedarf bei der Witwen- und Witwerrente in der gesetzlichen Rentenversicherung, SGb 2016, 241, 321.

detrimental to female spouses if social protection for spouses were eliminated altogether. Survivors' benefits are not designed to correct these shortcomings and achieve genuine equality in the workplace. An unequal labour market does not justify the continuation of survivors' benefits for spouses.

6. Splitting Pension Rights – Alternative to Survivors' Benefits?

In the event of divorce, pension rights can be split, similar to the division of assets acquired during their marriage. This division of pension rights follows the logic of family law, wherein jointly acquired property is divided equally between former partners. If the former spouses' pensions and assets accumulated during the marriage are combined and equally distributed between them, each party receives a fair share.[17] Pension splitting serves as an effective means to redistribute pension rights and facilitate a seamless separation between divorcing spouses.

The implications of splitting pension rights vary for married couples. Pension splitting does not yield any discernible advantages for spouses who live in the same household, since the shared household income as such is not affected. If the pension rights acquired by the couple during their marriage are split, however, it bridges the wage and pension gap between the two spouses.[18] This intervention increases the pension rights for the spouse who earned less, especially upon the death of the spouse with the higher income. Pension splitting might thus emerge as a potential alternative to survivors' benefits.

The rebalancing of pension rights does not have a significant impact on the spouses' living conditions if the household continues to function as a single consumption unit, because the transfer of pension rights from one spouse to the other inevitably comes at the expense of the other spouse. Consequently, while there may be a redistribution of pension rights, the overall amount of pension payments remains unchanged. While such a redistribution results in a fairer distribution of pension rights, it does not have a substantial impact on the couple's living conditions. In short, the splitting of pension rights is feasible in

---

[17] Freudenberg C / Kapuy K / Zwinger V (2022) How to design survivor' benefits in the 21st century? ISSA 2022, 32.
[18] James E (2009) Rethinking survivor benefits, Social Protection Discussion Papers and Notes from the World Bank No. 52019, Washington, D.C., 2009, 47.

cases of divorce but may not be practical when the household remains intact, as there is no change in the family's overall living conditions.

7. Survivors' Benefits – Benefits for the Future?

Survivors' benefits play a crucial role within the social security framework and have been firmly entrenched for over a century. This reflects the long-standing commitment by governments to uphold trust in existing social security legislation, which are only amended in response to compelling grounds that arise from far-reaching societal changes. Survivors' benefits face criticism because they are associated with substantial social expenditures,[19] the potential creation of disincentives to work and a violation of the equality between married and unmarried insured persons.[20] These arguments deserve careful consideration.

With the decreasing number of marriages, the rising labour market participation of women, and the growing entitlement of surviving men to social security benefits,[21] the question arises: should survivors' benefits be fully or partially be phased out in the foreseeable or distant future?

The criticism directed towards survivors' benefits does not uniformly apply to all categories, particularly concerning surviving children. The right to survivors' benefits is embedded in the family relationship between the principal beneficiary and the dependent. Children's dependence on their parents has not changed despite evolving family law and adaptations in the scope of family protection in recent decades; in fact, children's reliance on their parents has become even more relevant given that the phase of adolescence lasts longer. The untimely loss of a parent still causes significant economic hardship, i.e. orphans' benefits are a crucial subcategory of survivors' benefits and remain indispensable for the foreseeable future.

---

[19] In some states (Brazil, Italy, Greece, Spain and Germany) over 2% of GDP: Freudenberg C / Kapuy K / Zwinger V (2022) How to design survivor benefits in the 21st century? ISSA 2022, 6.
[20] Freudenberg C / Kapuy K / Zwinger V (2022) How to design survivor benefits in the 21st century? ISSA 2022, 10.
[21] Freudenberg C / Kapuy K / Zwinger V (2022) How to design survivor benefits in the 21st century? ISSA 2022, 17 et sequ.

A more sceptical approach is warranted when assessing the justification for survivors' benefits for spouses. Historically, a consumption unit typically consisted of a married couple. The death of the principal beneficiary does not necessarily reduce the couple's previous shared expenditures: the cost of housing and its maintenance are an ongoing expenditure, underscoring the need for ongoing protection for surviving spouses.

The underlying rationale of survivors' benefits is to maintain the previous standard of living during the transition from a shared to a single household, ensuring stability and protection.[22] Survivors' benefits for spouses serve to sustain the household's consumption capacity, particularly when the household income decreases following a spouse's death while household expenses largely remain unchanged.[23] Survivors' benefits bridge the gap between pre- and post-death standards of living and allow the surviving spouse to maintain her/his living standards, irrespective of her/his partner's death.[24]

However, the need for such support diminishes and eventually –ceases over time. Neither the relationship of dependence between parents and children nor that between spouses continues indefinitely. Consumption units are built on family relationships that evolve over time. Survivors' benefits should therefore be adjusted to align with these changes.

Pensions for widows and widowers should be treated and used as transitional support payments. Survivors' benefits could and should be restricted to assist the survivor in maintaining her/his independence for a certain period of time. Following this transitional period, widows and widowers should adjust their living conditions to their new circumstances.

In addition, the surviving spouse's economic status warrants consideration, particularly regarding whether her/his own income or social security benefits are adequate to sustain her/him.[25] Given that survivors' benefits are designed

---

[22] Fuchs M (2012) Rentenversicherung und Zivilrecht, in Eichenhofer E / Rische H / Schmähl W (Eds.) Handbuch der gesetzlichen Rentenversicherung, SGB VI, 2012, Kap. 31.

[23] James E (2009) Rethinking survivor benefits, Social Protection Discussion Papers and Notes from the World Bank No. 52019, Washington, D.C., 2009, 47.

[24] James E (2009) Rethinking survivor benefits, Social Protection Discussion Papers and Notes from the World Bank No. 52019, Washington, D.C., 2009, 35 et sequ.

[25] BVerfG 18.2.1998 - 1 BvR 1318/86, 1 BvR 1484/86, BVerfGE 97,271, Rn. 60 et sequ.

to assist those in need, they should not serve as a means of enrichment for individuals who are financially independent.

Hence, the need for support hinges on the degree of the surviving spouse's economic independence. If a widower already receives a decent pension based on his contributions, why should he receive his widower's pension upon his wife's death? Likewise, why should a childless wife, who earned a decent income throughout her marriage be entitled to a widow's pension despite being economically independent from her spouse prior to the spouse's death? In both scenarios, the surviving spouses undoubtedly experience economic losses upon their partner's death, but these setbacks do not qualify as a social need for compensation.

If the underlying notion of survivors' benefits is to assist family members who depended on the financial support provided by the deceased individual, and if such dependency between spouses was not one-sided but mutual according to the spouses' joint economic status and their individual economic independence, survivors' benefits should be subject to means- or income testing. By aligning benefits with the survivor's needs following the death of the spouse means no advantages would be extended to those who were never financially dependent on their partner. Survivors' benefits should reflect socioeconomic changes and be conceived as transitional benefits that are provided to the survivor to bridge the gap caused by the loss of the deceased spouse. Therefore, eligibility to the benefit should be contingent on meeting specific criteria of means-, wage- or social security protection testing.

Bibliography

Alvin L (1947) L'héritage social, salaire et sécurité social. Paris.

Borella M / De Nardi M (2023) Are Marriage-Related Taxes and Social Security Benefits Holding Back Female Labour Supply. Review of Economic Studies 90, 102-131.

Brosius-Gersdorf F (2016) Ehe- und familienverfassungsrechtlicher Reformbedarf bei der Witwen- und Witwerrente in der gesetzlichen Rentenversicherung. SGb 2016, 241-245; 321-328.

Bülow K (2021) Die eheähnliche Lebensgemeinschaft als sozialrechtliche Bedarfsgemeinschaft. NZFamR 2021, 400.

Dern S / Fuchsloch C (2017) Temporäre Bedarfsgemeinschaft im SGB II – wie soll es weitergehen? SGb 2017, 61.

Freudenberg C / Kapuy K / Zwinger V (2022) How to design survivor' benefits in the 21st century? ISSA Geneva 2022.

Fuchs M (2012) Rentenversicherung und Zivilrecht, in Eichenhofer E / Rische H / Schmähl W (Eds.) Handbuch der gesetzlichen Rentenversicherung, SGB VI, 2012, Kap. 31.

James E (2009) Rethinking survivor benefits, Social Protection Discussion Papers and Notes from the World Bank No. 52019, Washington D.C. 2009.

Jaenecke P (2011) Gesetzliche Grundlagen der Hinterbliebenensicherung im europäischen Rechtsvergleich, Baden-Baden: Nomos.

Rust U (1990) Familienlastenausgleich in der gesetzlichen Kranken-, Unfall- und Rentenversicherung, Berlin: Erich Schmidt.

Scheiwe K (2005) Soziale Sicherungsmodelle zwischen Individualisierung und Abhängigkeiten. Kritische Justiz Bd. 38 2005, 127-151.

Scheiwe K (2015) 100 Jahre Witwen- und Witwerrente – (k)ein Auslaufmodell, Baden-Baden: Nomos.

Shire K / Gottfried H (2021) Convergence and divergence in public gender regimes: Germany and Japan in national and world regional comparison, in: Scherger S / Abramowosk R / Dingeldey I / Hokema A / Schäfer A (Eds.) Geschlechterungleichheiten in Arbeit, Wohlfahrtsstaat und Familie, Frankfurt/New York: Campus, 85-108.

4 Minimum International and European Standards for Survivors' Benefits

Guido Van Limberghen

1. Introduction

European societies have witnessed substantial socioeconomic transformations, including increased female labour market participation, the prevalence of non-marital and same-sex partnerships, and rapidly rising divorce rates. These changes are having a significant impact on survivors' benefit schemes, which are designed to provide protection for surviving family members following the breadwinner's death. The increasing participation of women in the labour market makes it more challenging to determine who the family's (main) breadwinner is, and whether the surviving family members were in fact dependent on the deceased person. Likewise, the changing nature of partnerships further complicates the identification of surviving family members. In other words, it has become more difficult to accurately estimate the concrete (financial) implications of the breadwinner's death for surviving family members and consequently, to determine whether the consequences of this traditional social risk justify an introduction of new survivors' benefit schemes or whether to adapt existing ones.

A recent study sheds light on countries' varied responses to these societal changes and presents policy recommendations and administrative options for (re)designing survivors' benefit schemes. It also addresses international and

European instruments that establish legal guarantees which may limit the scope of feasible reforms.[1]

We examine the development of these legally established guarantees and assess to what extent they represent a barrier to (potential) adaptations of existing survivors' benefit schemes in response to contemporary socioeconomic trends.

We analyse the relevant instruments issued by the International Labour Organization (ILO) and the Council of Europe (CoE), namely ILO C039[2], ILO R043[3], ILO C102[4], ILO C128[5], ILO R 131[6], ECSS[7], Protocol ECSS[8] and Rev. ECSS.[9] These instruments can be categorised into three generations:

- First-generation instruments: ILO C039 and ILO R043, which are outdated and are therefore referred to in the past tense;
- Second-generation instruments; ILO C102, ECSS and Protocol ECSS; and
- Third-generation instruments: ILO C128, ILO R131 and Rev. ECSS.

---

[1] Freudenberg C / Kapuy K / Zwinger V (2022) *How to design survivor benefits in the 21st century?*. International Social Security Association, 44 ff.

[2] C039 – Survivors' Insurance (Industry, etc.) Convention, 1933 (No. 39), adopted in Geneva on 29 June 1933, ratified by 8 Member States and in force in 7 of them.

[3] R043 – Invalidity, Old-Age and Survivors' Insurance Recommendation, 1933 (No. 43), adopted in Geneva on 29 June 1933, withdrawn by decision of the International Labour Conference at its 92nd Session (2004).

[4] C102 – Social Security (Minimum Standards) Convention, 1952 (No. 102), adopted in Geneva on 28 June 1952, ratified by 65 Member States and in force in 63 of them.

[5] C128 – Invalidity, Old-Age and Survivors' Benefits Convention, 1967 (No. 128), adopted in Geneva on 29 June 1967, ratified by 17 Member States and in force in all of them.

[6] R131 – Invalidity, Old-Age and Survivors' Benefits Recommendation, 1967 (No. 131), adopted in Geneva on 29 June 1967.

[7] European Code of Social Security (ETS No. 048), adopted in Strasbourg on 16 April 1964, ratified by 21 Member States and in force in all of them.

[8] Protocol to the European Code of Social Security (ETS No. 048A), adopted in Strasbourg on 16 April 1964, ratified by 7 Member States and in force in all of them.

[9] European Code of Social Security (Revised) (ETS No. 139), adopted in Rome on 6 November 1990, ratified by 1 Member State and therefore not entered into force.

Furthermore, we take a closer look at the recent EU Recommendation on survivors' benefits which aims to guarantee adequate social protection for the surviving family members of all workers and self-employed persons.[10]

This chapter is divided into four sections. The first section focusses on the EU Recommendation, which does not define the contingency creating entitlement to survivors' benefits. By contrast, the ILO and CoE instruments define such contingency as the loss of support resulting from the death of the breadwinner.[11] This definition is discussed in more detail in Section 2. Survivors' benefits according to the ILO and CoE instruments, serve to compensate the surviving spouse and children for the loss of financial support normally provided by the deceased breadwinner.

The EU Recommendation, on the other hand, does not include any such provision. These two categories of beneficiaries, i.e. spouses and children, are analysed in Section 3. Section 4 takes a closer look at the duration of payment of survivors' benefits and how their amount is calculated. Finally, Section 5 presents concluding remarks.

2. The contingency covered

The death of a breadwinner entails two essential elements, namely the notion of death, which is analysed in Section 2.1, and that of breadwinner, which is discussed in Section 2.2.

2.1. The notion of death

The ILO and CoE instruments included in our analysis do not contain a clear definition of the notion of death. Consequently, this notion must be interpreted in accordance with its definition in national law or its common understanding.

A situation analogous to the death of the breadwinner, which is not addressed by any other contingency to which these Instruments apply, is the absence of an individual. It is therefore unclear whether that individual is still alive.

---

[10] Council Recommendation of 8 November 2019 on access to social protection for workers and the self-employed.
[11] Art. 6 ILO C039; Art. 60.1 ILO C102; Art. 60.1 ECSS; Art. 21.1 ILO C128; Art. 64.1 Rev. ECSS.

National legislation may stipulate whether a legal declaration of absence may be issued and whether the absence of this individual can be considered a presumption of the breadwinner's death for the purpose of awarding survivors' benefits to the breadwinner's surviving dependants.

The ILO and CoE instruments do not specify any particular causes of death of breadwinners. A breadwinner's death may thus result from an accident at work, for example, or from an occupational disease. In such cases, survivors may be eligible for both survivors' benefits and employment injury benefits The ILO and CoE instruments allow for a limitation to the cumulation of benefits, which in turn can be suspended by national legislation.[12] The EU Recommendation, on the other hand, stipulates that survivors and other benefits awarded in EU Member States must not only ensure that the beneficiaries can maintain a decent standard of living and are compensated for the loss of income previously provided by the breadwinner, but must also prevent the beneficiaries from falling into poverty. The total amount of survivors' benefits and employment injury benefits the deceased breadwinner's dependants receive may be taken into consideration when assessing whether the beneficiaries are adequately protected.[13]

On the other hand, the ILO and CoE instruments allow for the suspension of survivors' benefits in accordance with national law if the breadwinner's death resulted from specific causes, for example when the beneficiary caused the breadwinner's death through a criminal act or if the death resulted from the breadwinner's wilful misconduct.[14] In this respect, the term 'suspended' can be understood as "withheld" or "withdrawn"[15], as explicitly stipulated in the Revised ECSS.[16] The EU Recommendation allows for such safeguards to prevent abuse.[17]

---

[12] Art. 11.2(a) ILO C039; Art. 69 (c) ILO C102; Art. 68 (c) ECSS, Art. 33.2 ILO C128; Art. 22 ILO C121 regarding employment injury.
[13] Art. 11 EU Recommendation.
[14] Art. 11.1(a) ILO C039; Art. 69(e) and (f) ILO C102; Art. 68(e) and (f) ECSS; Art. 32(d) and (e) ILO C128.
[15] Korda M (2013) The Role of International Social Security Standards. An in-depth study through the case of Greece. Antwerp: Intersentia, 133.
[16] Art. 74.1(a) and (b) Rev. ECSS.
[17] Art. 9 EU Recommendation.

2.2. The breadwinner

Next, we turn to the concept of breadwinner (2.2.1). The mere fact that the deceased individual was the breadwinner does not automatically entitle his or her surviving dependants to survivors' benefits, unless they are protected due to their residence status[18] or because the breadwinner was a resident.[19] As is explained below, a deceased breadwinner must have also been socially insured (2.2.2) for his or her dependants to be entitled to survivors' benefits. Moreover, the breadwinner's dependent survivors must meet the conditions of eligibility for access to survivors' benefits (2.2.3).

2.2.1. The notion of breadwinner

None of the analysed ILO and CoE instruments explicitly defines the notion of breadwinner. According to common understanding, the breadwinner is typically considered to be the family member who contributes the largest share of household income and covers the family's needs.[20] This interpretation aligns with the intended definition of breadwinner in the instruments. It is also in line with the definition of 'widow', namely 'a woman who was maintained by her husband at the time of his death'[21] or 'a wife who is dependent on her husband'.[22]

The wording used in the instruments implies that the deceased individual is considered to have been the surviving dependants' sole breadwinner. However, the instruments only establish minimum standards, leaving room for national legislation to extend benefits under other circumstances as well, for instance when the beneficiary of survivors' benefits can be considered the family's breadwinner or when the deceased individual was not the household's primary wage earner.

---

[18] Art. 62 ILO C102; Art. 61 ECSS; Art. 22 ILO C128.
[19] Art. 65.1(c) and 65.2(b) Rev. ECSS.
[20] Cambridge Dictionary, https://dictionary.cambridge.org/dictionary/english/relaxation.
[21] Art. 1.1(d) ILO C102; Art. 1.1(g) ECSS; Art. 1(g) ILO C128; 1(e) ILO R131.
[22] Art. 1(f) ILO C128; 1(d) ILO R131; Art. 1(g) Rev. ECSS.

2.2.2. The socially insured breadwinner

According to the ILO and CoE instruments, beneficiaries of survivors' benefits – excluding individuals protected under social assistance schemes – typically include the spouse and children of the deceased breadwinner who was classified as a 'worker' in accordance with national legislation. National legislation can include other categories of persons as well.[23] For example, when apprentices are equated with workers, the deceased apprentice will not be considered the household's breadwinner per se but will be treated as a potential future breadwinner.

Moreover, the instruments seem to presuppose that the breadwinner was covered by social insurance at the time of his or her death, a circumstance that was clearly alluded to in the first-generation instruments.[24] While establishing minimum standards, the instruments allow national legislation to award survivors' benefits to dependants even if the breadwinner was no longer covered by social insurance at the time of his or her death, but had been (adequately) insured in the past, i.e. had accumulated sufficient periods of contributions, as explicitly provided for in the first-generation instruments.[25]

ILO C039 only applies to survivors' insurance schemes, while the other ILO and CoE instruments analysed cover social risks other than the death of the breadwinner. They do not require ratifying Member States to establish social security schemes for every contingency they cover.[26] Consequently, ratifying Member States can meet the obligations that arise under these instruments without actually implementing survivors' benefit schemes. Hence, the instruments do not guarantee the right for breadwinners covered by social insurance to participate in a survivors' benefit scheme. Participation in such a scheme ultimately depends on the legislation of the ratifying Member State.

---

[23] Art. 2 and 11 ILO C039; Art. 61 ILO C102; Art. 61 ECSS; 22.1 ILO C128; Art. 65 Rev. ECSS.
[24] Art. 5.2 ILO C039.
[25] Art. 3-5 ILO C039.
[26] Gómez Heredero A (2009) Social security. Protection at the international level and developments in Europe. Strasbourg: Council of Europe Publishing, 23-24; Nickless J (2002) Code européen de sécurité sociale: Vademecum. Strasbourg: Conseil de l'Europe, 19.

However, even if the ratifying Member State implements a survivors' benefit scheme, not all breadwinners will automatically be guaranteed access to it. The first-generation instruments, for instance, only targeted salaried workers. Although the instruments in principle sought to cover all individuals who were ordinarily engaged in a remunerated activity, they allowed national legislation to make exceptions for a large category of workers.[27] Moreover, as depicted in Figure 1, the Member States that ratified one or more second- and/or third-generation instruments can comply with the obligations stipulated in these instruments by providing access to survivors' benefit schemes for a specified percentage of employees only or for certain categories of workers among the economically active population.[28]

Figure 1. Percentage of employees or of the economically active population covered by protection

Protection for at least	ILO C102 (Art. 62)	ECSS (Art. 61)	ECSS + Protocol	ILO 128 (Art. 22)	Rev. ECSS (Art. 65)
Employees	50%	50%	80%	100%	100%
Economically active population	20%	20%	30%	75%	80%

ILO Member States are encouraged to gradually expand survivors' benefits – by stages, if necessary, and under specific conditions – to encompass the spouse and children of individuals engaged in casual employment or, alternatively, to include the spouse and children of *all* economically active persons.[29]

---

[27] Art. 2 ILO C039; Para. 1 ILO R131.
[28] Hermans K (2014) De WW en nieuwe sociale risico's Internationaalrechtelijke grenzen aan hervormingsvoorstellen. Deventer: Wolters Kluwer business, 221, 239, 277, 325 and 355-356; Praet B / Morsa M (2020) Le code européen de sécurité sociale : un étalon de valeur comme référence pour les systèmes de sécurité sociale européens? *Revue belge de sécurité sociale*, 607.
[29] Para. 3 ILO R131.

In this regard, the EU Recommendation in contrast to the ILO and CoE instruments, breathes (new) life into the right to survivors' benefits by expanding it to include surviving dependants of atypical workers and self-employed persons as well.[30] Within their own national contexts, EU Member States shall ensure that all workers residing in their territory, including atypical workers and self-employed persons, have access to survivors' benefit schemes.[31] If necessary, Member States shall expand social protection to cover workers or self-employed persons who were excluded from survivors' benefit schemes before the EU Recommendation came into effect.[32]

It is recommended for EU Member States to ensure access to adequate social protection for all self-employed persons, 'at least on a voluntary basis and where appropriate on a mandatory basis'.[33] While the European Commission supported compulsory affiliation to social protection schemes to enhance their financial sustainability, stakeholders advocated for voluntarily affiliation, especially as regards unemployment insurance, incapacity for work, and workplace accident insurance, given the heterogeneity of self-employed persons' activities and their fundamental freedom of choice.[34] P. Schoukens rightly cautions against the potentially negative drawbacks of voluntary affiliation with social insurance schemes. Self-employed persons with a high income might shirk

---

[30] Van Limberghen G (2023) Setting European Social Security Standards for the Self-Employed: The Interaction Between the European Code of Social Security and the EU Recommendation on Access to Social Protection. In: Jorens Y (Ed.) The Lighthouse Function of Social Law. Proceedings of the ISLSSL XIV European Regional Congress Ghent 2023, Cham: Springer, 284-288.

[31] Art. 1.1, 2 and 8 EU Recommendation.

[32] Van Limberghen G / Dumont D / Louckx F / Marchal S / Cantillon B (2021) Un regard critique et propositionnel sur les assurances sociales des salariés et des indépendants. Analyse au départ de la recommandation de l'Union européenne relative à l'accès des travailleurs à la protection sociale. *Revue belge de sécurité sociale*, 55.

[33] Art. 8 EU Recommendation.

[34] Observations (15) and (18) EU Recommendation; Lelie P (2021) La recommandation du conseil de l'union européenne relative à l'accès des travailleurs salariés et non-salariés à la protection sociale. Une occasion de préparer à l'avenir les systèmes de protection sociale des Etats membres de l'UE. *Revue belge de sécurité sociale*, 24-25 and 30-31; Schoukens P (2021) Building Up and Implementing the European Standards for Platform Workers. In: Becker U / Chesalina O (Eds.) Social Law 4.0. New Approaches for Ensuring and Financing Social Security in the Digital Age. Baden-Baden: Nomos Verlagsgesellschaft, 320-321.

the solidarity principle social protection schemes are built upon and thus jeopardise the financial sustainability of such schemes. Economically dependent self-employed persons, on the other hand, could (be forced to) opt out of affiliation with social insurance schemes and thus be left outside the scope of protection. With reference to the clause "and where appropriate on a mandatory basis", Schoukens calls for a restrictive interpretation of Member States' freedom to opt for voluntary affiliation of self-employed persons with social insurance schemes.[35] In line with this thinking, mandatory affiliation of self-employed persons with survivors' benefit schemes is highly recommended.

The ILO and CoE instruments, on the other hand, start from a mandatory affiliation of socially insured breadwinners[36] with survivors' benefit schemes, but allow for voluntary affiliation of both workers and of self-employed persons, under the condition that these schemes are supervised by public authorities or are administered by representatives of socially insured groups. Additionally, these schemes, in conjunction with other forms of protection where appropriate, should comply with the provisions of the relevant instrument and should protect a substantial share of low-wage socially insured breadwinners.[37]

Both the EU Recommendation and the ILO and CoE instruments allow for an expansion of the scope of existing schemes or the implementation of dedicated schemes, whether organised publicly or otherwise, to foster affiliation of socially insured breadwinners with social insurance schemes. However, the ILO and CoE instruments stipulate that workers' representatives and self-employed persons must be involved in the management of private schemes.[38]

2.2.3. The effectively insured breadwinner

According to Article 7, sub f) of the EU Recommendation, effective coverage for breadwinners' surviving dependants can be ensured when a Member

---

[35] Schoukens P (2021) Building Up and Implementing the European Standards for Platform Workers. In: Becker U / Chesalina O (Eds.) Social Law 4.0. New Approaches for Ensuring and Financing Social Security in the Digital Age. Baden-Baden: Nomos Verlagsgesellschaft, 324-326.
[36] Art. 3 ILO C039.
[37] Art. 6 ILO C102; Art. 6 ECSS; Art. 6 ILO C128; Art. 6 Rev. ECSS.
[38] Art. 13 ILO C039; Art. 72 ILO C102; Art. 71 ECSS; Art. 36 ILO C128; Art. 77 Rev. ECSS.

State's legislation or a collective agreement provides the breadwinner the possibility to accrue benefits and provides access to a given level of benefits to the breadwinner's surviving dependants following his or her death. In fact, a breadwinner's right to participate in a survivors' benefit scheme does not in itself suffice to guarantee entitlement of his or her surviving dependants to survivors' benefits.

According to the ILO and CoE instruments, entitlement to survivors' benefits can be contingent upon the completion by the breadwinner of a given qualifying period. The first-generation instruments stipulated that in such cases, the amount of survivors' benefits was to consist of a fixed sum or a fixed share of the benefit, unless a minimum rate was guaranteed, irrespective of the duration of the breadwinner's social insurance contributions.[39] The third-generation instruments, on the other hand, allow national legislation to make the payment of benefits to the widow contingent on her having fulfilled a specified period of residence in the country.[40] A previous proposal to make the widow's social assistance pension contingent upon the fulfilment of a specified period of residence by both her and her deceased husband was rejected. While a widow with children was expected to have resided in the country with her husband for a specific number of years, a widow without children could be required to have been married to the deceased breadwinner for a specified number of years before becoming eligible for survivors' benefits.[41]

Qualification periods for breadwinners can be included in national legislation, setting down several conditions such as contribution payments, employment, occupational activity, residence or a combination thereof for a specified period of time preceding the breadwinner's death.[42] Some ILO and CoE instruments prescribe or recommend, respectively, that certain periods such as compulsory military service, periods of paid unemployment, sick leave, incapacity for work or maternity leave are – under specific conditions – equated with the

---

[39] Art. 9.2 ILO C039.
[40] Art. 24.1(a) ILO C128; Art. 66.5(a) Rev. ECSS.
[41] Dijkhoff T (2011) International Social Security Standards in the European Union. The Cases of the Czech Republic and Estonia. Antwerp: Intersentia, 105.
[42] Compare Art. 4.1 ILO C039 with Art. 1(f) ILO C102; Art. 1.1(i) ECSS; Art. 1(i) ILO C128; Art. 1(g) ILO R131, and with Art. 1(e) Rev. ECSS.

breadwinner's contribution periods or years of employment.[43] The third-generation instruments allow for more advantageous provisions, i.e. national legislation can include additional qualification periods as well.[44]

The maximum duration of such qualifying periods in the ILO and CoE instruments are similar to those for eligibility for invalidity benefits.[45] According to the first-generation instruments, the qualifying periods could not exceed 60 contribution months, 250 contribution weeks or 1,500 contribution days.[46] The second-generation instruments extended the maximum duration of qualifying periods to 15 years of contributions, employment or occupational activity, or alternatively, to 10 years of residence.[47]

The duration of qualifying periods varies in countries depending on the breadwinner's age at the time of his or her death. According to the third-generation instruments, national legislation may only impose a qualifying period of contributions or years of employment that does not exceed 5 years at a prescribed minimum age. The duration of this period can be extended as the breadwinner grows older, without exceeding the prescribed maximum number of years.[48] This provision aims to balance shorter qualifying periods at a younger age against longer qualifying periods at an older age[49], thus increasing the flexibility of ILO C128 and facilitating its ratification. The requirement of a minimum age ensures that the qualifying periods in different countries remain proportionate to the Convention's maximum qualifying periods.[50]

---

[43] Art. 4.3 ILO C039; Para. 20-21 ILO R131.
[44] Art. 66.5(b) Rev. ECSS.
[45] Para. 19 ILO R131; Dijkhoff T (2011) International Social Security Standards in the European Union. The Cases of the Czech Republic and Estonia. Antwerp: Intersentia, 104 and 107; Korda M (2013) The Role of International Social Security Standards. An in-depth study through the case of Greece. Antwerp: Intersentia, 109-110; Myers R J / Yoffee W M (1966) Social Security Issues: Fiftieth International Labour Conference. *Social Security Bulletin*. November 1966: 28, https://www.ssa.gov/policy/docs/ssb/ v29n11/29n11p20.pdf (last consulted on 5 February 2024).
[46] Art. 4.2 ILO C039; Para. 6 ILO R043.
[47] Art. 63.1(a) ILO C102; Art. 63.1(a) ECSS; Art. 24.1(a) ILO C128; Art. 66.5(a) Rev. ECSS.
[48] Article 24.5 ILO C128; Art. 67.2 Rev. ECSS.
[49] Dijkhoff T (2011) International Social Security Standards in the European Union. The Cases of the Czech Republic and Estonia. Antwerp: Intersentia, 104.
[50] Korda M (2013) The Role of International Social Security Standards. An in-depth study through the case of Greece. Antwerp: Intersentia, 96-97 and 100.

The EU Recommendation also allows for the application of qualifying periods, provided they are justified by legitimate objectives such as preventing abuse of survivors' benefit schemes or ensuring their financial sustainability.[51] While other legitimate policy goals may also justify the implementation of qualifying periods, they must be relevant and proportional to the objective being pursued.[52] Unlike the ILO and CoE instruments, the EU Recommendation does not specify a maximum duration of qualifying periods. However, it limits Member States' autonomy in this matter. It requires for eligibility regulations for atypical workers and self-employed persons, which differ from those applicable to ordinary workers, to be proportionate and align with atypical workers and self-employed persons' specific conditions.[53] Member States should adapt initially identical eligibility criteria if they disproportionately disadvantage atypical workers, self-employed persons or individuals who are atypical self-employed persons or are transitioning from one employment status to the other.[54] Furthermore, in line with their national contexts, Member States should ensure that the qualifying periods fully or partially acquired within the scope of mandatory or voluntary survivors' benefit schemes, are preserved, accumulated and/or transferred, when individuals combine or transition between the status of

---

[51] Art. 9 EU Recommendation.

[52] Schoukens P / Bruynseraede C (2021) Access to social protection for self-employed and non-standard workers. An analysis based upon the EU Recommendation on access to social protection. Leuven: Acco, 63-64.

[53] Art. 5 and 9 EU Recommendation.

[54] Observation (19) EU Recommendation; European Commission, Staff Working Document. Impact Assessment, Accompanying the document Proposal for a Council recommendation on access to social protection for workers and the self-employed, 26-27, https://eur-lex.europa.eu/legal-content/EN/ALL/?uri=CELEX%3A52018SC0070 (accessed on 5 February 2024); Lelie (2021) La recommandation du conseil de l'union européenne relative à l'accès des travailleurs salariés et non-salariés à la protection sociale. Une occasion de préparer à l'avenir les systèmes de protection sociale des Etats membres de l'UE. *Revue belge de sécurité sociale,* 31; Schoukens P / Bruynseraede C (2021) Access to social protection for self-employed and non-standard workers. An analysis based upon the EU Recommendation on access to social protection. Leuven: Acco, 68-74; Van Limberghen G / Dumont D / Louckx F / Marchal S / Cantillon B (2021) Un regard critique et propositionnel sur les assurances sociales des salariés et des indépendants. Analyse au départ de la recommandation de l'Union européenne relative à l'accès des travailleurs à la protection sociale. *Revue belge de sécurité sociale,* 55-56.

worker and self-employed or transition from one status to the other.[55] The EU Recommendation also affords EU Member States the freedom of policymaking, thereby limiting the enforceability of these principles. In other words, EU Member States are not required to apply these principles and are thus not obligated to guarantee the transfer of rights accumulated under survivors' benefit schemes to workers and self-employed persons. It was argued that a transferability of rights could potentially cause severe financial strain or administrative burdens.[56]

3. Beneficiaries of survivors' benefits

In contrast to the EU Recommendation, which does not contain any provisions on the beneficiaries of survivors' benefits, the ILO and CoE instruments stipulate that survivors' benefits must provide protection to the breadwinner's surviving dependent widow and children. We first examine the notion of dependant widow (3.1), followed by that of dependent children (3.2). The instruments only establish minimum standards, that is, national legislation can include additional categories of dependants as beneficiaries[57], as explicitly provided for in some third-generation instruments.[58]

3.1. The dependant widow

According to the ILO and CoE instruments, the only adult specifically mentioned as being entitled to protection is the deceased breadwinner's widow as the beneficiary of survivors' benefits. We first, examine the definition of 'widow' in these instruments (3.1.1), and then analyse the extent of the widow's dependence on the deceased breadwinner for eligibility to survivors' benefits (3.1.2).

---

[55] Art. 10 EU Recommendation.
[56] Lelie P (2021) La recommandation du conseil de l'union européenne relative à l'accès des travailleurs salariés et non-salariés à la protection sociale. Une occasion de préparer à l'avenir les systèmes de protection sociale des Etats membres de l'UE. *Revue belge de sécurité sociale*, 25.
[57] Korda M (2013) The Role of International Social Security Standards. An in-depth study through the case of Greece. Antwerp: Intersentia, 60.
[58] Art. 22 ILO C128; Para. 3 ILO R131.

3.1.1. The notion of widow

The ILO and CoE instruments only require ratifying Member States to provide protection to the deceased breadwinner's spouse.[59] This restriction does not violate the prohibition of discrimination enshrined in the European Convention on Human Rights. The European Court of Human Rights (ECtHR) ruled that the legal status of marriage differs from that of *de facto* cohabitation which, according to the Court, is not necessarily reflected in the duration of the family relationship but in the acknowledgement of obligations arising from marriage.[60] The ILO and CoE instruments allow national legislation to make a childless widow's right to survivors' benefits conditional upon a minimum duration of her marriage to the breadwinner to preclude potential abuse.[61] Apparently, the risk of abuse is considered less likely when the breadwinner's widow has children.[62]

The requirement of marriage implies that the instruments do not recognise registered or *de facto* cohabiting partners as beneficiaries of survivors' benefits. However, the instruments allow national legislation to extend these benefits to surviving partners.

The requirement of marriage as outlined in the instruments may therefore imply that the breadwinner's former wife is no longer considered to be a beneficiary if the spouses are divorced or separated at the time of the breadwinner's death. In this respect, the first-generation instruments stipulated that a widow's pension rights could be withheld if the marriage had been dissolved or a separation legally pronounced due to marital misconduct on the part of the wife at the time of the insured or retired person's death.[63] Although the question whether divorced or separated spouses should be entitled to (certain) social security benefits has been discussed in some countries[64], later ILO and CoE

---

[59] Art. 2, 6 and 7 ILO C039; Art. 1.1(d) ILO C102; Art. 1.1(g) ECSS; Art. 1(g) ILO C128; Par. 1(e) ILO R131.
[60] ECtHR appl. No. 3976/05, Şerife Yiğit, 2 November 2010; ECtHR appl. No. 9957/08, Taddeucci and McCall, 10 February 2011.
[61] Art. 7.3 ILO C039; Art. 63.5 ILO C102; Art. 63.5 ECSS; Art. 21.4 ILO C128; Art. 64.4 Rev. ECSS.
[62] *Cf.* Cour constitutionnelle belge No. 138/99, 22 December 1999; Cour constitutionnelle belge No. 94/2001, 12 July 2001.
[63] Art. 7.4 ILO C039.
[64] Korda M (2013) The Role of International Social Security Standards. An in-depth study through the case of Greece. Antwerp: Intersentia, 87.

instruments do not contain any relevant provisions. Nonetheless, it follows from the definition of 'widow' in these instruments that the marriage between the breadwinner and his wife must be intact at the time of his death. In the absence of any contrary provisions in the instruments, which only establish minimum standards, national legislation may award survivors' benefits to the divorced or separated spouse of the deceased breadwinner. The breadwinner may have remarried and may thus have a new spouse. Only one instrument explicitly stipulates that in such cases, the amount of survivors' benefits for all adult beneficiaries can be limited to a single pension.[65] In the absence of specific regulations in other instruments, national legislation has discretion to decide on this matter.

With the exception of the Revised ECSS, the ILO and CoE instruments only mention widows as beneficiaries of survivors' benefits.[66] Given the traditional roles of men and women at the time, ILO C102 did not include a specific provision for ratifying countries to include widowers in survivors' benefit schemes. It was later proposed to include disabled and dependent widowers as beneficiaries to align ILO C128 with Article 18, para. 1 of ILO C121 on employment injury. Despite support for this proposal by most countries, this provision was rejected due to concerns that it might jeopardise many Member States' willingness to ratify ILO C128.[67] In contrast, the Revised ECSS promotes a gender-neutral approach, aiming to eliminate discrimination based on sex. It distances itself from the traditional view of women as homemakers[68], stating that each Contracting Party shall take appropriate measures to ensure equal treatment for protected persons of both sexes.[69] As regards survivors' benefits, "surviving spouses" rather than "surviving widows" are explicitly designated as beneficiaries of survivors' benefits. Member States may only temporarily reserve benefits

---

[65] Art. 7.5 ILO C039.
[66] Art. 3 ILO C039.
[67] Korda M (2013) The Role of International Social Security Standards. An in-depth study through the case of Greece. Antwerp: Intersentia, 87-88.
[68] Nickless J (2002) Code européen de sécurité sociale : Vademecum. Strasbourg: Conseil de l'Europe, 12-13.
[69] Art. 3.6 Rev. ECSS.

for widows only if their legislation specified that widows only are entitled to survivors' benefits at the time of consenting to the obligation of equal treatment.[70] As the Revised ECSS has not yet entered into force, it only serves as a policy guideline for national legislators. Survivors' benefit schemes are thus not required to protect widowers to comply with the ILO and CoE instruments.[71] Nonetheless, they allow for the implementation of more advantageous provisions, i.e. national legislation may grant widowers the same entitlement as widows to survivors' benefits, an approach that is recommended for all ILO Member States.[72]

The EU Recommendation does not contain any provision explicitly prohibiting unequal treatment on the basis of gender or sex. While Observation 25 recalls that Union law prohibits any form of direct or indirect discrimination on the basis of sex in all matters of social protection, it only refers to the relevant EU Directive. Yet, this Directive does not apply to statutory survivors' benefits.[73]

National constitutions and Article 14 of the European Convention on Human Rights, in conjunction with Article 8 or Article 1 of the First Protocol to the Convention, may require national legislation to treat widowers and widows equally.[74]

3.1.2. The dependant widow

The ILO and CoE instruments do not automatically guarantee widows entitlement to survivors' benefits. In fact, widows must fulfil certain conditions to qualify for these benefits. One instrument recommends ILO Member States to grant an allowance for a fixed period or to provide a lump sum benefit to widows who

---

[70] Art. 70 Rev. ECSS.
[71] Dijkhoff T (2011) International Social Security Standards in the European Union. The Cases of the Czech Republic and Estonia. Antwerp: Intersentia, 101.
[72] Para. 21 ILO R043; Para. 12 ILO R131.
[73] Art. 3.2 Directive 79/9 of 19 December 1978 on the progressive implementation of the principle of equal treatment for men and women in matters of social security.
[74] Cf. ECtHR, appl. No. 78630/12, Beeler v. Switzerland, 11 October 2022; cf. De Becker E (2023) Overview of recent cases before the European Court of Human Rights (October 2022 – December 2022). *European Journal of Social Security*, 87-94; Slingenberg L / Leijten I (2023) Social security in the case law of the European Court of Human Rights. In: Pennings F / Vonk G (Eds.) Research Handbook on European Social Security Law, Cheltenham: Edward Elgar Publishing Limited, 48-51, see also the contribution of Thomas Gächter in this book.

do not meet the necessary conditions, provided that the deceased breadwinner fulfilled the prescribed qualifying conditions.[75]

The first-generation instruments allowed national legislation to specifically reserve pensions for widows who had reached a specified age or suffered from invalidity.[76] Widows who did not meet these criteria were not automatically entitled to survivors' benefits. It was recommended, however, that if eligibility for survivors' benefits was contingent on conditions other than the completion of qualifying periods by the breadwinner, such benefits were to also be awarded to widows with a school-age dependant or a child under the age of 17, who is still enrolled in general or vocational education.[77]

The second-generation instruments allow an awarding of survivors' benefits to widows who are not capable of supporting themselves, in line with national legislation.[78] At the time, the criteria for awarding survivors' benefits varied considerably from one country to another. The new instruments therefore did not contain a specific provision outlining the circumstances under which a widow was considered incapable of supporting herself.[79] The supervising committees carefully assessed whether national legislation had exceeded the boundaries of their discretion in this matter.[80] For instance, they examined *what social protection measures were available to a widow who was manifestly incapable of supporting herself due to her advanced age and the virtual impossibility of finding employment after depending on her husband for many years.*[81] Relying on such an abstract concept renders it more difficult to define the precise scope of the contingency covered.[82]

---

[75] Para. 10 ILO R131.
[76] Art. 7.1 ILO C039.
[77] Para. 20(b) ILO R043.
[78] Art. 60.1 ILO C102; Art. 60.1 ECSS.
[79] As regards ILO C102, see Dijkhoff T (2011) International Social Security Standards in the European Union. The Cases of the Czech Republic and Estonia. Antwerp: Intersentia, 100-101.
[80] Dijkhoff T (2011) International Social Security Standards in the European Union. The Cases of the Czech Republic and Estonia. Antwerp: Intersentia, 189 and 293-294.
[81] Nickless J (2002) Code européen de sécurité sociale: Vademecum. Strasbourg: Conseil de l'Europe, 107; *cf.* Cour constitutionnelle belge No. 135/2017, 30 November 2017.
[82] Dijkhoff T (2011) International Social Security Standards in the European Union. The Cases of the Czech Republic and Estonia. Antwerp: Intersentia, 106.

Consequently, the third-generation instruments replaced the notion of 'incapability of supporting oneself' with more specific provisions. While the instruments still require the widow or spouse, respectively, to have been dependent on the deceased person at the time of the latter's death[83], they allow national legislation to award survivors' benefits to widows or spouses respectively who have reached a specified age which, however, may not exceed the maximum age prescribed for entitlement to old-age benefits.[84] Furthermore, they prohibit the application of the statutory pension age as prescribed by national law to surviving dependants who are invalid or incapacitated for work respectively, or who are caring for a dependent child belonging to the deceased breadwinner.[85] To be eligible to survivors' benefits, a widow must meet at least one of three conditions, namely she must have reached a specific age, suffer from invalidity, be incapacitated for work or have child care responsibilities.[86] Survivors' benefits must be awarded as long as the widow continues to suffer from invalidity, is incapacitated for work, or as long as she provides care for the deceased breadwinner's dependent child.[87] It is recommended for national legislation to provide all forms of assistance and access to all facilities, including training and job placement services alongside the payment of survivors' benefits, where appropriate, to help dependants find suitable employment.[88] Survivors' benefits should only be awarded when these eligibility criteria are met at the time of the

---

[83] Art. 1(f) ILO C128; Art. 1(g) Rev. ECSS.
[84] Art. 21.2 ILO C128; Art. 64.2 Rev. ECSS.
[85] Art. 21.3 ILO C128; Art. 64.3 Rev. ECSS.
[86] Korda M (2013) The Role of International Social Security Standards. An in-depth study through the case of Greece. Antwerp: Intersentia, 86.
[87] Art. 69 Rev. ECSS; CEACR, Direct Request, adopted 2007, published 97th ILC session (2008), Invalidity, Old-Age and Survivors' Benefits Convention, 1967 (No. 128) – Netherlands, https://www.ilo.org/dyn/normlex/en/f?p=1000:13100:0::NO:13100:P13100_COMMENT_ID,P11110_COUNTRY_ID,P11110_COUNTRY_NAME,P11110_COMMENT_YEAR:2279564,102768,Netherlands,2007; Korda M (2013) The Role of International Social Security Standards. An in-depth study through the case of Greece. Antwerp: Intersentia, 85.
[88] Para. 9 ILO R131; Art. 66.4 Rev. ECSS.

breadwinner's death. Not all countries have introduced provisions to that effect.[89] According to the ILO Bureau, widows expecting the deceased breadwinner's child should be afforded the same rights as widows who are caring for the deceased breadwinner's child(ren).[90]

Finally, the ILO and CoE instruments allow ratifying Member States to suspend – or according to Article 74.1 (j) Revised ECSS to withhold or withdraw – survivors' benefits, if the beneficiaries are engaged in a gainful activity in line with national law. Alternatively, Member States may opt to reduce the amount of contributory benefits if the beneficiaries' income exceeds a specified amount, or to reduce non-contributory benefits if the beneficiaries' income and/or other financial means exceed a specified amount.[91] This provision also applies to the beneficiaries of other types of benefits. This possibility is as an additional indication of the principle that survivors' benefits can be exclusively reserved for beneficiaries who are not capable of supporting themselves or who were financially dependent on the deceased breadwinner.

3.2. The child(ren)

The ILO and CoE instruments, in addition to the widow, also include the deceased breadwinner's children as beneficiaries of survivors' benefits. We first examine the definition of 'child' in these instruments (3.2.1) and then explore under what conditions children are presumed to be dependent on the deceased breadwinner (3.2.2).

3.2.1. The notion of child

The ILO and CoE instruments designate the breadwinner's children as beneficiaries of survivors' benefits, without a distinction being made between half and full orphans.[92]

---

[89] Korda M (2013) The Role of International Social Security Standards. An in-depth study through the case of Greece. Antwerp: Intersentia, 86-87.
[90] Korda M (2013) The Role of International Social Security Standards. An in-depth study through the case of Greece. Antwerp: Intersentia, 86.
[91] Art. 11.2(e) and 21.1 ILO C039; Art. 60.2 ILO C102; Art. 60.2 ECSS; Art. 31.1 ILO C128.
[92] Art. 6 C039; Art. 61 ILO C102; Art. 61 ECSS; ECSS Protocol; Art. 22 ILO C128; Art. 65 Rev. ECSS.

The first-generation instruments explicitly allowed children of either parent to qualify as beneficiaries, provided that their right to survivors' benefits was contingent on the child's mother having contributed to the child's support or that she was a widow at the time of her own death.[93] Despite later proposals for the breadwinner's child to be entitled, as a general rule, to survivors' benefits, regardless whether the deceased breadwinner was the child's father or mother,[94] neither the second- nor the third-generation instruments include an explicit provision addressing this issue. As the instruments only establish minimum standards, national law may stipulate that children are entitled to survivors' benefits if their mother was the main breadwinner, even if the surviving widower himself does not qualify as a beneficiary.

The first-generation instruments focussed exclusively on the legitimate children of the deceased breadwinner. This follows from a provision that explicitly allowed national legislation to specify cases in which children other than the breadwinner's legitimate ones might also be entitled to survivors' benefits.[95] Later instruments do not include a similar provision, however. They only mention the deceased breadwinner's widow and children as beneficiaries of survivors' benefits. Despite the use of the terms "the widow" and "the children", one might be inclined to think that only the breadwinner's legitimate children qualify as beneficiaries. However, national law may award survivors' benefits to children born outside the breadwinner's marriage, as explicitly stipulated in ILO C128, which allows for the protection of dependants other than the deceased breadwinner's widow and children. As the ILO and CoE instruments only establish minimum standards, they allow national legislation to award survivors' benefits to the deceased breadwinner's children born outside of wedlock. Survivors' benefits may in fact even be extended to children who are not direct descendants of the deceased breadwinner or his spouse, such as, for instance, the breadwinner's younger siblings or a child of his deceased sibling.

---

[93] Art. 8 ILO C039.
[94] Dijkhoff T (2011) International Social Security Standards in the European Union. The Cases of the Czech Republic and Estonia. Antwerp: Intersentia, 101.
[95] Art. 8.3 ILO C039.

3.2.2. Dependent child(ren)

As is the case for widows, the deceased breadwinner's surviving children are not automatically entitled to survivors' benefits. Survivors' benefits may be denied to orphans who have reached a specific age. Initially, this age was set at 14 years,[96] and later raised to 15 years,[97] while it is set at 16 years in another instrument.[98]

The third-generation instruments introduced an adjustable higher age alongside the set age limits. The instruments require national legislation to award survivors' benefits to children up to the specified (higher) age, if the children are students, apprentices, suffer from a chronic illness or have a disability that prevents them from engaging in a gainful activity.[99] To offer greater flexibility, ILO C128 expanded the conditions outlined in ILO C102 according to which children must be considered as being dependent on the breadwinner to be eligible for survivors' benefits. The instrument's provisions were aligned with those of ILO C121 on employment injury, which had already considerably broadened the notion of children compared to ILO C102. Therefore, and given that only few countries at the time awarded survivors' benefits to orphans without imposing any age limit, the proposal to extend survivors' benefits to disabled children without a given age restriction was rejected.[100] In this respect, the ECSS Protocol holds a special position and sets the maximum age at 16 years, but grants the Contracting Parties the possibility to reduce the age limit to 15 years, provided that this lower age threshold is raised to 18 years for children who are pursuing a higher education or an apprenticeship, or have a disability.

4. Survivors' benefits

The EU Recommendation does not explicitly define the nature of survivors' benefits. According to the ILO and CoE instruments, survivors' benefits must

---

[96] Art. 8.1 ILO C039),
[97] Art. 1.1(d) ILO C102; Art. 1.1(h) ECSS; Art. 1(h) ILO C128; 1(f) ILO R131.
[98] Art. 1(h) Rev. ECSS.
[99] Art. 1(h) ILO C128; 1(f) ILO R131; Art. 1(h) Rev. ECSS.
[100] Korda M (2013) The Role of International Social Security Standards. An in-depth study through the case of Greece. Antwerp: Intersentia, 91-92.

be regularly paid[101], meaning that payments of a set amount must be made at regular intervals.[102] The periodic nature of survivors' benefits thus, in principle, excludes lump sum payments which might signal uncertainty to beneficiaries in terms of the amount they will receive or what they will be able to afford at a given time.[103] The next section analyses the duration of payment of survivors' benefits in the ILO and CoE instruments and the EU Recommendation (4.1), and how those benefits must be calculated (4.2).

4.1. Duration of payment of survivors' benefits

The EU Recommendation allows Member States to limit the duration of payment of benefits to prevent abuse of survivors' benefits schemes and to safeguard their financial sustainability. Other policy goals may also justify limitations to the duration of payment of survivors' benefits. The EU Recommendation does not, however, specify a minimum duration of payment of survivors' benefits.[104] In contrast, the ILO and CoE instruments require survivors' benefits to be paid throughout the contingency[105], meaning that the payment of benefits may not be limited for reasons other than the end of the contingency.[106] As a result, survivors' benefits are often paid over an extended period. Therefore, with the exception of the first-generation instruments, the ILO and CoE instruments require regular adjustments to the amount of the benefits to ensure they continue to be in line with current economic conditions, especially in the face of substantial changes in the cost of living.[107]

---

[101] Art. 62 ILO C102; Art. 62 ECSS; Art. 23 ILO C128; Art. 66 Rev. ECSS.
[102] Cf. Nickless J (2002) Code européen de sécurité sociale: Vademecum. Strasbourg: Conseil de l'Europe, 8-9.
[103] Korda M (2013) The Role of International Social Security Standards. An in-depth study through the case of Greece. Antwerp: Intersentia, 111-112.
[104] Van Limberghen G (2023) Setting European Social Security Standards for the Self-Employed: The Interaction Between the European Code of Social Security and the EU Recommendation on Access to Social Protection. In: Jorens Y (Ed.) The Lighthouse Function of Social Law. Proceedings of the ISLSSL XIV European Regional Congress Ghent 2023, Cham: Springer, 289.
[105] Art. 64 ILO C102; Art. 64 ECSS; Art. 25 ILO C128; Art. 68 Rev. ECSS.
[106] Art. 69 Rev. ECSS; Dijkhoff T (2011) International Social Security Standards in the European Union. The Cases of the Czech Republic and Estonia. Antwerp: Intersentia, 103.
[107] Art. 65.10 and Art. 66.8 ILO C102; Art. 65.10 and Art. 66.8 ECSS; Art. 29.1 ILO C128; Para. 24 ILO R131; Art. 71.12 Rev. ECSS.

The contingency clearly comes to an end when the beneficiary dies or when the dependent child exceeds the prescribed age limit or is no longer a student or an apprentice. It can be argued that widowhood ceases when a widow remarries. Nonetheless, it was deemed appropriate to explicitly address this issue in the ILO and CoE instruments. According to the first-generation instruments, survivors' benefit schemes should, at a minimum, confer pension rights to widows who have not remarried.[108] Later instruments also stipulated that survivors' benefits could be suspended if the widow was cohabiting with a man as his registered partner or in case she remarried,[109] in line with national law either more generally or with social security regulations specifically. The phrase 'living with a man as his wife' suggests that national legislation can opt to suspend survivors' benefits in case of cohabitation as well.[110]

The concept of suspension as explicitly stipulated in Art. 74.1(i) of the Revised ECSS is to be understood as denying the payment of or withdrawing of benefits. However, the terms 'at minimum' and 'may' imply that national legislation does not have to deny, suspend or withdraw benefits in case the widow remarries, since the legislation of some countries did not at the time include such provisions. It can thus be concluded that national legislation has enjoyed considerable leeway with respect to consequences related to the widow's remarriage and may, for instance, decide whether a widow's rights based on her first marriage should be reinstated in the event of the death of her second husband, particularly if this second marriage did not entitle her to survivors' benefits.[111]

4.2. Calculation of the amount of survivors' benefits

Article 11 of the EU Recommendation calls on Member States to ensure that survivors' benefit schemes provide an adequate level of protection to the breadwinner's dependants, with the aim of maintaining a decent standard of

---

[108] Art. 6 ILO C039; Para. 20(a) ILO R043.
[109] Art. 74.1(i) Rev. ECSS.
[110] Art. 11.2(d) ILO C039; Art. 69(j) ILO C102; Art. 68(j) ECSS; Art. 32. (g) ILO C128).
[111] Korda M (2013) The Role of International Social Security Standards. An in-depth study through the case of Greece. Antwerp: Intersentia, 80-90.

living and offering adequate income replacement while also preventing beneficiaries from falling into poverty. Hence, the EU Recommendation clearly outlines the targets to be achieved by the Member States. Yet the targeted level of benefits is described in an abstract way. This does not necessarily come as a surprise, given that Article 1, para. 1 of the EU Recommendation does not intend to prejudice Member States' autonomy to organise their social protection system. Consequently, the EU Recommendation neither defines what constitutes a decent standard of living or an adequate income replacement, nor does it outline how Member States should assess whether beneficiaries are sufficiently protected from falling into poverty.[112] Article 11 of the EU Recommendation only stipulates that Member States must assess the adequacy of their social protection system as a whole. Hence, social assistance schemes may be included in assessments of the adequacy of a Member State's overall social protection system, while according to its Article 4, the EU Recommendation does not apply to social assistance schemes as such. Social insurance benefits that are based on equating social contributions with benefits does not always prevent low-income beneficiaries from falling into poverty. Member States should therefore align their social protection schemes to ensure coherence across all Member States. Verifying whether the recommended level of benefits is ensured becomes more complex when benefits provided by social assistance schemes must be taken into consideration as well.[113]

In contrast, from the outset,[114] the ILO and CoE instruments have allowed national legislation to independently determine the method of calculation of survivors' benefits, provided that the benefits provided meet at least the minimum level specified in the instruments. This makes it easier to verify whether

---

[112] Cf. Aranguiz A / Bednarowicz B (2019) Access to social protection, for some, 4, https://socialeurope.eu/access-to-social-protection-for-some (accessed on 5 February 2024); Schoukens P / Bruynseraede C (2021) Access to social protection for self-employed and non-standard workers. An analysis based upon the EU Recommendation on access to social protection. Leuven: Acco, 83-84.

[113] Lelie P (2021) La recommandation du conseil de l'union européenne relative à l'accès des travailleurs salariés et non-salariés à la protection sociale. Une occasion de préparer à l'avenir les systèmes de protection sociale des Etats membres de l'UE. *Revue belge de sécurité sociale*, 31; Schoukens P (2020) Digitalisation and social security in the EU. The case of platform work: from work protection to income protection?, *European Journal of Social Security*, 445-449.

[114] Art. 9 C039.

survivors' benefits meet the required minimum level. Next, we examine how the ILO and CoE instruments establish the required minimum level of survivors' benefits within the scope of social insurance schemes (4.2.1). We then focus on the relationship between the required minimum level of such social insurance benefits and the duration of qualification periods (4.2.2). Finally, we take a look at how the instruments establish the minimum level of survivors' benefits within the scope of social assistance schemes (4.2.3).

4.2.1. Minimum level of survivors' benefits within the scope of social insurance schemes

The amount of survivors' benefits must at the very least represent a specified percentage of the deceased breadwinner's previous earnings, depending on the relevant instrument, as presented in Figure 2.[115]

Figure 2. Prescribed percentage of the deceased breadwinner's previous earnings

Prescribed ratio	40%[116]	45%	55%	65%
Instrument(s)	ILO C102 ECSS	ILO C128 Protocol ECSS	ILO R131	Rev. ECSS

Only one instrument stipulates that the deceased breadwinner's previous earnings must be reviewed under specific conditions, in response to changes in the beneficiary's overall level of earnings or in the cost of living.[117] By not imposing a fixed amount of survivors' benefits in a specific currency, the ILO and CoE

---

[115] Art. 66-67 ILO C102; Art. 65-67 ECSS; Protocol ECSS; Art. 26-29 ILO C128; Par. 22 ILO R131; Art. 71-73 Rev. ECSS.
[116] The proposed rate of 30 per cent was ultimately raised to 40 per cent, which is also the prescribed rate for old-age pensions, invalidity benefits and employment injury benefits, because this minimum rate may be lowered for schemes that require qualifying periods of no more than five years (Dijkhoff T (2011) International Social Security Standards in the European Union. The Cases of the Czech Republic and Estonia. Antwerp: Intersentia, 103).
[117] Art. 71.11 Rev. ECSS.

instruments acknowledge the differences in the standard of living across Member States. Moreover, the application of a replacement rate aims to ensure that surviving dependants can maintain a certain standard of living, an approach that is generally recommended for ILO Member States.[118]

The replacement ratio applies to standard beneficiaries to ensure equivalent benefit levels across all types of survivors' benefit schemes. A widow with two children is considered the standard beneficiary of survivors' benefits. If the widow does not have a pension of her own, her two children must be awarded at least the same minimum benefit amount.[119] From a practical point of view, the sum of survivors' benefits for a widow with two children and any additional family allowance should be at least equal to the fixed percentage of the sum of the deceased breadwinner's previous earnings and any applicable family allowance provided prior to the breadwinner's death.[120] The benefit provided to other beneficiaries, for instance for widows without children or with more than two children, should be reasonably proportional to the standard amount of survivors' benefits provided. With one exception, the ILO and CoE instruments do not explicitly specify what is to be understood as reasonably proportional. The Revised ECSS's Schedule to Part IX sets the minimum level for widows at 50 per cent and 20 per cent for a child, whereas the replacement ratio for the standard beneficiary is 65 per cent.

To provide more flexibility, the ILO and CoE instruments allow survivors' benefits to be calculated on the basis of capped wages, provided that the wage

---

[118] Para. 23 ILO R131.
[119] Dijkhoff T (2011) International Social Security Standards in the European Union. The Cases of the Czech Republic and Estonia. Antwerp: Intersentia, 103; Protocol ECSS.
[120] Gómez Heredero A (2009) Social security. Protection at the international level and developments in Europe. Strasbourg: Council of Europe Publishing, 98-102 and 156-166; Nickless J (2002) Code européen de sécurité sociale: Vademecum. Strasbourg: Conseil de l'Europe, 63-67; cf. as to ILO C102, Dijkhoff T (2011) International Social Security Standards in the European Union. The Cases of the Czech Republic and Estonia. Antwerp: Intersentia, 53-62 and 112-119, Korda M (2013) The Role of International Social Security Standards. An in-depth study through the case of Greece. Antwerp: Intersentia, 112-119; Praet B / Morsa M (2020) Le code européen de sécurité sociale: un étalon de valeur comme référence pour les systèmes de sécurité sociale européens?. *Revue belge de sécurité sociale*, 635-638.

ceiling meets the minimum replacement ratio relative to a skilled labourer's average wage. Member States may also provide flat rate benefits as long as these meet at least the prescribed replacement ratio relative to an unskilled labourer's average wage. As a result, the stipulated minimum level of flat rate benefits is lower than the minimum level of benefits calculated as a percentage of capped wages. By establishing the required minimum levels for both flat-rate benefits and benefits calculated on the basis of capped wages, the ILO and CoE instruments suggest that survivors' benefits should protect beneficiaries from falling into poverty. However, these minimum levels do not guarantee that the beneficiaries will remain out of poverty, since the instruments do not directly refer to any poverty threshold.[121]

In this respect, the European Committee of Social Rights monitors the application of the (Revised) European Social Charter which in Article 12 stipulates that Member States' social security system must safeguard an adequate level of protection that is at least equivalent to that required for the ratification of the European Code of Social Security. The Committee calls for the amount of social insurance benefits to be at least equal to the national poverty line, which it set at 50 per cent of the equivalised median income determined by Eurostat. However, the Committee acknowledges that if a benefit amounts to at least 40 per cent of the equivalised median income, the standard set by the Committee can be achieved by providing complementary benefits, such as those granted by social assistance schemes.[122]

---

[121] Van Limberghen G / Dumont D / Louckx F / Marchal S / Cantillon B (2021) Un regard critique et propositionnel sur les assurances sociales des salariés et des indépendants. Analyse au départ de la recommandation de l'Union européenne relative à l'accès des travailleurs à la protection sociale. *Revue belge de sécurité sociale*, 66.

[122] Council of Europe (2022) Digest of the case law, 120-121 and 126-127, https://rm.coe.int/digest-ecsr-prems-106522-web-en/1680a95dbd (accessed on 5 February 2024); Mikkola M (2015) The development of European social security standards. In: Pennings F / Vonk G (Eds.) Research Handbook on European Social Security Law. Cheltenham: Edward Elgar Publishing Limited, 154-157.

4.2.2. Setting minimum levels of social insurance benefits based on the duration of qualifying periods

As already discussed above,[123] entitlement to survivors' benefits can be made conditional on the completion of a qualifying period by the breadwinner, the maximum duration of which is specified in the ILO and CoE instruments. If national legislation applies such qualifying periods, it must ensure that survivors' benefits reach the amount prescribed by the applicable instrument if the breadwinner has fulfilled the maximum duration of the applicable qualifying period established by the given instrument. According to the first-generation instruments, only a minimum benefit rate had to be guaranteed in case survivors' benefits were awarded without the requirement for breadwinners to complete a specific qualifying period.[124]

Later instruments stipulated that the guaranteed benefit amount could be reduced if the deceased breadwinner had only completed a 5-year qualifying period (instead of a minimum of 15 years) of contributions or years of employment in line with the prescribed regulations.[125] If the spouse and children of all economically active persons are protected, the same applies when the breadwinner has only completed a qualifying period of 3 years of contributions and has only contributed half of the yearly average (instead of the yearly average) number of required contributions.[126] In that case, national legislation may award benefits to the breadwinner's beneficiaries at a reduced rate up to a maximum of 10 per cent less than the prescribed standard rate.[127]

Throughout the negotiations leading up to the adoption of ILO C128, agreeing on a greater reduction proved challenging, whereas the proposed 10 per cent decrease corresponded to that already established in ILO C102.[128] National legislation may apply a proportional reduction of the normally prescribed minimum percentage for qualifying periods of over 5 years but less than 15

---

[123] *Supra*, 2.2.3. The effectively insured breadwinner.
[124] Art. 9.2 ILO C039.
[125] Art. 63.2(a) ILO C102; Art. 63.2(a) ECSS; Art. 24.2 ILO C128.
[126] Art. 63.2(b) ILO C102; Art. 63. (b) ECSS; Art. 24.2 ILO C128.
[127] Art. 63.3 ILO C102; Art. 24.3 ILO C128.
[128] Korda M (2013) The Role of International Social Security Standards. An in-depth study through the case of Greece. Antwerp: Intersentia, 99.

years of contributions or years of employment.[129] The Revised ECSS offers even greater flexibility by allowing benefits to be reduced in proportion to the completed qualifying period if it is shorter than the maximum duration of the qualifying periods set by the Revised ECSS.[130] When national legislation awards benefits that are calculated independently of the qualifying period, the benefit amount must be at least equal to 90 per cent of the standard rate if the breadwinner has completed a qualifying period of no more than 12 months in accordance with prescribed rules.[131]

4.2.3. Minimum level of survivors' benefits within the scope of social assistance schemes

The ILO and CoE instruments allow Member States to provide survivors' benefits through a social assistance scheme to protect resident widows and children whose financial means fall below a specified threshold. According to the first-generation instruments, national legislation had to establish this threshold, taking the minimum cost of living into account and determining up to what level the beneficiaries' means were to be excluded from an assessment of the general threshold. The amount of benefits, in addition to any means exceeding the exempted income, had to adequately cover the beneficiaries' essential needs.[132]

Later instruments stipulated that the benefit rate must be established in accordance with a prescribed scale or a scale determined by the competent public authority in conformity with applicable regulations. The instruments only required the beneficiary's means to be exempt if they exceeded the threshold determined by national legislation. The sum of the awarded benefits and the beneficiary's non-exempted means must be sufficient to maintain the beneficiary's livelihood and may at the same time not be less than the benefit calculated as the required percentage of wage of an ordinary adult male worker. Furthermore, the instruments provided Member States with the option of conducting an overall assessment of the beneficiary's overall income. Accordingly,

---

[129] Art. 63.4 ILO C102; Art. 24.4 ILO C128.
[130] Art. 66.6 Rev. ECSS.
[131] Art. 66.7 Rev. ECSS.
[132] Art.21-22 ILO C039; Para. 22 and 24 ILO R043.

the prescribed benefit level is deemed to have been reached if the total amount of survivors' benefits paid exceeds the total amount of benefits by at least 30 per cent, which would have been obtained if the benefits had been calculated in accordance with the calculation outlined above under a scheme that covers 20 per cent of all residents (in line with ILO C102 or ECSS) or 75 per cent of the economically active population (in line with ILO C128).[133]

5. Concluding remarks

The socioeconomic transformations that are having a profound impact on survivors' benefit schemes in European countries began unfolding after the adoption of the international and European instruments analysed here, which set minimum standards for survivor benefit schemes. It therefore does not come as a surprise that these instruments largely disregard the ongoing societal developments that countries are responding to or are planning to respond to by adapting their survivors' benefit schemes. The Revised ECSS no longer designates widows as the beneficiary of survivors' benefits but refers to the 'surviving spouse'. This, however, is only a minor adaptation following from the European Convention on Human Rights in conjunction with Article 8 or Article 1 of the First Protocol to the Convention, as well as from many countries' constitutions. Moreover, the Revised ECSS has not yet entered into force. The recent EU Recommendation fails to directly address the socioeconomic shifts that are having a significant impact on survivors' benefit schemes. Instead, it invites EU Member States to adapt their social protection schemes to accommodate contemporary labour market shifts, particularly the rise of atypical and self-employed work. Viewed from this perspective, the Recommendation breathes new life into entitlements to survivors' benefits.

The ILO and CoE instruments, with the exception of the Revised ECSS, have centred around a family structure consisting of the deceased male breadwinner and his surviving wife, and have not been adjusted to increasing female

---

[133] Art. 67 ILO C102; Art. 67 ECSS; Art. 28 ILO C128; Art. 73 Rev. ECSS; see Korda M (2013) The Role of International Social Security Standards. An in-depth study through the case of Greece. Antwerp: Intersentia, 117-118; Nickless J (2002) Code européen de sécurité sociale : Vademecum. Strasbourg: Conseil de l'Europe, 63-65.

employment. As regards surviving adults, the marriage requirement neglects the rapidly growing number of divorced spouses, as well as registered and *de facto* partnerships. This, however, does not mean that the instruments prevent national legislation from adapting survivors' benefit schemes to the changing circumstances. By establishing minimum standards only, the instruments allow national legislation to award benefits in case the deceased person was not a male breadwinner, nor the family's only or the primary breadwinner, or in case the breadwinner was no longer socially insured at the time of his or her death. They also do not prevent other categories of dependants in addition to widows from qualifying as beneficiaries of survivors' benefits, as explicitly stipulated in some third-generation instruments. National legislation may also deny, suspend or withdraw benefits in case of remarriage or cohabitation. Furthermore, the instruments allow national legislation to award survivors' benefits to the breadwinner's children who were born outside of wedlock, and even to children who are neither direct descendants of the deceased breadwinner nor of his or her spouse.

None of the instruments requires national law to grant an unconditional right to survivors' benefits. Surviving children, as well as adult dependants must fulfil certain conditions which can depend on the amount of the breadwinner's income at the time of his or her death. The second-generation instruments allow survivors' benefits to be exclusively reserved for widows who are not capable of supporting themselves in line with national legislation. In this respect, Dijkhoff argues that a broad interpretation of the notion of incapability of supporting oneself conflicts with a far-reaching individualisation of social security rights.[134] Nonetheless, such an abstract concept renders it more difficult to define the precise scope of the contingency covered. Therefore, the third-generation instruments have replaced the notion of incapability of supporting oneself with more specific provisions, which allow survivors' benefits to be reserved for widows who meet specific criteria, such as having reached a prescribed age, being incapacitated for work or caring for the deceased breadwinner's dependent

---

[134] Dijkhoff T (2011) International Social Security Standards in the European Union. The Cases of the Czech Republic and Estonia. Antwerp: Intersentia, 194.

child. Yet the ban on imposing an age requirement for widows who are caring for a dependent child seems to be at odds with the widespread phenomenon of single mothers with children, who are engaged in professional work.

The ILO and CoE instruments are not immutable laws of nature. Their provisions often reflect the greatest common denominator of national social security laws at a given time, and they are regularly adapted to reflect the developments in the respective field. The adaptation or interpretation of treaty provisions should therefore ensure that national legislation is not prevented from adapting the Member State's survivors' benefit schemes to changing social circumstances and from removing inconsistencies related to survivors' benefits. Denying survivors access to social protection following the breadwinner's death would be at odds with the instruments' provisions. Moreover, even in contemporary society, there are compelling reasons to continue to uphold statutory social security benefits aimed at mitigating the financial repercussions of the loss of the breadwinner.[135] Yet lifelong survivors' pensions should not be automatically granted in all cases.

---

[135] See e.g. Alofs E / Hoop R (2009) The sustainability of survivor and divorce benefits in the adult worker model: incorporation of new social risks. In: Verschraegen B (Ed.) Family Finances. Vienna: Jan Sramek Verlag, 49-70.

Bibliography

Alofs E and Hoop R (2009) The sustainability of survivor and divorce benefits in the adult worker model: incorporation of new social risks. In: Verschraegen B. (Ed.) Family Finances. Vienna: Jan Sramek Verlag, 49-70.

Aranguiz A and Bednarowicz B (2019) Access to social protection, for some, https://socialeurope.eu/access-to-social-protection-for-some (last consulted on 5 February 2024).

De Becker E (2023) Overview of recent cases before the European court of human rights (October 2022 – December 2022). *European Journal of Social Security*, 87-94.

Dijkhoff T (2011) International Social Security Standards in the European Union. The Cases of the Czech Republic and Estonia. Antwerp: Intersentia, 448 ff.

Freudenberg C, Kapuy K and Zwinger V (2022) *How to design survivor benefits in the 21st century?*. International Social Security Association, 44 ff.

Gómez Heredero A (2009) Social security. Protection at the international level and developments in Europe. Strasbourg: Council of Europe Publishing, 241 ff.

Hermans K (2014) De WW en nieuwe sociale risico's Internationaalrechtelijke grenzen aan hervormingsvoorstellen. Deventer: Wolters Kluwer business, 467 ff.

Korda M (2013) The Role of International Social Security Standards. An in-depth study through the case of Greece. Antwerp: Intersentia, 763 ff.

Lelie P (2021) La recommandation du conseil de l'union européenne relative à l'accès des travailleurs salariés et non-salariés à la protection sociale. Une occasion de préparer à l'avenir les systèmes de protection sociale des Etats membres de l'UE. *Revue belge de sécurité sociale*, 5-48.

Mikkola M (2015) The development of European social security standards. In: Pennings F. and Vonk G (Eds.) Research Handbook on European Social Security Law. Cheltenham: Edward Elgar,149-160.

Myers RJ and Yoffee WM (1966) Social Security Issues: Fiftieth International Labour Conference. *Social Security Bulletin*. November 1966: 20-37, https://www.ssa.gov/policy/docs/ssb/v29n11/v29n11p20.pdf (last consulted on 5 February 2024).

Nickless J (2002) Code européen de sécurité sociale: Vademecum. Strasbourg : Conseil de l'Europe, 81 ff.

Praet B and Morsa M (2020) Le code européen de sécurité sociale : un étalon de valeur comme référence pour les systèmes de sécurité sociale européens ?. *Revue belge de sécurité sociale*, 603-650.

Schoukens P (2020) Digitalisation and social security in the EU. The case of platform work: from work protection to income protection?, *European Journal of Social Security*, 434-451.

Schoukens P (2021) Building Up and Implementing the European Standards for Platform Workers. In: Becker U and Chesalina O (Eds.) Social Law 4.0. New Approaches for Ensuring and Financing Social Security in the Digital Age. Baden-Baden: Nomos, 309-334.

Schoukens P and Bruynseraede C (2021) Access to social protection for self-employed and non-standard workers. An analysis based upon the EU Recommendation on access to social protection. Leuven: Acco, 159 ff.

Slingenberg L and Leijten I (2023) Social security in the case law of the European Court of Human Rights. In: Pennings F and Vonk G (Eds.) Research Handbook on European Social Security Law, Cheltenham: Edward Elgar Publishing Limited, 30-63.

Van Limberghen G (2023) Setting European Social Security Standards for the Self-Employed: The Interaction Between the European Code of Social Security and the EU Recommendation on Access to Social Protection. In: Jorens Y (Ed.) The Lighthouse Function of Social Law. Proceedings of the ISLSSL XIV European Regional Congress Ghent 2023, Cham: Springer, 281-298.

Van Limberghen G, Dumont D, Louckx F, Marchal S and Cantillon B (2021) Un regard critique et propositionnel sur les assurances sociales des salariés et des indépendants. Analyse au départ de la recommandation de l'Union européenne relative à l'accès des travailleurs a la protection sociale. *Revue belge de sécurité sociale*, 49-134.

5 How to Design Survivors' Benefits in the 21st Century?

Verena Zwinger and Christoph Freudenberg

1. Introduction[1]

Survivors' benefits[2] are an essential component of social security in many countries. Nearly 10 per cent of women aged 20 years and older receive survivors' benefits in selected OECD countries.[3] The impact of these benefits is also evident from a fiscal perspective. OECD countries spend around 0.8 per cent of their gross domestic product (GDP) on survivors' benefits, which is more than the amount spent on unemployment benefits (around 0.6 per cent of GDP).

This chapter explores major international trends in the design of survivors' benefits and compares key parameters of the current legal frameworks in around 50 countries worldwide. These include the design of survivors' benefits in terms of eligibility age, coverage and replacement rates. Based on these legal parameters, empirical findings are presented on the impact of survivor benefit regulations on the adequacy of survivors' income and labour market participation of survivors. Moreover, the study's results highlight changes in socio-economic trends that affect the financial position of survivors – such as female labour market participation – over time and across different countries.

---

[1] This chapter is based on a project conducted by the Pension Insurance Institution (PVA) and the German Federal Pension Insurance (DRV) within the 2020–2022 triennium of the International Social Security Association (ISSA), and represents selected and, where necessary, slightly modified sections of the project's report (full version) in English. See Freudenberg / Kapuy / Zwinger, How to design survivor benefits in the 21st century?, Technical Commission on Old-Age, Invalidity and Survivors' Insurance, ISSA, 2022.

[2] Benefits for orphans are not covered in this chapter.

[3] Own calculations based on OECD figures.

Finally, the chapter outlines recent reforms in survivor benefit schemes in response to these socio-economic trends.

2. Historical aspects: When and why were survivors' benefits introduced?

The introduction of survivors' benefits sought to improve the financial situation of widows at a time when the traditional male (sole) breadwinner model was prevalent.[4] Historically, the primary purpose was to prevent survivors from falling into poverty following the loss of the family's breadwinner. Today, however, the focus has shifted towards ensuring that both widows and widowers[5] can maintain their standard of living after the death of the spouse (partner).[6] Consequently, the initial objective of poverty prevention has become less important taken a backseat and is now increasingly addressed by measures that seek to fight poverty, such as social assistance benefits.

---

[4] The first benefits for widows date back to the 17th century, with an expansion beginning in the mid-20th century.
[5] Considering current socio-economic developments, such as gender equality of women and men based on the realization of individual entitlements.
[6] See also James, Rethinking Survivor Benefits, The World Bank, 2009.

3. How are survivor benefit schemes structured globally?

We compared 47 countries based on selected criteria to identify similarities between existing survivors' benefit schemes. The selection of countries followed a three-stage approach, namely by world region,[7] population size and World Bank income category.[8] The parameters compared included, among others, the minimum eligibility age for permanent benefits (3.1), the personal scope of survivors' benefits (3.2), and the gender distribution among recipients (3.3). Simulations were used to determine the average replacement rate in 40 countries (3.4). The results are based on database research,[9] our own calculations, and responses to a questionnaire distributed to 30 International Social Security Association (ISSA) members.

3.1. Minimum eligibility age for permanent benefits

No minimum eligibility age for permanent survivors' benefits applies in around two-thirds (29) of the 47 countries analysed. This figure increases to nearly 90 per cent in case of dependent children for the countries included in this specific analysis (41 countries). Various age limits apply to both women and men in a total of six countries (including e.g. Saudi Arabia or Moldova).

3.2. Personal scope of application

In 45 of the 47 countries, the spouse is entitled to survivors' benefits.[10] Registered partners are entitled to survivors' benefits in 12 of the 47 countries (e.g. Honduras, Italy). Divorced spouses/separated partners can claim survivors' benefits in nine countries (e.g. Egypt, Spain), while maintaining a joint household may be a sufficient condition to qualify for permanent survivors' benefits in five countries (e.g. Hungary, Mexico). In 35 countries, other close relatives of the deceased (e.g. parents, siblings) are also entitled to survivors' benefits. Such arrangements are particularly common in Arabic countries (e.g. Oman).

---

[7] The nomenclature of ISSA's world regions was used (America, Europe, Africa, Asia).
[8] These are classified as "high", "upper middle", "lower middle" and "low".
[9] ISSA country profiles, MISSOC, World Bank.
[10] In the remaining two countries, i.e. Kenya and Nepal, it is customary to name a surviving dependant who is entitled to survivors' benefits.

Since 2000, there has been a tendency to extend the scope of personal coverage.

3.3. Distribution of recipients by sex

Although four out of five survivor benefit recipients are (still) female,[11] a notable trend seems to be emerging: according to data derived from the ISSA questionnaires, the share of male survivor benefit recipients between 2000 and 2019 increased in 16 of 18 countries (where sufficient data were available). On average, there was a 4.1 percentage point (pp) increase, reaching 15.7 per cent in 2019.[12] This trend is even more pronounced when considering the new male beneficiaries in 2019 only, accounting for 18.7 per cent. This development is most likely due to the inclusion of male spouses/partners in the group of eligible persons; a reduction in age differences among couples, and an increasing share of women who have their own pension entitlements.

3.4. Replacement rates and calculation of survivors' benefits

Another important indicator in international comparisons is benefit amount and replacement rate. To ensure comparability, simulations for standardized widows' cases were conducted. The key indicator used was the *survivor replacement rate*, which measures survivors' benefits as a share of benefits paid to the deceased prior to his or her death.[13]

To determine the *survivor replacement rate*, it was assumed that both partners were aged 70 years and that the spouse or partner's death occurred in 2019, with all national requirements for eligibility to survivors' benefits having been met. In this scenario, the fictional (female) surviving dependant received 50 per cent of the deceased's (male) old-age pension, which corresponded to

---

[11] United Nations, Estimates and Projections of Women of Reproductive Age Who Are Married or in a Union: 2020 Revision, https://www.un.org/en/development/desa/population/theme/marriage-unions/marriage_estimates.asp (accessed on 9.2.2024).

[12] The highest increase was recorded in Peru (+29 PP), Spain (+28 PP) and Chile (+23 PP).

[13] Due to national calculation methods and data availability, the "survivor replacement rate" exclusively considers the share of the deceased's pension income. Additional calculations, including other social benefits based, for example, on periods of residence measured against average income for selected countries, can be found in the full version of the project report.

the average pension in 2019 (i.e. in the year of death) in the respective country (*basic scenario*).

We find that the level of the *survivor replacement rate* necessary to maintain the standard of living depends on the distribution of household income between the partners prior to the other's death. The higher the surviving dependant's own income, the lower the survivor replacement rate. Additionally, economies of scale should also be considered, as singles have a higher per capita expenditure than couples, given that costs such as housing, electricity and other fixed costs cannot be shared. Taking these factors into account, we estimate that a replacement rate of 50-56 per cent of the deceased's pension would be necessary in our base scenario to maintain the living standards following the spouse's death, while 66-71 per cent of the deceased's pension would be required in more traditional couple formations where the deceased was the sole breadwinner.

In around half of the countries included in our analysis, a *survivor replacement rate* of 50-60 per cent is provided, which is deemed sufficient to maintain the living standards in our base scenario. Some countries have a much higher replacement rate of well over 60 per cent (e.g. Brazil, Iran and Colombia). The standard of living following the death of a spouse may even improve, while in countries with a comparatively low replacement rate of far below 50 per cent (e.g. Belgium, Hungary or Japan), the survivor's living standards may deteriorate if no additional (social) benefits are provided.

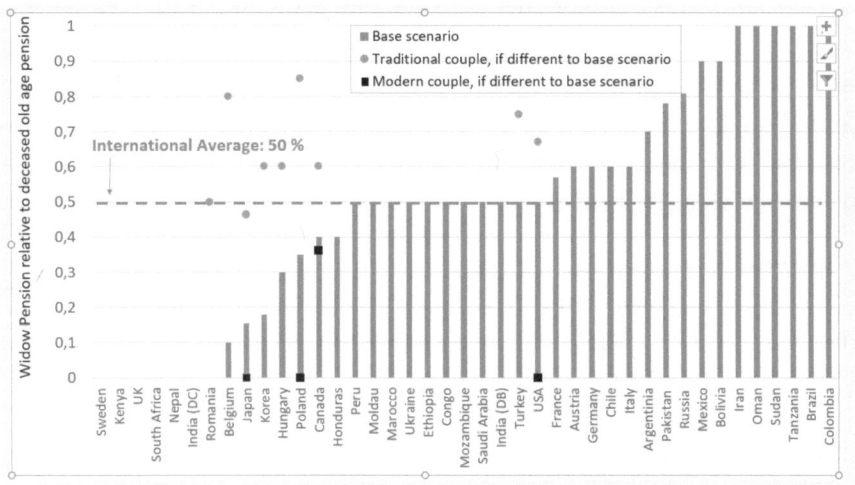

The international overview reveals a variety of designs for survivor benefit formulas. In the majority of countries, survivor benefits are calculated as a share of the pension the deceased received or would have received.[14] Some systems make distinctions based on the survivor's age (e.g. in Germany) and number of surviving children (e.g. in Spain), whereby younger survivors are presumed to be better able to adjust their level of labour market participation, while a greater need for protection is assumed in case of surviving children. Any additional income of surviving dependants is partially offset against the survivor benefit. This typically involves reductions above a certain income limit or benefit cap (e.g. in Hungary). The Austrian calculation formula stands out in this regard, as the surviving dependant's income is directly related to the deceased's income. The lower the surviving spouse's own income relative to that of the deceased, the higher the replacement rate. In Lithuania and Pakistan, on the other hand, a flat-rate benefit is provided. The calculation formula is equally unusual in Poland and Romania, where only the higher of the two, i.e. the old-age or the survivor's pension, is granted.[15]

4. Which socio-economic developments are particularly relevant for existing survivor benefit schemes?

4.1. Do women (still) live longer than men?

Life expectancy has been on the rise in recent years, in part due to medical advancements and improved living conditions. One particularly interesting question with regards to survivor benefits is whether women live longer than men and are therefore more likely to receive survivors' benefits. When comparing data from between 1990 and 1995 and between 2015 and 2020,[16] we find that the overall life expectancy of men and women at the age of 60 has not

---

[14] Depending on whether the system is based on contributions or periods of residence and whether it provides for a basic benefit/basic pension.
[15] It might not be favourable for surviving dependants to engage or continue to engage in the labour market.
[16] United Nations, World Population Prospects 2022, https://population.un.org/wpp/ (accessed on 4.2.2024).

converged. In fact, the gap in life expectancy has slightly widened from an average of 2.9 years in1990–1995 to 3.1 years in 2015–2020. This trend is particularly evident in middle- and low-income countries.[17] In high-income countries,[18] on the other hand, this gap has started to narrow.[19]

Data on age at first marriage reveals that women are, on average, three years younger than their male spouses.[20] This age difference, coupled with women's higher life expectancy, increases the likelihood that women will outlive their spouse.

4.2. Female labour force participation

In most countries, women's labour force participation has increased significantly in recent years. Between 1990 and 2019, 70 per cent of the 44 countries (with sufficient data) recorded a rise in female labour force participation. This trend is particularly pronounced in Latin American and Western European countries.[21] Only a small minority of countries have witnessed strong declines in the labour force participation of women.[22] On average, it has increased by 11 per cent over the last three decades in our sample countries.

---

[17] More than five years at the age of 60, e.g. in Mozambique and Indonesia.

[18] For example Canada or Sweden.

[19] The largest gender gaps were reported for countries of the former Soviet Union (such as Kazakhstan). According to the United Nations, the gender gap in middle-and low-income countries is expected to develop similarly to that in high-income countries. Nevertheless, equalisation will not be achieved in the near future.

[20] United Nations, Estimates and Projections of Women of Reproductive Age Who Are Married or in a Union: 2020 Revision, https://www.un.org/en/development/desa/population/theme/marriage-unions/marriage_estimates.asp (accessed on 9. 2. 2024).

[21] The largest increase was reported for Peru (+29 percentage points [PP]), Spain (+28 PP) and Chile (+23 PP).

[22] In China, for example, female labour force participation fell from 79 per cent in 1990 to 69 per cent in 2019.

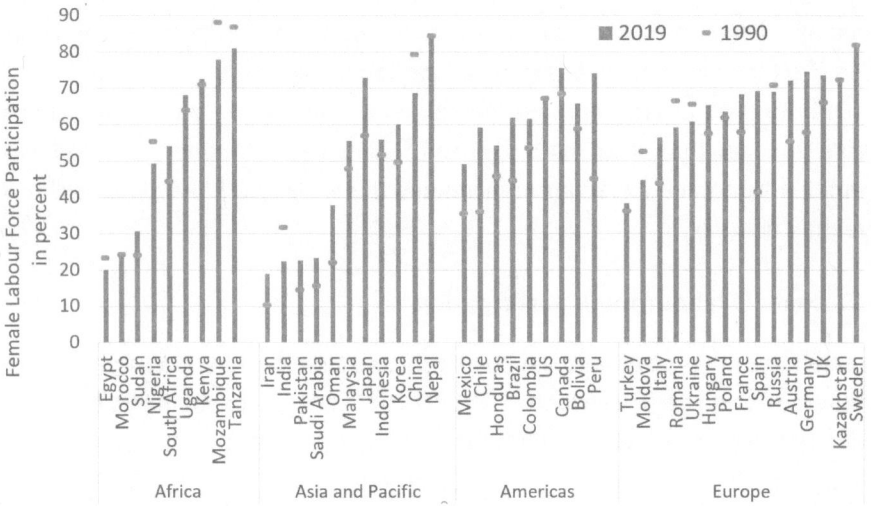

Increasing the labour force participation of women can help reduce gender-specific differences in pension levels (so-called gender pension gap), which are primarily due to women's comparatively shorter or interrupted periods of employment and insurance.[23] A trend towards a reduction in the gender pension gap has been reported in several countries (particularly in Canada, Brazil and Argentina),[24] a trend that is likely to continue in coming decades. Assuming that survivors' benefits are primarily intended to secure survivors' standard of living, the need for such benefits might decrease in the long term. At present, however, survivors' benefits still play an important role in reducing the gender pension gap.

---

[23] In addition to labour force participation, the inclusion of child-raising periods or periods of (informal) care and support also contribute to narrowing the gap. See, e.g. European Commission, 2021 Pension Adequacy Report: current and future income adequacy in old age in the EU, Volume I.

[24] European Commission, 2021 Pension Adequacy Report: current and future income adequacy in old age in the EU, Volume I, Figure 52. The same observations were made by the PVA for its insured persons, showing that the gender pension gap according to the status of old-age pensions between 2000 and 2021 has narrowed from 45.4 per cent to 42.3 per cent.

Many countries have successfully maintained the standard of living as the primary objective of survivors' benefits. Studies from France,[25] Switzerland,[26] the Netherlands,[27] Canada,[28] the USA[29], and an analysis by the Pensionsversicherungsanstalt (PVA – Pension Insurance Institution) for Austria indicates that the standard of living remains relatively stable or decreases by less than 10 per cent following the death of a spouse/partner. A 2020 study, which examined the financial situation of widows in 17 European countries using survey data, supports these findings. Only around 3 per cent of the widows surveyed reported having experienced severe financial difficulties since their partner's death.[30] However, the disparity in maintaining one's standard of living varies across different population groups. In general, male recipients of survivors' benefits, who, on average, have higher individual pension entitlements are in a more favourable financial position. In some cases, a male beneficiary's standard of living may even improve if he receives a permanent survivors' benefit, as his own pension entitlements are enough to support him after his spouse's death. In contrast, younger recipients of survivors' benefits often face greater reductions[31] due to their usually shorter insurance periods and the resulting lower (notional) pension of the deceased. This has been empirically demonstrated for the Netherlands as well as in our calculations for Austria.[32] Younger

---

[25] Bonnet/Hourriez, Veuvage, pension de réversion et maintien du niveau de vie suite au décès du conjoint: une analyse sur cas types, Retraite et société 2008/4 (n° 56), 71.

[26] Burkhard, Allocation of Expenditures in Elderly Households and the Cost of Widowhood, Schweizerische Zeitschrift für Wirtschaft und Statistik, 2017/153, 371.

[27] see Van de Vaart / Alessie / van Ooijen (2020) Economic Consequences of Widowhood, Netspar Design Paper 160.

[28] Li (2004) Verwitwung: Consequences on Income for Senior Women, Analytical Paper, Statistics Canada; Bernhard / Li (2006) Death of a Spouse: The Impact on Income for Senior Men and Women, Analytical Paper, Statistics Canada.

[29] Fadlon / Ramnath / Tong (2019) Market inefficiency and household labour supply: Evidence from social security's survivors benefits, NBER working paper 2558.

[30] Hanemann / Rausch (2020) Poor Survivors? Economic Consequences of Death of Spouse, MEA Discussion Paper No 20.

[31] See Van de Vaart / Alessie/van Ooijen, Economic Consequences of Widowhood Netspar Design paper 160; Hanemann / Rausch, Poor Survivors?, MEA Discussion Paper No. 20, 20.

[32] For details see Van de Vaart et al. (2020) and Freudenberg / Kapuy / Zwinger (2022) How to design survivor benefits in the 21st century?, Technical Commission on Old-Age, Invalidity and Survivors' Insurance, ISSA, 24.

working-age groups, however, are usually more adaptable to their new situation as survivors and adjust their labour market activity (see below) and are also more likely to enter into a new partnership compared to survivors that belong to older age groups.

4.3. Labour market effects of survivors' benefits

Against the backdrop of an ageing population, various measures have been discussed or implemented internationally to mitigate labour shortages by increasing labour force participation and extending the duration of individuals' total labour market activity. In this context, the design of survivor benefit schemes can have a significant impact on the labour market and should not be underestimated. The following literature review presents international findings on the effect of survivors' benefits on labour market participation.

Empirical studies demonstrate that the level of survivors' benefits and income tests, in particular, can lead to a decline in labour market participation among younger recipients (or those of working age). For example, in Brazil, the likelihood of participating in the labour market drops by 67 per cent when receiving survivors' benefits.[33] In Italy, a study[34] assessed the effects of the 1995 pension reform, which resulted in an average 21 per cent reduction in benefits. It reveals that the earned income of survivor benefit recipients who are of working age increased by the same amount by which the replacement rates were reduced, with labour force participation rising, particularly at the beginning and end of the survivors' working careers. In addition, a 10 pp reduction in the effective retirement age of surviving dependants and a 4 pp increase in labour force participation were observed.[35] Similar observations were made in Austria[36] and the US.[37]

---

[33] Constanzi / Ansiliero / Bichara (2017) Survivors' pensions and their impact on the Brazilian labor market, ISSR 2017, 19.

[34] Giupponi (2019) When income effects are large: Labor supply responses and the value of welfare transfers, CEP discussion paper 1651, LSE.

[35] The labour market effect was again greatest for younger recipients of survivor benefits.

[36] Böheim / Topf (2020) Unearned Income and Labor Supply: Evidence from Survivor Pensions in Austria, 2020.

[37] Fadlon / Ramnath / Tong (2019) Market inefficiency and household labour supply: Evidence from social security's survivors benefits, NBER working paper 25586.

It is worth mentioning in this context that income tests can have a particularly negative impact, reducing the amount of survivors' benefits when a given threshold of the survivor's own (earned) income is reached. When such income tests were introduced in the Netherlands in 1996, it was estimated that survivors with a high (own) income or existing assets were more likely to reduce their working hours. This consequence highlights a potential conflict between the objectives of means-testing through income imputation and the negative work incentives it creates.

Additionally, the design of survivors' benefits can also have an impact on the labour force participation of the non-widowed population. Some U.S. studies[38] suggest significant positive employment effects if survivors' benefits were hypothetically abolished. Women's overall employment rate would increase by an average of 1 to 6 pp in the long term.[39] However, because men might become less active in the labour market as a result of the hypothetical abolition of survivors' benefits, the U.S. study estimates that overall economic income could increase by 0.3 - 2 per cent.

In summary, the literature indicates that changes in the design of survivors' benefits within social security can have substantial aggregate labour market effects. Accordingly, it seems worthwhile to summarise the reforms already being implemented in the countries studied.

5. Selected reform options and legal framework considerations

Various trends have been observed in the organisation of survivors' benefits across the 30 countries analysed based on the received questionnaires:

The assumption that the male spouse is the main breadwinner and that a widow's benefit should be paid to prevent the widow from falling into poverty is increasingly being abandoned. Societal changes, such as the increased par-

---

[38] Nishiyama (2015) The Joint Labor Supply Decision of Married Couples and the Social Security Pension System, Economics Working Paper Series 2015/017, Lancaster University; Sanchez-Marcos / Bethencourt (2018) The effect of public pensions on women's labour market participation over a full life cycle, Quantitative Economics, 2018/9, 707.

[39] As no substantial state survivors' benefits are expected in the event of a spouse's death, the focus would shift towards realising one's own entitlements.

ticipation of women in the labour market and their ability to accumulate sufficient pension entitlements, have influenced the design of survivors' benefits in many countries.

In some countries (e.g. France, Sweden), the retirement age for eligibility to permanent benefits has been raised (usually in alignment with the statutory retirement age), while other countries have introduced transitional benefits (particularly for younger beneficiaries). In Greece and Hungary, for example, benefits are provided for two to five years if the recipient has not yet reached the retirement age for an old-age pension.[40] Another recent example is Finland, which, since 2022, has been providing a temporary survivor's pension to cohorts born after 1975 for either a period of ten years or until the youngest child reaches the age of 18. In addition to taking a child-centred approach, the reform's main objectives were to provide a sufficient adaptation period and at the same time, take the (increasing) labour force participation of women into account. More far-reaching reforms have been introduced in Sweden,[41] the United Kingdom, Australia and New Zealand, among others. Survivors' benefits have been completely abolished in these countries or the payment of survivors' benefits is discontinued if the recipient is in receipt of another social benefit.[42] In addition to the introduction of income tests (which studies have shown do not necessarily always yield positive outcomes, see above), increased labour force participation following the partner's death is being facilitated through alternative support benefits. In Norway, for instance, there is a growing focus on facilitating labour market access by providing benefits for children in connection with vocational education and training.

In this context, it is important to mention the introduction of pension splitting in addition to the "classic" survivors' benefits model of widows' and widowers' pensions. In line with the analysis of the questionnaire, different models exist in four out of 30 countries, with entitlements being split during the qualifying

---

[40] Norway from 2024 onwards.
[41] A 2018 evaluation of the 1990 reform in Sweden suggests that either all surviving dependants should be granted a transitional benefit, regardless of their age, or that the state should not grant a transitional benefit to surviving dependants without children.
[42] It should be noted in this context that all the countries mentioned provide other social benefits for older persons to ensure a certain minimum income (e.g. residence-based basic pension in the case of Sweden).

phase (Austria, Switzerland), at the time of separation (Japan) or upon retirement (Germany). To avoid the creation of any negative incentives to end a partnership, the splitting should take place during the entitlement phase. At present, Switzerland is the only country that prescribes mandatory pension splitting during marriage.[43] Moreover, alternative family forms, including same-sex or registered partnerships, as well as divorced persons have increasingly been added to the group of persons entitled to survivors' benefits.[44]

Compliance with international minimum social security standards, both at the global and regional levels, must be ensured before considering amendments to a country's survivors' benefits scheme. For instance, ILO Convention No. 128 on Invalidity, Old-Age and Survivors' Benefits has been ratified by 17 states.[45] The Convention's provisions include the personal scope of survivors' benefits, age limits, benefit amounts, waiting periods and benefit duration. Given this holistic approach, some argue that a (complete) abolition of survivors' benefits could violate Convention No. 128 (if ratified).[46] Similarly, Part X. of ILO Convention No. 102 establishes "minimum standards of social security" for its 62 ratifying states, including provisions for survivors' benefits.[47] (FN 62) In Europe, the Code of Social Security, a Council of Europe convention signed by 21 states, also sets minimum standards that are modelled after those in the ILO conventions.

Apart from international social security standards, human rights must also be observed: at the universal global level, the Convention on the Elimination of All Forms of Discrimination against Women (CEDAW) has been ratified by nearly 200 UN member states.[48] According to this convention, the effects on women's old-age security must be considered when reforming survivor benefits schemes to avoid any disadvantages. In Europe, the European Social Charter

---

[43] Similar political intentions exist in Austria as well.
[44] In seven out of 30 questionnaires returned.
[45] https://www.ilo.org/wcmsp5/groups/public/---ed_norm/---normes/documents/normativeinstrument/wcms_c128_de.pdf (accessed on 9.2.2024).
[46] Frey/Scheiwe/Wersig, 100 years of widows' and widowers' pensions - (k)ein Auslaufmodell?, 2015, 17 ff.
[47] https://www.ilo.org/wcmsp5/groups/public/---ed_norm/---normes/documents/normativeinstrument/wcms_c102_de.pdf (accessed on 9.2.2024).
[48] https://tbinternet.ohchr.org/_layouts/15/TreatyBodyExternal/download.aspx (accessed 9.2.2024).

must be observed as well, which, in addition to a general "right to social security", guarantees the "right of older people to social protection" (1st Additional Protocol) and "measures to combat poverty" (revised version).

Survivors' benefits are also safeguarded by the right to property, assuming this right is derived from the deceased's original entitlement to a (pension) benefit (derivative right).[49] In Europe, Article 1 of the 1st Additional Protocol to the ECHR serves as the relevant legal basis in this regard. This article does not establish a right to acquire property, nor does it guarantee entitlement to a specific benefit level. However, the reduction or discontinuation of a benefit may constitute a justifiable interference with the freedom of ownership. In relevant case law, the ECtHR examines whether: 1) the claimant's entitlement to certain benefits has been violated in a way that impairs the essence of his or her entitlement; 2) there is a legitimate expectation of receiving benefits, or 3) a statutory measure affects entitlement to a future pension benefit or current payments; 4) the measure applies to a larger group of people, or 5) any benefit reductions are attributable to an exceptional crisis, and 6) transitional periods have been provided. At the individual level, it is also decisive whether the respective benefit is or was the only source of income and whether opportunities exist for finding new employment.[50]

6. Conclusion

The question of how widows' and widowers' pensions should be designed in the 21st century largely depends on national circumstances. Our study shows that the regulations governing survivors' benefits, socio-economic trends (such

---

[49] This is generally the case in most legal systems, although there are considerations in some countries about which surviving dependants shall receive benefits independently of the deceased person's original or individual entitlement. Surviving dependants are therefore entitled to benefits because conditions that take the surviving dependant's individual situation (e.g. own income) into account are met instead of the deceased's accumulated insurance periods or periods of residence. In Australia, for example, derived rights to survivors' benefits have been abolished. See also James, Rethinking Survivor Benefits, The World Bank, 2009.

[50] See Freudenberg / Kapuy / Zwinger (2022) How to design survivor benefits in the 21st century?, Technical Commission on Old-Age, Invalidity and Survivors' Insurance, ISSA, 33 et seq for individual references from the case law of the ECtHR and Van Limberghen, in this book.

as women's labour force participation) and policies vary across countries. Consequently, the motivations and objectives for implementing reforms are equally varied. Nevertheless, global reform trends can be identified, such as the extension of the personal scope of survivors' benefits or an increase in the age at which survivors' benefits become payable (permanently).

Bibliography

Bernhard A / Li C (2006) Death of a Spouse: The Impact on Income for Senior Men and Women, Analytical Paper, Statistics Canada.

Bonnet C / Hourriez J-M (2008) Veuvage, pension de réversion et maintien du niveau de vie suite au décès du conjoint: une analyse sur cas types, Retraite et société 2008/4 (n° 56).

Böheim R / Topf M (2020) Unearned Income and Labor Supply: Evidence from Survivor Pensions in Austria, IZA DP No. 13994.

Burkhard D (2017) Allocation of Expenditures in Elderly Households and the Cost of Widowhood, Schweizerische Zeitschrift für Wirtschaft und Statistik, 2017/153, 371.

Constanzi R / Ansiliero G / Bichara J (2017) Survivors' pensions and their impact on the Brazilian labor market, ISSR 2017, 19.

European Commission (2021) Pension Adequacy Report: current and future income adequacy in old age in the EU, Volume I.

Fadlon I / Ramnath S / Tong P (2019) Market inefficiency and household labour supply: Evidence from social security's survivors benefits, NBER working paper 2558.

Frey W / Scheiwe K / Wersig M (2015) 100 Jahre Witwen- und Witwerrenten - (k)ein Auslaufmodell?, Baden-Baden: Nomos.

Freudenberg C / Kapuy K / Zwinger V (2022) How to design survivor benefits in the 21st century?, Technical Commission on Old-Age, Invalidity and Survivors' Insurance, ISSA.

Giupponi G (2019) When income effects are large: Labor supply responses and the value of welfare transfers, CEP discussion paper 1651, LSE.

Hanemann F / Rausch J (2020) Poor Survivors? Economic Consequences of Death of Spouse, MEA Discussion Paper No 20.

James E (2009) Rethinking Survivor Benefits, The World Bank.

Li C (2004) Verwitwung: Consequences on Income for Senior Women, Analytical Paper, Statistics Canada.

Nishiyama S (2015) The Joint Labor Supply Decision of Married Couples and the Social Security Pension System, Economics Working Paper Series 2015/017, Lancaster University.

Sanchez-Marcos V / Bethencourt C (2018) The effect of public pensions on women's labour market participation over a full life cycle, Quantitative Economics, 2018/9 707.

United Nations (2020) Estimates and Projections of Women of Reproductive Age Who Are Married or in a Union: 2020 Revision, https://www.un.org/en/development/desa/population/theme/marriage-unions/marriage_estimates.asp (accessed on 9.2.2024).

United Nations (2022) World Population Prospects 2022, https://population.un.org/wpp/ (accessed on 4.2.2024).

Van de Vaart J / Alessie R / van Ooijen R (2020) Economic Consequences of Widowhood: Evidence from a survivor's benefits reform in the Netherlands, Netspar Design paper 160.

6 Survivors' Benefits and Divorce

Hans-Joachim Reinhard

---

1. Introduction

While Germany's population is projected to decline slightly by 2040, the number of households in the country continues to rise – particularly single households, which are already the most common household type in Germany. According to the Federal Statistical Office, in 2022, single-person households accounted for about 41 per cent (16.8 million) of all households.[1] BBSR projections suggest that this figure will increase to around 44 per cent by 2040. In the city states (Berlin, Hamburg and Bremen), over half (52 per cent) of all households will by then be single-person households.[2] Similar trends are observed in other industrialized countries and are even beginning to emerge in less developed countries.

These figures should not obscure the fact that most people still live in multiple-person households for various periods of time. Partners typically support each other financially, but no partnership lasts forever. Partners may separate or divorce and ultimately, every partnership, regardless how stable, ends with the death of one of the partners. This raises the question about the surviving partner's financial situation, a question that was especially pressing when the primary breadwinner of a traditional household died. The loss of the primary source of income in traditional family structures often resulted in financial hardship for the surviving partner and disproportionately affected women who earned little or no income in such structures.

---

[1] Federal Statistical Office, https://www.destatis.de/DE/Presse/Pressemitteilungen/2023/06/PD23_N037_12_63.html
[2] Bundeszentrale für politische Bildung, https://www.bpb.de/kurz-knapp/zahlen-und-fakten/soziale-situation-in-deutschland/61590/entwicklung-der-haushaltstypen/

Social security schemes were quick to address such cases of financial vulnerability by introducing survivors' insurance.[3] A fixed percentage[4] of the deceased primary breadwinner's old-age pension entitlement is usually provided to the surviving partner. Most social security schemes include calculation mechanisms to ensure that survivors receive a higher rate of survivors' benefits in case of the breadwinner's premature death at a young age.[5]

However, social security provisions in the event of divorce were either not addressed at all in most social security schemes or were tied to conditions that women in particular were unable or not willing to fulfil. There were several reasons for this. Legal divorce was not possible in many countries. In Catholic countries in particular, divorce was only introduced in the 1970s or 1980s[6], with Ireland legalising divorce in 1991 following a referendum, and Malta in 2011. Today, apart from the Vatican, the Philippines remains the only country where divorce is still not legally possible.

Countries where divorce has been legalised usually tied social security benefits to the fault principle. The partner who was considered to be at fault for the breakdown of the marriage was no longer entitled to any derived social security benefits. This made it nearly impossible for women, in particular, to file for divorce. If they were found to be responsible for the divorce, they were left without access to social security benefits, leading to poverty in old age. As a result, their only alternative was to remain in a failed marriage, becoming eligible for survivors' benefits only after their spouse's death.

2. Limitations of survivors' benefits

Survivors' benefits come with notable limitations. No social security scheme provides the survivors the full pension the deceased would have been entitled to. A working individual does not suffer a major financial loss in the event of the death of his or her partner who earned less or did not have an income. The amount of survivors' benefit is typically between 50 per cent and 60 per cent of

---

[3] Historically, the main breadwinner was male.
[4] In most countries, the percentage fluctuates between 50 per cent and 60 per cent, with an additional percentage in case of joint children.
[5] This is achieved by upgrading earnings or extending contribution periods
[6] E.g. Spain, Italy, Portugal.

the deceased's pension. This benefit is often contingent upon meeting certain conditions such as reaching a specific age[7], the marriage lasting a minimum duration,[8] or the payments being time-limited.[9] Some schemes also factor in the survivor's own income.[10] If the deceased was previously married, the benefits are often divided between the survivors.

Survivors' benefits are usually only provided in the case of a legally recognised marriage in the country where the social benefits are being claimed. This can lead to complications if the marriage was contracted abroad or in a religious ceremony. A marriage that does not observe legal prohibitions (e.g. marriage between close relatives or violations of the minimum age for marriage) will not be legally recognised. The provision of social benefits may also become problematic when the beneficiary's country of origin allows polygamous marriage, as is the case in some Arab countries (although there is a growing trend towards imposing restrictions on such arrangements).[11]

Recent developments in some countries have extended survivors' benefits to unmarried partners.[12] The prerequisite for eligibility is typically proof of cohabitation for at least five years or an official registration of the partnership. These requirements may be less stringent if the couple has a child together. Moreover, several countries now also recognise same-sex partnerships for the purpose of granting social security benefits.

Benefits are provided to surviving dependants under two circumstances, namely upon the partner's confirmed death or in the event of an official declaration of death in case of disappearance due to an accident (e.g. shipwreck, avalanche, etc.).

---

[7] E.g. 45 years in Germany.
[8] At least one year in Germany.
[9] E.g. 24 months for survivors under the age of 45.
[10] E.g. Germany, France.
[11] Maghreb Post 12, November 2022, https://maghreb-post.de/marokko-polygamie-soll-weiter-eingeschraenkt-werden/
[12] E.g. Spain, Canada.

3. Survivors' benefits and divorce[13]

What happens to survivors' benefits in the event of divorce? First, as in the case of marriage, the divorce must be recognised in the country where the benefits are claimed. However, not all countries require marriages to be divorced in court. In some countries, a private divorce or a divorce before a public authority (e.g. a registry office) is accepted. With increasing digitalization, some countries allow such documents to be delivered via WhatsApp, which may, however, complicate recognition of the divorce in some countries.[14] Today, the principle of fault is rarely applied in divorce proceedings. Instead, it is now assumed that neither partner is unilaterally at fault when a marriage breaks down. This has made it much easier to get a divorce. Moreover, unlike a few decades ago, divorce no longer carries the same social stigma. Two trends are evident: on the one hand, the number of formal marriages is decreasing significantly, while on the other, divorce rates are disproportionately rising. Around one-third of marriages are divorced on average, though in some countries, half or more of all marriages end in divorce. An increasing number of long-term marriages are dissolved at an advanced age after many years of marriage. Retirement no longer guarantees that couples will remain together for the rest of their lives; instead, it often prompts either one or both spouses to pursue a new direction in life.

Although no data are available, it is reasonable to assume that separation trends in non-formal or same-sex partnerships are similar to those in formal marriages, i.e. such partnerships, just like formal ones, are not immune to relationship crises.

This makes the financial question of social security following separation or divorce even more relevant, especially for the partner who earned less due to childcare duties or household responsibilities. The traditional social security model for surviving dependants becomes ineffective when an existing marriage or partnership is not dissolved by death but by divorce or separation.

---

[13] For a comparative approach, see Reinhard H-J (1995) Rechtsordnungen mit Versorgungsausgleich im Sinne des Art. 17 Abs. 3 EGBGB, Baden-Baden: Nomos (Studien aus dem Max-Planck-Institut für ausländisches und internationales Sozialrecht, Band 14).

[14] Oberlandesgericht Frankfurt/Main, Beschluss v. 22.11.2021 – 28 VA 1/21.

Unlike the dissolution of a marriage or partnership by death, when the surviving partner typically receives a percentage of the deceased's old-age pension, varying social security regulations apply to cases of divorce in different countries. The financial security of divorced partners is therefore difficult to predict. Women who divorced in the past often found themselves without adequate old-age provisions. While family law has abolished the principle of fault, thus making it far easier to end an unhappy marriage, social security laws have not kept pace with this development. In practice, this means that partners who earn a low income still face the difficult choice about whether to accept the financial disadvantages of a divorce.

Moreover, benefits for surviving dependants are not paid from the survivor's own social insurance account, but from the deceased's account. This is not necessarily a disadvantage, especially if the deceased earned a higher income than the surviving partner. Divorced partners, on the other hand, only have access to their ex-partner's social security through maintenance payments which often become a contentious issue in divorce proceedings. Enforcing regular payments is often a very time-consuming and complicated procedure, especially when the relationship ends acrimoniously.

Additionally, maintenance payments cease with the ex-partner's death, which creates a gap in the social security scheme for the surviving divorced partner. This gap predominantly affects women. In addition to the fact that women's income level is usually lower than men's, in many marriages, the male is older. Another decisive factor is that men's life expectancy is generally around five years shorter than women's, which significantly increases the probability of a divorced woman outliving her ex-partner by several years. The following section outlines measures social security schemes have implemented to address these gaps.

4. Entitlements of the divorced partner under social security law

4.1. Inheritance law solution

The solution under inheritance law assumes that social security claims are included in the deceased's estate. Since divorced spouses are generally not entitled to the deceased's inheritance, they are left without access to any related social security benefits. The inheritance law solution can primarily be found in private insurance schemes, such as capital-based life insurance policies or retirement savings plans, but not in public social security schemes. The scaling back of public social security schemes and the growing emphasis on private pension plans, encouraged through tax incentives is becoming increasingly problematic for divorced spouses.

The worst possible outcome for a divorced spouse is when they are excluded from such private savings plans through a settlement. However, even if the former partner agrees to transfer part of his or her private savings, this typically results in significant losses in tax benefits, often preventing the parties from reaching such an agreement.

4.2. Maintenance solution

Under the maintenance solution,[15] the surviving divorced partner can receive survivors' benefits from the social security scheme, similarly to those provided for spouses in a marriage that has been dissolved by death. However, the prerequisite is that the surviving divorced partner was entitled to maintenance payments from his or her deceased ex-partner. Survivors' benefits are thus intended as compensation for the loss of maintenance payments. Yet, this model has notable drawbacks. First, as already mentioned, it requires the existence of an entitlement to maintenance. In legal systems still rooted in the principle of fault, courts may not grant maintenance payments to the partner who is considered to be at fault for the divorce. In practice, it is also not uncommon for the weaker partner to waive a maintenance claim to end the failed marriage as quickly as possible. In marriages characterised by a significant financial disparity, a waiver of maintenance obligations is sometimes even included in a prenuptial agreement. This is usually the case when one partner possesses significantly more wealth than the other.

An additional condition for the maintenance solution is proof that maintenance payments have actually been made in the past. If the deceased only made few maintenance payments, entitlement to survivors' benefits is reduced or completely eliminated. This situation is not always attributable to the ex-

---

[15] E.g. Austria.

partner's unwillingness to pay maintenance. In the case of remarriage, child support payments, unemployment or illness, the divorced partner's maintenance claim may not be realisable.

4.3. "Surviving spouse" solution

In some social security systems, a divorced spouse is treated as a surviving dependant, regardless of the divorce.[16] The divorce itself, therefore, initially has no negative impact on the divorced spouse's social security entitlement. However, as with other surviving dependants, benefits are only provided once the ex-partner dies. Until then, the divorced spouse can only seek financial support through maintenance claims.

A further disadvantage arises if the ex-partner remarries after the divorce. Several scenarios are possible in this case. In some systems, the survivors' benefit is exclusively paid to the second spouse, leaving the ex-partner to negotiate with the couple for a share of the survivors' benefit. This, of course, is a very sensitive matter.

For this reason, most social security schemes divide survivors' benefits equally among the current and any former spouses. It is less common to divide the benefits by individual headcount. In case of two former spouses, each receives half of the benefit amount. A more common – and arguably fairer – approach is to allocate survivors' benefits based on the duration of each marriage. For example, if the deceased insured person was married to the first partner for 30 years and only 10 years to the second, the former partner receives 30/40 and the second only 10/40 of the benefit amount.

4.4. "Divorced spouse" solution

One particularly generous solution entitles divorced spouses to survivors' benefits, regardless of the ex-spouse's death.[17] The benefit amounts to 50 per cent of the higher-earning spouse's retirement pension. The former spouse does

---

[16] E.g. France.
[17] US-Social Security System, cf. Reinhard H-J (2015) US-amerikanische Altersrenten im Versorgungsausgleich, in: Devetzi S / Janda C (Eds.) Freiheit – Gerechtigkeit – Sozial(es) Recht, Festschrift für Eberhard Eichenhofer, Baden-Baden: Nomos, 528-539.

not have to already be receiving an old-age pension to be eligible to the survivors' benefit. The only decisive factor is whether the divorced spouse has reached retirement age. It is not only the pension entitlements accrued by the higher-earning partner during the marriage that are considered, but their lifetime insurance contributions, which is a highly favourable solution for the divorced spouse.

However, this approach is not without limitations. The marriage must have lasted at least 10 years for the divorced spouse to qualify for benefits. No survivors' benefits are provided if the marriage was of a shorter duration. This regulation puts divorced spouses who do not meet the 10-year threshold at a disadvantage. On the other hand, it can be assumed that in cases of short marriages, the divorced partner still has sufficient time to accrue his or her own pension entitlements. Another disadvantage is that that the divorced spouse's pension cannot be combined with a separate old-age pension. If the divorced spouse was gainfully employed, his or her own entitlement to an old-age pension is lost. If his or her own old-age pension is higher, he or she loses entitlement to the divorced spouse's pension, i.e. both benefits cannot be claimed simultaneously, and the higher pension amount takes precedence. This may discourage divorced spouses from pursuing gainful employment after divorce.[18]

This model represents a major financial burden for the social security system. The insured person receives 100 per cent of his or her pension, while the divorced spouse is entitled to an additional 50 per cent of that amount. A divorced couple thus receives 150 per cent from one insurance account. Ironically, from a financial perspective, a couple could be advised to get divorced when reaching the required age threshold because it is financially very advantageous in terms of social security benefits.

---

[18] Ausländische Rentenanwartschaften im Versorgungsausgleich. Schwierigkeiten und Tücken ihrer Bewertung am Beispiel US-amerikanischer Anrechte, in: Zeitschrift für das gesamte Familienrecht (FamRZ) 37 (1990) 11, 1194-1197.

5. Different solutions in family law

5.1. Compensation payment

Old-age pension entitlements are many couples' most important asset. This becomes particularly apparent when a pension entitlement is capitalised. A monthly pension of EUR 100 roughly corresponds to a capitalised value of EUR 23 000. An average old-age pension of EUR 1 200 can reach the equivalent of the purchase price of a flat or small house. However, the calculation of this capital value is only theoretical, as social security systems do not usually offer lump-sum payments. Should this be the case in exceptional circumstances, however, the total amount would be subject to a substantial reduction.

In case of compensation for old-age pension entitlements, the higher-earning spouse often cannot afford to make such a payment. This is why family courts in some countries have started combining compensation payments for old-age pension claims with other assets (e.g. property, cars, boats, jewellery). While this approach does not directly guarantee the divorced spouse's pension security, selling these assets can significantly improve his or her financial situation. In practice, this solution is straightforward, especially in proceedings before the family court, but presupposes that further assets are available to compensate the pension claim. This is usually not the case for couples with an average or low income. Another problem is that there is no binding formula for determining the interest rate when calculating the assets' capital value, which is why the result can vary greatly from case to case.

5.2. Partial sharing

In this model, the divorced spouse receives a share of the ex-spouse's old-age pension directly from the social insurance scheme. This share is earmarked in the former spouse's insurance account.[19] The advantage is that the divorced partner receives social security benefits immediately. In addition, unlike maintenance payments, he or she is not dependent on the good will of his or her ex-partner, i.e. the payments are made automatically by the authorities each month.

---

[19] U.S. military pensions.

This model's disadvantage is that the payments continue to be made from the ex-spouse's insurance account. If his or her entitlement to benefits ends due to death, the payments to the divorced partner cease as well. Theoretically, it would be possible for the payments to continue as a survivors' benefit after the insured person's death, but this solution is not widespread.

5.3. Pension sharing

The most complex model grants divorced partners direct entitlement to their own retirement pension, independent of their ex-partner's circumstances. In principle, it is similar to splitting a joint bank account. Let us presume the higher-earning spouse is entitled to a monthly pension of EUR 1 000 per month. In the divorce proceedings, a claim of EUR 500 per month would be transferred to the divorced spouse's account, with the insured person being left with a pension entitlement of EUR 500 per month. The divorced spouse's situation might improve considerably but both partners may also be left to live on a low retirement pension. The equalisation claim is always limited to maximum half of the insured person's pension and only covers the duration of marriage. If the partner was insured for 40 years, for instance, but insured for only 20 years during the marriage, the pension EUR 1 000/40*20 = EUR 500 is divided and the divorced partner is thus only credited EUR 250. The amount of the divorced partner's own old-age pension entitlement is also taken into account. In the above example, if the lower-earning partner acquired an entitlement of EUR 200 during the marriage, he or she will receive EUR 1 000 - EUR 200 = EUR 800 / 2 = EUR 400 as compensation. Consequently, each partner has a separate entitlement to an old-age pension of EUR 600 after the divorce.

This model has the advantage of dividing pension rights between divorced partners into two independent claims to an old-age pension. From a fairness perspective, this solution seems reasonable. The ultimate consequence of a divorce is that the assets earned are divided fully and permanently.

While the model of dividing old-age pensions in the event of divorce sounds appealing and is straightforward, only few systems have introduced it so far. One legal obstacle lies in the fact that it involves two distinct areas of law, namely family law (divorce proceedings) and social security law (old-age provision). Another challenge is the increasing diversification of social security in old age. Public social security systems only provide a partial contribution to financial security in old age. There have been increasing calls since the 1990s to supplement or even replace social security and public pensions with occupational or private pension schemes.

Furthermore, in nearly all countries, certain occupational groups (e.g. civil servants, liberal professions, self-employed persons, military personnel) are covered by special pension schemes. Each system has its own regulations. Moreover, these schemes are limited to members of the respective occupational group, i.e. divorced partners cannot be included in them. If these schemes are not considered in the pension calculation in the event of divorce, a significant imbalance in the distribution of benefits arises. Although pension splitting is being discussed in some countries, it has so far only been implemented in Canada, Switzerland and Germany, albeit in different ways.

a) Canada

Canada was one of the first countries to introduce pension splitting on 1 January 1978. Pension splitting is limited to entitlements from the public Canada Pension Plan[20] or the Province of Quebec's Quebec Pension Plan.[21] Membership in these schemes is mandatory for employees, with benefits amounting to only 25 per cent of the average earned income, i.e. the level of social protection is not very high. The more financially lucrative private pension plans in old age are shared by both divorced partners under family law[22] in line with the compensation principle described above.

b) Switzerland

Under the Swiss public social security scheme (AHV), the level of benefits is not proportionally dependent on the individual's previously earned income from gainful employment. Even those without an earned income can qualify for benefits. Since 1 January 1997, divorced couples can request the splitting and

---

[20] Sec. 55, Sec. 55.1 CPP "Division of unadjusted pensionable earnings".
[21] Art. 102 QPP "Partition of unadjusted pensionable earnings".
[22] Each province has its own family law. This makes it difficult to predict the outcome. In general, dividing assets and how this is done is at the discretion of the court. In most cases, private or occupational pension plans are not divided as such, but parties agree on a compensation payment.

equalisation of earned incomes. Even if the couple does not request pension splitting, it is automatically applied once both partners reach pensionable age.[23] Since 1 January 2000, occupational pension entitlements (BVG) must be divided in the event of divorce.[24] Only employees with an annual income of CHF 22 050 (approx. EUR 23 200) are required to participate. Pension entitlements from other private pension plans are not included. Their division is based on the rules of the matrimonial property regime.[25]

c) Germany

Germany was the first country to introduce pension splitting on 1 July 1977.[26] The scheme includes all forms of old-age provision into the equalisation procedure.[27] The principle of dividing all pension entitlements acquired during marriage in half is one of the procedure's pillars. This principle intends to promote fair equalisation in the event of divorce but makes the process very complex and lengthy. It becomes even more complicated if one of the ex-spouses has pension entitlements from abroad.

Migrants who return to their home country face additional challenges. When pension splitting was introduced, survivors' pensions for divorced persons were abolished. Pension equalisation must therefore be carried out in any case.

When divorce proceedings are initiated in Germany, the family court carries out pension equalisation before finalising the divorce. If one of the spouses worked abroad during the marriage, their foreign pension entitlements must be determined. Unfortunately, cooperation from foreign social security systems is often inadequate, as many systems are unfamiliar with pension splitting and fail to provide the necessary information. Additionally, there is no EU-wide regulation requiring foreign social security systems to share such information.

---

[23] https://www.ahv-iv.ch/p/1.02.d
[24] Art. 122 ZGB; https://kutterlaw.com/der-versorgungsausgleich-in-der-schweiz/
[25] Entscheidungen des Bundesgerichts BGE 137 III 337 E. 2.1.1; BGE 129 III 257.
[26] § 1587 BGB; Versorgungsausgleichsgesetz (Pension Equalisation Act).
[27] Reinhard H-J / Blenk-Knocke E / Eichenhofer E (1987) Comparative study on credit splitting in the Federal Republic of Germany and Canada and arrangements in selected other countries. Vol. 1-4. Munich: Max-Planck-Institut für ausländisches und internationales Sozialrecht.

However, if the divorce is finalised abroad, the foreign court has no jurisdiction to carry out pension equalisation. As a result, the divorced spouse will not be eligible for survivors' benefits because the marriage has been dissolved. To claim his or her share of his or her ex-partner's pension, proceedings must be initiated before a German family court. This process can be challenging for migrants, who may face language barriers and lack access to specialised lawyers. The proceedings may take 2-3 years or even longer. However, the divorced spouse only starts receiving social security benefits after the final ruling on pension equalisation. This means that many migrants – especially women – face financial hardship. If their ex-partner dies before the proceedings have been concluded, they do not receive a survivors' pension and also do not receive their own pension share as long as the pension equalisation proceedings have not been concluded.

In practice, this means that many migrant women do not receive the share of their ex-partner's pension to which they are entitled, leaving many in a very precarious financial situation in old age. In certain cases, this might also affect German couples who live abroad, as EU law applies the principle of habitual residence.[28] For example, if a German wife follows her German husband to China, where he is employed in an international company, Chinese law will govern the divorce, and she will not be entitled to survivors' benefits. Similarly, if a German couple retires to Spain and later divorces under Spanish law, the wife may be left without a pension entitlement.[29]

---

[28] Art. 8 Rom III-Regulation.
[29] Reinhard H-J (2024) Gewöhnlicher Aufenthalt und Alterssicherung geschiedener Frauen, SGb 2024, 469-472.

Bibliography

Brosius-Gersdorf F (2016) Ehe- und familienverfassungsrechtlicher Reformbedarf bei der Witwen- und Witwerrente in der gesetzlichen Rentenversicherung (Teil I) SGb 2016, 241-245.

Eichenhofer E (2023) Sozialrechtliche Hinterbliebenenleistungen – zeitgemäß?, DRV 2023, 253-265.

Government of Canada (Date modified: 2024-06-03) Your public service pension – Benefits for survivors. https://www.tpsgc-pwgsc.gc.ca/remuneration-compensation/services-pension-services/pension/pubs/survv-01-index-eng.html

Hohnerlein E M (2003) Eigenständige und abgeleitete soziale Sicherung der Frauen in Deutschland vor und nach der Rentenreform von 2001, Reform der Sozialen Sicherungssysteme in Japan und Deutschland, 143-173 (JDZB documentation, Band 3).

Jaenecke P (2011) Gesetzliche Grundlagen der Hinterbliebenensicherung im europäischen Rechtsvergleich. Bochumer Schriften zum Sozial- und Gesundheitsrecht, Band 10, Baden Baden: Nomos.

Köbl U (2002) Reform der Hinterbliebenenrenten, Ausbau der eigenständigen Sicherung der Frauen und der Familienkomponente in der Rentenversicherung ZFSH/SGB 2002, 594-602.

Reinhard H-J (1990) Ausländische Rentenanwartschaften im Versorgungsausgleich. Schwierigkeiten und Tücken ihrer Bewertung am Beispiel US-amerikanischer Anrechte in: Zeitschrift für das gesamte Familienrecht (FamRZ) 37 (1990) 11, 1194-1197.

Reinhard H-J (1995) Rechtsordnungen mit Versorgungsausgleich im Sinne des Art 17 Abs 3 EGBGB, Eine vergleichende Untersuchung unter besonderer Berücksichtigung des kanadischen, niederländischen, belgischen und spanischen Rechts, Studien aus dem Max-Planck-Institut für ausländisches und internationales Sozialrecht Bd 14.

Reinhard H-J (2008) Dokumentation der Tagung "Eigenverantwortung, Private und öffentliche Solidarität – Rollenleitbilder im Familien- und Sozialrecht im Europäischen Vergleich", 114-134 (Forschungsreihe / Bundesministerium für Familie, Senioren, Frauen und Jugend, Band 3).

Reinhard H-J (2015) US-amerikanische Altersrenten im Versorgungsausgleich, in: Devetzi S / Janda C (Eds.) Freiheit – Gerechtigkeit – Sozial(es)

Recht, Festschrift für Eberhard Eichenhofer, Baden-Baden: Nomos, 528-539.

Reinhard H-J (2024) Gewöhnlicher Aufenthalt und Alterssicherung geschiedener Frauen, SGb 2024, 469-472.

Reinhard H-J / Blenk-Knocke E / Eichenhofer E (1987) Comparative study on credit splitting in the Federal Republic of Germany and Canada and arrangements in selected other countries. Vol. 1–4. Munich: Max-Planck-Institut für ausländisches und internationales Sozialrecht.

Steinmeyer H-D (1994) Die Alters-, Invaliditäts- und Hinterbliebenensicherung Selbständiger in den Mitgliedstaaten der Europäischen Gemeinschaft, Bestandsanalyse und Entwicklungsmöglichkeiten, NZS 1994, 103-109.

Stegmann M / Bieber U (2012) Alters- und Renteneinkommen von Witwen und Witwern in Deutschland – Ein Überblick über die Leistungen der GRV und empirische Ergebnisse, DRV 2012, 45-68.

7 Survivors' Benefits in Switzerland

Thomas Gächter

Switzerland has always considered itself a unique case. It remains outside the European Union, following its own independent path in social policy development. With family policy and social security provisions for families evolving over time, Switzerland has been moving at its own pace, at times even in a different direction.

This chapter focuses on survivors' benefits. The differences between survivors' benefits in Switzerland and in other European countries[1] are less pronounced than, for example, with regard to paternity leave or maternity protection. Switzerland's peculiarity is highlighted in a recent European Court of Human Rights[2] ruling in Strasbourg against Switzerland for discriminating against widowers compared to widows (see Section 3 below).

1. Overview of the Swiss system of survivors' benefits

Switzerland has a mixed system of social security schemes that incorporates elements of benefit entitlement and benefit levels based on the basic social security framework in line with universal schemes (Beveridge model). One key distinction is that these schemes are primarily financed from contributions rather than from tax revenues and are structured like an insurance. This frame-

---

[1] Swiss legislation on survivors' benefits is in line with international standards and principles that apply in this area, see Pieters D (2006) Social Security: An Introduction to the Basic Principles. Alphen an den Rijn: Kluwer Law International, 59-63.
[2] ECHR Case 78630/12 (2022), Beeler v Switzerland.

work, which to some degree ensures a basic level of security for all, is supplemented by class insurance consistent with the Bismarck model,[3] which primarily covers employees.[4] One notable feature is that basic benefits are often supplemented by additional benefits from class insurance schemes.

Survivors' benefits specifically are accumulated,[5] i.e. a surviving dependant may receive benefits from up to three different schemes at the same time. However, legal provisions prevent overcompensation.

In Switzerland, the protection of survivors is a component of the social security system. Along with old-age and disability protection, the protection of survivors, therefore, lies at the core of the country's social security system.[6]

As in the case of other countries, Switzerland has a three-pillar model[7] of social security.[8]

- Basic insurance (first level): covers the entire population and includes old-age, survivors' and disability insurance. Contributions to this system are made by all, even those not gainfully employed.
- Occupational insurance (second level): standard insurance for employees, as they are its only compulsorily insured group. Covers the bulk of social security. However, only incomes of at least CHF 22,050 are covered under this scheme,[9] which corresponds to slightly less than one-third of the average Swiss income (2023). Accident insurance also takes over part of this function of the second pillar. It supplements the benefits of the first pillar if disability or survivorship occurs due to an insured accident.

---

[3] Gächter T and Tremp D (2019) Social Security Law in Switzerland. Bern: Stämpfli Publishers, N 863 ff.
[4] Gächter T and Tremp D (2019) Social Security Law in Switzerland. Bern: Stämpfli Publishers, N 880 ff.
[5] Gächter T and Tremp D (2019) Social Security Law in Switzerland. Bern: Stämpfli Publishers, N 946 ff.
[6] Swiss Federal Constitution (Bundesverfassung der Schweizerischen Eidgenossenschaft/BV), 111.
[7] It may, however, be more accurate to refer to three levels rather than to three pillars.
[8] Swiss Federal Constitution (*Bundesverfassung der Schweizerischen Eidgenossenschaft/BV*), 111, 112, 113. Gächter T and Tremp D (2019) Social Security Law in Switzerland. Bern: Stämpfli Publishers, N 863 ff.
[9] Occupational Pensions Law (Bundesgesetz über die berufliche Alters-, Hinterlassenen- und Invalidenversicherung/BVG), 7 (1).

- Voluntary insurance (third level): voluntary protection by way of individual savings that are granted tax benefits.[10]

The three-tiered system's performance targets are structured differently: the first pillar aims to provide adequate coverage of basic needs.[11] However, this goal is rarely met due to the extremely high cost of living in Switzerland. The maximum old-age pension in the first pillar, for example, is currently CHF 2,450 per month, which roughly corresponds to the cost of renting a modest flat in an urban area.

The second pillar, therefore, plays a crucial role for most insured persons. It aims to ensure the continuation of one's own accustomed standard of living.[12] Without this second level, old-age, disability and survivors' benefits would hardly sufficiently cover living costs. Lastly, the third voluntary pillar aims to ensure coverage of individual needs.

Understanding the Swiss system requires not only knowledge of its basic structure but also of the purpose of survivors' benefits: they are primarily designed to replace family law obligations that can no longer be fulfilled by the deceased person.[13] In this context, one generally speaks of the "service function of social security" in relation to family law. That is, social security steps in to serve as a substitute for family law obligations in cases where the obligated person no longer exists.[14]

Social security encompasses various areas of protection independent of family law, with social security law providing additional benefits in certain aspects.[15] One area where social security law clearly extends beyond family law – an area that is quite important from a socio-political perspective – is found in

---

[10] Gächter T and Tremp D (2019) Social Security Law in Switzerland. Bern: Stämpfli Publishers, N 876.
[11] Swiss Federal Constitution (Bundesverfassung der Schweizerischen Eidgenossenschaft/BV), 112 (2).
[12] Swiss Federal Constitution (Bundesverfassung der Schweizerischen Eidgenossenschaft/BV), 113 (2).
[13] Hürzeler M (2014) System und Dogmatik der Hinterlassenenversicherung im Sozialversicherungs- und Haftpflichtrecht. Bern: Stämpfli Publishers, 51 ff.
[14] Hürzeler M (2014) System und Dogmatik der Hinterlassenenversicherung im Sozialversicherungs- und Haft-pflichtrecht. Bern: Stämpfli Publishers, 174f.
[15] Gächter T and Schwendener M (2005) Nichteheliche Lebensgemeinschaften im Sozialversicherungsrecht. FamPra.ch. 2005(4), 861-869.

the second pillar: pension funds may cover individuals who do not have a legally established family relationship with the deceased, meaning they are treated as survivors and are eligible for survivors' benefits.[16] This possibility covers the need for protection in practice. The system thus aligns the treatment of unmarried, cohabiting partners – an atypical legal status – with that of married spouses in terms of survivors' benefits.[17]

2. Survivors' benefits in Switzerland

Death or being left behind are treated as standard social risks.[18] However, it is not the death of the insured person him- or herself that is covered by survivors' benefits. Instead, the insurance covers the economic losses resulting from the insured person's death. This is especially relevant if the deceased person was the primary breadwinner of the surviving dependants.[19]

However, the compensation provided is not intended to cover the survivors' actual financial loss, but the "typical" losses in such cases. Standard situations that warrant protection under the social insurance system and for which a lump-sum compensation is provided in case of an insured person's death are to some extent mapped out. Whether this compensation meets survivors' actual financial loss is not verified.[20]

The biggest problem of the current survivors' benefit scheme is that the Swiss social security system is built on the traditional family model with one primary breadwinner, who is typically male.[21] The social security system is thus designed to provide protection for survivors in this (formerly) conventional

---

[16] Occupational Pensions Law (Bundesgesetz über die berufliche Alters-, Hinterlassenen- und Invalidenversiche-rung/BVG), 20a.
[17] Gächter T and Schwendener M (2005) Nichteheliche Lebensgemeinschaften im Sozialversicherungsrecht. Fa-mPra.ch. 2005(4), 849-850.
[18] E.g. Pieters D (2006) Social Security: An Introduction to the Basic Principles. Alphen an den Rijn: Kluwer Law international, 59.
[19] E.g. Pieters D (2006) Social Security: An Introduction to the Basic Principles. Alphen an den Rijn: Kluwer Law international, 59.
[20] E.g. Pieters D (2006) Social Security: An Introduction to the Basic Principles. Alphen an den Rijn: Kluwer Law international, 61-62.
[21] Gächter T and Schwendener M (2005) Nichteheliche Lebensgemeinschaften im Sozialversicherungsrecht. Fa-mPra.ch. 2005(4), 862-863.

case. Social insurance systems are often described as "conservative systems"[22] because they essentially 'freeze' a given social condition, which is 'preserved' in legal provisions for decades.

The 'freezing point' in the Swiss system can be traced back to the middle of the 20th century. Since the reform of family law in the 1980s, however, the traditional family structure has changed. The most recent major reform of the first pillar in 1997 acknowledged that the husband is no longer necessarily the family's only or primary breadwinner. Nevertheless, the husband is still assigned the main role in the family, and gender equality has yet to be fully implemented.

Remnants of the traditional family model can be found across all insurance schemes that provide survivors' benefits. These remnants are most evident in the first pillar and in accident insurance, whereas in the second pillar, legal equality has largely been achieved.

That last point in particular, however, creates inequalities, as the minimum threshold for insurance coverage[23] in the second pillar excludes many part-time employees. Switzerland, together with the Netherlands, has the highest share of part-time workers in Europe,[24] the vast majority of whom are women.[25] Accordingly, insurance coverage for part-time female workers is inadequate.

That being said, this needs to be put into perspective: married women are usually covered by their spouse's insurance to protect against the risk of being left behind without having to make contributions towards that insurance. Conversely, insurance coverage for male spouses is usually inadequate, as women are often either not insured at all or only have limited coverage through occupational pension schemes.

---

[22] Esping-Andersen G (1990) The three worlds of welfare capitalism. Cambridge: Polity Press, p. 27.

[23] CHF 22,050; Occupational Pensions Law (Bundesgesetz über die berufliche Alters-, Hinterlassenen- und Invalidenversicherung/BVG), 7 (1).

[24] Approx. 40 per cent. See Eurostat. Part-time and full-time employment statistics, https://ec.europa.eu/eurostat/statistics-explained/index.php?title=Part-time_and_full-time_employment_-_statistics#Worker_profile_and_countries: (visited 4 April 2024).

[25] Over 60 per cent of employed women work part time compared to less than 20 per cent of employed men. See Eurostat. Part-time and full-time employment statistics, https://ec.europa.eu/eurostat/statistics-explained/index.php?title=Part-time_and_full-time_employment_-_statistics#Worker_profile_and_countries: (visited 4 April 2024).

The current law states that *widows and widowers* are entitled to a survivor's pension under the applicable old-age, survivors' and disability insurance scheme if they have children at the time of the spouse's death.[26] The children's age does not affect this entitlement. Moreover, the concept of children is interpreted very broadly.[27] It is evident that the legislator intended to create a generous and favourable provision. The underlying assumption is that where children are involved, the surviving partner will have to take care of them and will face some form of financial hardship. While this approach may be generous, it no longer necessarily reflects the current realities of life.

Until 1997, only women were entitled to a widow's pension. When the widower's pension was introduced on the path towards equal rights, full equal rights was not achieved, primarily due to concerns over the associated costs. Moreover, despite recognition of the principle of legal equality, women were perceived to be more reliant on survivors' benefits than their male spouses.[28] Widowers, therefore, face two disadvantages in the first pillar: first, they only receive a widower's pension until their youngest child turns 18. Second, widowers are not entitled to receive a widower's pension in situations in which women are eligible for a widow's pension, that is to say, when a widow is over the age of 45 at the time of her spouse's death and they had been married for more than five years.[29] The latter provision, in particular, seems rather outdated. The legislator clearly assumes that women aged 45+ can no longer be integrated into the labour market. This may be true if the woman has never been gainfully employed. And yet, that matter of fact is not a requirement, only the duration of her marriage (five years) and her age (over 45 years) are of relevance.[30]

---

[26] Old Age and Survivors Insurance Law (Bundesgesetz über die Alters- und Hinterlassenenversicherung/AHVG), 23 (1).

[27] Gächter T and Tremp D (2019) Social Security Law in Switzerland. Bern: Stämpfli Publishers, N 947.

[28] Cardinaux B (2023) Das EGMR-Urteil Beeler und seine Folgen. SZS. 67(3),117-120.

[29] Old Age and Survivors Insurance Law (Bundesgesetz über die Alters- und Hinterlassenenversicherung/AHVG), 24. Gächter T and Tremp D (2019) Social Security Law in Switzerland. Bern: Stämpfli Publishers, N 948.

[30] Gächter T and Tremp D (2019) Social Security Law in Switzerland. Bern: Stämpfli Publishers, N 948.

The regulation for *divorcees* in the first pillar is also quite generous. Both divorced men and women are eligible to receive a widower/widow's pension if they have children with the deceased and were married for at least ten years; if they were married for at least ten years and the divorce occurred after the divorced surviving spouse's 45th birthday; if the youngest child has not yet turned 18 by the time of the divorced surviving spouse's 45th birthday; or as long as the divorced surviving spouse has children under the age of 18.[31] Interestingly, it is not necessary for the divorced surviving spouse to actually still receive family law benefits from the divorce to qualify for the widower/widow's pension. That is, even if the divorced surviving spouse is no longer entitled to alimony, the widower/widow's pension is provided.

Compared to other benefits available under the old-age, survivors' and disability insurance schemes, widower/widow's pensions are quite generous. They amount to 80 per cent of the old-age pension that the deceased would have been entitled to,[32] with a maximum of CHF 1,960.

An important point to consider in this context is that over 95 per cent of the total amount of all survivors' benefits granted to widows and widowers are paid out to widows. This disparity is due to the more straightforward eligibility criteria for widows, as well as the higher mortality rate among men.[33]

A brief look at provisions for *orphans* reveals that children are, in principle, entitled to receive an orphan's pension from each parent, whereby the benefit's total amount is capped at one and a half times the value of one orphan's pension. That is, an orphan's pension may amount to maximum 40 per cent of the old-age pension to which the deceased parent would have been entitled,[34] i.e. a maximum of CHF 980. If both of the child's parents are deceased, or if he or she is a foundling or has only one parent, he or she will receive 60 per cent of

---

[31] Gächter T and Tremp D (2019) Social Security Law in Switzerland. Bern: Stämpfli Publishers, N 949.
[32] Old Age and Survivors Insurance Law (Bundesgesetz über die Alters- und Hinterlassenenversicherung/AHVG), 36.
[33] Cardinaux B (2023) Das EGMR-Urteil Beeler und seine Folgen. SZS. 67(3), 120.
[34] Old Age and Survivors Insurance Law (Bundesgesetz über die Alters- und Hinterlassenenversicherung/AHVG), 37 (1).

the old-age pension to which the deceased parent would have been entitled,[35] i.e. a maximum of CHF 1,470.[36] These amounts seem reasonable compared to the benefit amount provided in other European countries. However, they are insufficient to cover the costs of living in Switzerland. As previously mentioned, these amounts must be considered in conjunction with benefits provided under other social insurance schemes: they are either supplemented by benefits from other social insurance schemes, such as occupational pension schemes, or through a special means-tested system which offers additional support up to the subsistence level. The benefit from this latter system is referred to as 'supplementary benefits' ("Ergänzungsleistungen") and is financed through taxes. Without this supplementary system, the constitutional mandate of the first pillar, namely ensuring an adequate subsistence level for all, could not be fulfilled.

Next, we will focus on the *second pillar, the occupational pension system*. Only employees who earn more than CHF 22,050 annually (working for one employer) are insured under this insurance scheme. This branch of insurance was introduced in 1985 and is therefore strongly influenced by the equality efforts implemented in family law at the time. The insurance benefits are legally equal, i.e. both surviving women and men are treated equally.[37] The benefit conditions are slightly more restrictive than in the first pillar. Moreover, the benefits are geared more towards survivors' actual needs than is the case in the first pillar. Widows and widowers who are raising at least one child, or who are older than 45 at the time of becoming widowed and whose marriage lasted at least five years are entitled to survivors' benefits.[38]

The second pillar also provides for survivors' benefits for *divorced spouses* if the marriage lasted at least ten years. Unlike in the first pillar, however, there is *a close connection to family law claims*. Only in the now rare cases in which

---

[35] Old Age and Survivors Insurance Law (Bundesgesetz über die Alters- und Hinterlassenenversicherung/AHVG), 37 (2).

[36] Gächter T and Tremp D (2019) Social Security Law in Switzerland. Bern: Stämpfli Publishers, N 951-953, 957.

[37] Occupational Pensions Law (Bundesgesetz über die berufliche Alters-, Hinterlassenen- und Invalidenversiche-rung/BVG), 19.

[38] Occupational Pensions Law (Bundesgesetz über die berufliche Alters-, Hinterlassenen- und Invalidenversiche-rung/BVG), 19.

the divorced spouse has been awarded a lifelong support benefit or a one-off settlement does this claim arise.[39] This is no longer a frequent occurrence.

As already mentioned, most pension funds treat not only divorced spouses as survivors, but *unmarried partners* as well.[40]

The benefits provided under the second pillar are quite generous. Together with the benefits provided under the first pillar, sufficient coverage is provided to survivors in most cases. It should be noted, however, that even if survivors' benefits are basically structured equally under law, women benefit far more from them than men do. Because the number of women who work part time is very high, their wages are usually too low for them to be insured, or they are only minimally insured under the second pillar. Survivors thus hardly have access to any benefits.

Despite the fact that both men and women are treated equally under the second pillar, it still, to some extent, reflects the traditional family model of the sole breadwinner, who is fully insured and whose income sustains the entire family, because ultimately, only full-time employees are fully covered by insurance.

3. The special case of widower's pension and recent ECHR case law

The case of Beeler v. Switzerland made waves in Switzerland around two years ago.[41] This case was not only about a widowed father of two daughters but also intersected with the political debate in Switzerland at the time regarding women's retirement age. Specifically, a proposal was made to align the retirement age of women with that of men, i.e. increasing it from 64 to 65 years. A referendum was held, resulting in the approval of alignment by a very narrow majority.[42] During the political debate, the disadvantage women face in terms

---

[39] Ordinance No. 2 on Occupational Pensions Law (Verordnung über die berufliche Alters-, Hinterlassenen- und Invalidenvorsorge/BVV 2), 20 (2) b.
[40] Occupational Pensions Law (Bundesgesetz über die berufliche Alters-, Hinterlassenen- und Invalidenversicherung/BVG), 20a.
[41] ECHR Case 78630/12 (2022), Beeler v Switzerland.
[42] Cardinaux B (2022) AHV 21: Welche Änderungen bringt die Reform? SZS. 66(6), 340-341.

of wages and pensions was raised, which ought to justify a lower retirement age for women. Shortly after the referendum, the decision was made to equalise the retirement age of both women and men, thereby also ensuring legal equality, albeit by aligning women's position with the less favourable position of men.

In 1994, Max Beeler's wife died in a hiking accident, leaving behind two daughters, aged two and four. Mr Beeler gave up his gainful employment to care for his daughters full time. The family lived on survivors' benefits consisting of old-age, survivors and disability insurance in addition to supplementary benefits. When the younger daughter turned 18, the widower's pension and supplementary benefits to old-age and survivors' benefits were discontinued. Mr. Beeler was 57 years old at the time and had not been gainfully employed for 16 years. His objections were unsuccessful at the national level. Although the Federal Supreme Court recognised the unequal treatment, it cannot, due to a peculiarity of Swiss law, deviate from laws, even if they contradict the Constitution.[43] Consequently, the Court confirmed the termination of Mr. Beeler's widower's pension.[44] He appealed this decision to the European Court of Human Rights (ECtHR).

Given the clear legal situation, it was no surprise that Switzerland was convicted. Criticism arose within the country's Supreme Court that the ECtHR was interfering in national social security matters. This is significant because Switzerland has not signed the 1st Additional Protocol to the ECHR, which contains the property guarantee. Social security issues are typically dealt with in connection with this Protocol. In this, as in previous cases, the Court opted for a combined application of the broad protection provided under Art. 8 ECHR and Art. 14 ECHR, a practice that has already been criticised in previous court decisions.

The Swiss government has contended that the eligibility criteria for survivors' pensions differ due to the varying standards of living and earned income between widows and widowers, which it argues justifies unequal treatment.

---

[43] Swiss Federal Constitution (Bundesverfassung der Schweizerischen Eidgenossenschaft/BV), 190.
[44] Cardinaux B (2023) Das EGMR-Urteil Beeler und seine Folgen. SZS. 67(3), 125-126.

The ECtHR acknowledges that valid reasons may exist for a difference in treatment between men and women with regard to survivors' pensions. However, in the specific case of Mr. Beeler, the Court determined that the unequal treatment was no longer justified, as his situation was comparable to that of a woman.

This decision established that Mr. Beeler had been wrongfully denied his widower's pension, entitling him to demand the corresponding back payment, a substantial sum. However, recent media reports indicate that Mr Beeler has been unable to reach an agreement with the insurance company on the amount owed to him, suggesting that another legal dispute may be imminent.

For all other insured individuals and widowers, the following decision will be implemented: since the Court's ruling, widowers' pensions will continue even after the youngest child turns 18. However, pensions that have already ceased to be paid will not be reinstated. Other cases of unequal treatment of widowers regarding old-age and survivors or accident insurance remain. Significant work still needs to be done to achieve full equality.

The Court's decision was generally well-received by the Swiss public and seen as a step towards greater equality. However, it soon sparked questions about the legislation's direction: would the more favourable conditions for widows' pensions be extended to all widowers, or would widows' entitlements be aligned with those of widowers?

It is not particularly surprising that the legislator opted for the second option. Survivors' benefits had already been identified as a potential area for cost saving a few years ago, considering that they are sometimes paid even when beneficiaries do not face economic hardship. The Federal Council is preparing the following amendments:[45] widows' and widowers' pensions will be paid to parents, regardless of marital status, until the child's 25th birthday. Married or divorced widows and widowers who no longer have to care for dependent children receive a survivor's pension for two years instead of a lifelong pension to allow for time to adjust to their new financial situation, provided the deceased person had a maintenance obligation. Pensions are thus reserved for persons

---

[45] Swiss Federal Council, Media information, 28 June 2023 (www.admin.ch/gov/de/start/dokumentation/medienmitteilungen.msg-id-96171.html, visited 4 April 2024).

with children. Survivors' pensions for widows or widowers who have not yet reached the age of 55 and who do not have dependent children will cease after a two-year period (transitional provision). For older widows and widowers, a grandfathering guarantee will apply to survivors' pensions.

Switzerland has not been among the pioneers of gender equality in recent decades. Universal women's suffrage at the federal level was only introduced in 1971, one of the last democracies in the world to do so. The gender roles embedded in the social security system have also been slow to change. Nonetheless, some progress has been made recently: in 2022, the Swiss electorate (very narrowly) approved the equalisation of women's retirement age with that of men. The equalisation of widows' and widowers' benefits has been pursued for a long time and is now set to be implemented, extending beyond cases such as Mr Beeler's. For economic reasons, this will more likely be a "downward" adjustment, which is characteristic of the cautious Swiss social legislation.

4. Further developments

In summary, there is significant pressure to adapt survivors' benefits in Switzerland.

The social reality of families and family law have diversified and have moved away from the single-earner model. Civil law on the post-marital maintenance obligation following divorce, in particular, has changed considerably. Social security law will eventually follow suit, albeit with a relatively long delay, with spouses' survivors' benefits adjusted downwards. Only orphans' pensions remain unchallenged.

Bibliography

Cardinaux B (2023) Das EGMR-Urteil Beeler und seine Folgen. SZS. 67(3): 115–133

Cardinaux B (2022) AHV 21: Welche Änderungen bringt die Reform? SZS. 66(6): 339–354

Esping-Andersen G (1990) The three worlds of welfare capitalism. Cambridge: Polity Press

Gächter T and Schwendener M (2005) Nichteheliche Lebensgemeinschaften im Sozialversicherungsrecht. FamPra.ch. 2005(4): 844–869

Gächter T and Tremp D (2019) Social Security Law in Switzerland. Bern: Stämpfli Publishers

Hürzeler M (2014) System und Dogmatik der Hinterlassenenversicherung im Sozialversicherungs- und Haftpflichtrecht. Bern: Stämpfli Publishers

Pieters D (2006) Social Security: An Introduction to the Basic Principles. Alphen an den Rijn: Kluwer Law international

8 Survivors' Benefits in Sweden: Social Security Developments, Collective Agreements and Gender Aspects[1]

Martina Axmin and Jenny Julén Votinius

1. Introduction

The Swedish public welfare system is built on the premise that both spouses are employed. It is also premised that both spouses are covered by an occupational welfare scheme. This assumption, which in fact reflects reality, has been a cornerstone of Sweden's gender equality policy for over 50 years. Female participation in the workforce has increased significantly since the 1970s from an already high level. By the mid-1980s, the difference in employment rates between men and women had decreased significantly, with 77 per cent of women and 80.5 per cent of men in employment in 2023.[2] This development corresponds to the gradual introduction of reforms that sought to increase women's participation in the labour market. These included gender-neutral parental leave, the expansion of public childcare, and individual income taxation. Sweden's welfare state centres around the individual, with every adult expected to be able to sustain themselves and their children with support from public services, benefits and additional supplementary assistance, if neces-

---

[1] This research has partly been carried out within the framework of the research project 'Prolonged Working Lives, Older Workers, and Dismissals. A Study of the Dynamics between Employment Protection, Non-discrimination, and Collective Bargaining', funded by the Swedish Research Council for Health, Working Life, and Welfare (Forte).
[2] Swedish Statistics, Labour Force Surveys, September 2023, population aged 16–64 years.

sary. In this context, the need for survivors' benefits is thus limited; social security benefits associated with the death of a spouse are only provided temporarily, with the intention of easing the transition to the new economic reality (single income household).

This chapter is structured as follows. The first section provides a brief overview of both the Swedish welfare and the occupational welfare systems. In the following two sections, the social insurance and occupational insurance schemes, as well as the public and occupational pension schemes are presented. The next section focuses on the limited role survivors' benefits play in Sweden's public and occupational schemes. The final section of this chapter examines how the interplay between public and occupational schemes for survivors aligns with the social security system's fundamental principles, especially in terms of gender.

2. The Swedish Welfare System

The Swedish welfare system is characterised by its universality and equitable income redistribution. It has traditionally provided benefits on an individual basis. Sweden has a comprehensive range of welfare systems and benefits, with responsibilities for providing these benefits shared among the local, regional and central government.[3] Local governance in Sweden is deeply rooted in tradition, characterised by self-governance and clearly defined responsibilities.[4]

Social welfare services, including social assistance and long-term care for older persons, are managed locally across 290 municipalities. There has been an increasing shift in recent years towards privatising care services within these municipalities.[5] Healthcare services and dentistry, on the other hand, fall under

---

[3] Chapter 1, paragraphs 1 and 7 of the Instrument of Government (1974:152).
[4] Chapter 14, paragraph 4 of the Instrument of Government (1974:152).
[5] Meagher G and Szebehely M (2013) Marketisation in Nordic eldercare: a research report on legislation, oversight, extent and consequence. Stockholm: Stockholm University. See also Pettersson H and Katzin M (2017) Legal approaches to private and public responsibilities for elder care. In: Numhauser Henning A (Ed.) Elder Law. Evolving European Perspectives. Cheltenham: Edward Elgar Publishing, 287-308.

the responsibility of 21 regions. Eligibility for social welfare services is contingent on residency. By the same token, each region assumes responsibility for residents within its territory.

Social security is administered at the state level, with the exception of unemployment benefits, which are administered by 24 autonomous unemployment insurance funds. These funds are economic associations, often closely affiliated with a trade union.

In addition to the public welfare system, the majority of the workforce are also protected by collective agreements that include occupational insurance for social risks. In the Swedish legal context, collective agreements are treated as private contracts; the occupational welfare scheme and the public one are two separate systems. Collectively bargained pension provisions as well as financial assistance in case of sickness, invalidity and unemployment, have been in place for 100+ years. Today's occupational schemes also include provisions on parenthood.[6]

Occupational benefits were initially provided at the firm level only, with no sector-wide schemes in place. Consequently, many workers were not covered at all. Over time, the system expanded, with occupational benefits becoming a matter of collective bargaining; occupational pension schemes were introduced in collective agreements in the 1970s in all sectors. As the welfare state evolved, the role of occupational benefits shifted from being the primary protection against social risks to serving as an important supplement and enhancement to the overall compensation provided by the public welfare system.[7] In recent years, occupational schemes covering risks that fall under the public social security system have gained increasing importance. Social science literature attributes this development to a combination of the strong influence of

---

[6] Jansson O et al (2018) Sweden: Supplementary Occupational Welfare with Near Universal Coverage. In Natali D and Pavolini E (Eds.) Occupational Welfare in Europe: Risks, Opportunities and Social Partner Involvement. European Trade Union Institute (ETUI) and European Social Observatory (OSE), 55–77.

[7] Johansson C (2020) Occupational Pensions and Unemployment Benefits in Sweden. *International Journal of Comparative Labour Law and Industrial Relations*. 36 (3): 339–366.

the social partners and a general decline in the statutory welfare system, including the erosion of statutory benefits that began in the early 1990s.[8]

3. Swedish Social Security

3.1. Public Welfare System

The public welfare system is administered by the Social Insurance Agency (*Försäkringskassan*) and the Pension Agency (*Pensionsmyndigheten*), and is regulated in the Social Insurance Code (2010:110). Unlike in most European countries, healthcare and unemployment insurance are not considered components of social security in the Swedish context. Social security falls within the scope of the Social Insurance Agency and the Pension Agency.[9]

The guiding principles of the Swedish public social security system are universality, equal treatment and just redistribution. Most benefits provided by the social security system are financed through employer contributions,[10] with other benefits financed through state taxes. Individuals are insured on an individual basis, irrespective of their occupation and civil status. This means that family members do not acquire any rights to social security benefits through a working person; each individual must independently meet the insurance conditions to qualify for benefits.

Some benefits are work-based, meaning that eligibility is contingent on working in Sweden.[11] These benefits are intrinsically linked to the labour market, with entitlement associated with economic activity. The level of compensation is determined by level of income. Entitlement to other benefits, in turn,

---

[8] Blomqvist P and Palme J (2020) Universalism in Welfare Policy: The Swedish Case Beyond 1990, *Social Inclusion*. 8(1): 114–123. Compare Greve B (2018) At the Heart of the Nordic Occupational Welfare Model: Occupational Welfare Trajectories in Sweden and Denmark. *Social Policy & Administration*. 52(2): 508–518.

[9] See chapter 1, paragraph 1 and chapter 2, paragraph 2 of the Social Insurance Code (2010:110).

[10] Government Inquiry Report SOU 2017:05, 197.

[11] Chapter 6, paragraph 6 of the Social Insurance Code (2010:110) lists work-based benefits.

is based on residence in Sweden.[12] These benefits are paid at a flat rate. Still other benefits, such as pensions, are both work and residence-based.

The concept of residence is defined in the Social Insurance Code (2010:110). According to this law, anyone who resides in Sweden for at least one year is considered a resident and thus eligible for residence-based social security benefits.[13] Even if an individual temporarily moves abroad, he or she is still considered a resident of Sweden as long as that stay is intended to last less than one year.

3.2. Occupational Insurance[14]

The national industrial relations system is rooted in self-regulation, cooperation between the social partners and autonomous collective bargaining.[15] It operates as a single channel system, with employees exclusively represented by their unions. There are no parallel forms of representation within companies, such as work councils.[16] About 70 per cent of all employees are union mem-

---

[12] Chapter 5, paragraph 9 of the Social Insurance Code (2010:110) lists residence-based benefits.

[13] Chapter 5, paragraph 2 of the Social Insurance Code (2010:110).

[14] In this article, the sections on occupational insurance partly build on findings in Julén Votinius J (2020) Collective Bargaining for Working Parents in Sweden and Its Interaction with the Statutory Benefit System. *International Journal of Comparative Labour Law and Industrial Relations.* 36 (3) 367-386.

[15] For a comprehensive introduction to Swedish labour law, see Numhauser Henning A (2022) Labour Law and Non-Discrimination. In: Bogdan M and Wong C (Eds.) Swedish Legal System. Stockholm: Norstedts Juridik, 295-324.

[16] Compare Biagi M and Tiraboschi M (2010) Forms of Employee Representational Participation. In Blanpain R (Ed.) Comparative Labour Law and Industrial Relations in Industrialized Market Economies. Alphen aan den Rijn: Wolters Kluwer; and Rosen E J (2009) Workplace Representation in Europe – are there any Single-Channel Systems Left? In Blanke T, Roze E, Voogsgeerd H, Zondag W (Eds.) Recasting Worker Involvement? Recent Trends in Information, Consultation and Codetermination of Worker Representatives in a Europeanized Arena. Deventer: Kluwer. Compare Weiss M (2004) The Future of Workers' Participation in the EU. In Barnard C, Morris G S and Deakin S (Eds.) The Future of Labour Law: Liber Amicorum Bob Hepple QC. London: Hart, 229-252 and Bamber G J and Lansbury R D (1998) An Introduction to International and Comparative Employment Relations. In Bamber G J, Russell D and Lansbury R D (Eds.) International and Comparative Employment Relations: A Study of Industrialised Market Economies. London: Sage.

bers, although significant differences exist between sectors and groups of employees. Collective agreement coverage in Sweden is high, with approximately 90 per cent of all employees covered, including all public sector employees and around 83 per cent of private sector employees.[17] Employers bound by a collective agreement are required to apply its terms and conditions to all employees, regardless whether the employees are union members or not.

A collective agreement is a private law contract defined by law as 'an agreement in writing between an organisation of employers or an employer and an organisation of employees about conditions of employment or other type of relationship between employers and employees'.[18] While there is no system that extends collective agreements to all workers, the fact that collective bargaining coverage in Sweden is around 90 per cent results in a de facto *erga omnes* effect.[19] Trade unions are responsible for supervising the implementation of collective agreements, particularly the terms and conditions of employment in statutory law.

Collective agreements are concluded at three different levels. Sectoral-level agreements often delegate authority to the local level to decide on derogations from semi-mandatory legislation. In addition to sectoral- and local-level agreements, collective agreements exist at the national intersectoral level as well. Although few in number, such agreements are crucial as they establish the general framework for cooperation between the social partners and for the collective bargaining process. There are around 670 industry-wide sectoral collective agreements, covering all sectors of the Swedish economy.[20] However, collective agreements on occupational welfare are typically concluded at the intersectional level.[21] Consequently, each of these agreements covers a large share of the labour market, including all private sector blue- and white-collar

---

[17] Swedish National Mediation Office (2023) Medlingsinstitutets årsrapport 2022, 149.
[18] Section 23 of the Co-determination Act (1976:580).
[19] Swedish National Mediation Office (2023) Medlingsinstitutets årsrapport 2022.
[20] Fahlbeck R (2008) Employee Participation in Sweden: Union Paradise and Employer Hell or-? Lund: Juristförlaget. Swedish National Mediation Office (2023) Medlingsinstitutets årsrapport 2022.
[21] Jansson O et al (2018) Sweden: Supplementary Occupational Welfare with Near Universal Coverage. In Natali D and Pavolini E (Eds.) Occupational Welfare in Europe: Risks, Opportunities and Social Partner Involvement. European Trade Union Institute (ETUI) and European Social Observatory (OSE), 55-77.

employees, and all municipal and state employees. The social partners have established joint insurance companies within these intersectoral agreements and disputes are resolved through bipartite arbitration tribunals. This comprehensive occupational welfare system, which supplements the public welfare system, includes all employees who are covered by a collective agreement, i.e. around 90 per cent of the entire workforce.

4. Pensions

4.1. The Public Pension System

The Swedish pension system is often depicted through a cone model. The lower section of the cone, which is described below, represents the public pension system. The central part of the cone consists of major occupational pension schemes, which are discussed in the subsequent section. The top and smallest section of the cone represents private pension savings schemes, which lie outside the scope of this chapter.

A new public pension system was adopted in Sweden in 1999. It covers all individuals who have worked or resided in the country. It consists of an earnings-related component based on notional accounts, a private mandatory contribution system, and an income-tested minimum top-up benefit.[22]

The public pension system's main component is a state-organised, notional defined-contribution system, the pensionable income. The contribution rate of this pay-as-you-go system is set at 16 per cent of pensionable earnings. An individual's pension is thus based on his or her lifetime income.

The public system's second component consists of a mandatory, fully funded defined contribution, the premium pension. The system is administered by the state and financed through a contribution rate of 2.5 per cent of pensionable income. Individuals can choose among over 800 funds to invest in. The rate of return on the funded part is determined by the rate of return on the chosen funds.

---

[22] The discussion on the public pension system is primarily drawn from Section E of the Social Insurance Code (2010:110) labelled 'Old-age Benefits'.

The contributions are paid by both the employer and employee, with the former contributing 10.21 per cent on the employee's full income and the latter paying 7 per cent as gross pensionable income.

There is a ceiling on income qualifying for pension credits. Income earned above this threshold does not yield additional pension benefits. In other words, this income ceiling caps the maximum amount payable from the public pension system. In 2019, 12.5 per cent of women and 25.4 per cent of men had incomes that exceeded this ceiling.[23] Consequently, the system redistributes income from high earners to low-wage earners by imposing a ceiling on earnings for determining benefits but levying employers' contributions on employees' full earnings.

In addition to the income pension and the premium pension, the public pension system provides a minimum threshold known as the guaranteed pension, financed through general taxes. The purpose of the guaranteed pension is to ensure a minimum standard of living in retirement for those with a low or no earnings-related pensions within the public scheme. It is means-tested against the pension drawn from the two other parts within the public welfare system, i.e. the income pension and the premium pension, but not against other incomes, such as work-related income or an occupational pension.

The public pension system covers all persons across all occupational sectors, i.e. it applies to both employees and self-employed persons. The two earnings-related pension schemes within the public pension system, namely the income pension and the premium pension, are work-based pensions. The guaranteed pension is contingent on residency in Sweden. To be eligible for the full guaranteed pension, an individual must have resided in Sweden for at least 40 years.

No statutory retirement age applies in the Swedish public pension system. Individuals can start drawing their pensions from the age of 63 without an upper age limit. However, income-tested pensions cannot be drawn before the age of 66. Starting in 2026, the retirement age will be indexed to a new 'indicative' age, which will increase in line with life expectancy.

---

[23] Social Insurance Inspectorate (2023) Löneväxling till tjänstepension. En redovisning av löneväxlingens omfattning och fördelning, Rapport 2022:3, 26.

4.2. Occupational Pensions

Sweden has a total of seven occupational pension schemes which together cover 90 per cent of employees.[24] The majority are covered by one of four intersectoral schemes, which are described below.[25] In addition, three sectors have their own individual schemes: the banking, insurance and cooperative sector. In all seven occupational schemes, employers contribute 4.5 per cent of the employee's earnings up to the statutory pension scheme's income ceiling. For earnings above that ceiling, employers pay a contribution of 30 per cent on the employee's earnings. Some sectoral agreements include an additional contribution.[26]

The impact of the occupational pension on total pension payout depends on two factors: income and age. For incomes exceeding the public pension system's income ceiling, the occupational pension system provides full compensation. In other words, higher incomes result in a larger share of the total pension drawn from the occupational pension scheme. Age also plays an important role due to the public pension scheme's design to gradually adjust to demographic changes: the later a person is born, the lower his or her public pension will be, and the greater the share of his or her total pension that will be drawn from the occupational pension scheme.

---

[24] Åmark K (2019) De svenska tjänstepensionsavtalen 1947–2017. *Tidskrift för samhällsanalys* (11): 7–40.

[25] Collective Agreement on ITP and TGL. Confederation of Swedish Enterprise – Council for Negotiation and Cooperation for Salaried Employees in the Private Sector PTK, 2023-01-01; Collective Agreement on Occupational Pension SAF–LO, 1996. Confederation of Swedish Enterprise - The Swedish Trade Union Confederation LO, 2021; Collective Agreement on AKAP-KR and KAP-KL. Swedish Municipalities and Regions (SKR) along with the Organisation of Employers in Municipal Companies (Sobona) and The Swedish Municipal Workers' Union (Kommunal), Public Employees' Negotiation Council (OFR) and Negotiation Council for Academics in the Municipal and County Sectors (AkademikerAlliansen), 2022-12-14; Collective Agreement PA–KFS 09 for employees in Municipal Companies; Collective Agreement PA 16 on pensions for State sector employees.

[26] Ferm E (2018) Skydden till efterlevande inom tjänstepensionen. Valen och valbeteendet. Swedish Pension Agency.

5. Survivors' Benefits

5.1. Survivors' Benefits in the Public Welfare System

The widow's pension was abolished in 1999[27] and replaced by a new, gender-neutral benefit, known as the adjustment allowance.[28] Survivors receive this adjustment allowance for 12 months, with payments continuing if the survivor has children younger than 12 years. The amount of the allowance is based on the deceased person's earnings. The amount of pension is set at 55 per cent of the deceased person's actual or hypothetical old age pension from the earnings-related pension system.

This revision was based on the rationale that working-age individuals are expected to support themselves, aligning with the goal of implementing a model where individuals are insured on an individual basis. The preparatory works emphasized that the allowance is intended to help individuals adjust to their new circumstances. It was discussed how long the state should contribute to this adjustment allowance, ultimately resulting in the decision to provide it for a period of 12 months.[29]

The adjustment allowance's upper age limit is currently set at 66 years, which corresponds to the age at which the means-tested guaranteed pension can be drawn. The rationale behind this, according to the preparatory works, was that older persons' working situation would not need to change. However, this age limit has faced criticism for being ageist.[30] The Pension Agency advocated for the age limit to be abolished.[31] Older persons, just like their younger counterparts, also need time to adjust to new circumstances.

A survivor protection component can be included in the premium pension, i.e. the smaller share of the public pension system, which grants a surviving

---

[27] Due to the transition rules for women born before 1944, the widow's pension will continue to be paid for several decades.
[28] The section on survivors' benefits in the public pension system mainly builds on Section F of the Social Insurance Code (2010:110) labeled 'Survivors' Benefits'.
[29] Government Bill 1999/2000:91.
[30] Eriksson A (2022) Efterlevandeskydd - Finns ett behov hos pensionärer idag och ska det finnas en övre åldersgräns? The Swedish Association for Senior Citizens.
[31] Kirs K and Ferm E (2018) Analys av efterlevandeskyddet. Svar på regeringsuppdrag. The Pension Agency.

partner the right to the accrued funds. In this case, the pension is adjusted downward to account for the expected longer payout period.

Survivors' benefits in the public pension system also include a children's pension, which depends on the accrued capital in the deceased person's pension account. A notional additional capital is calculated for the remaining years until the deceased person would have turned 64 years. The child receives around 35 per cent of the deceased person's notional old-age pension. In case of multiple children, each child receives around 20-25 per cent, though the total payout cannot exceed 100 per cent of the notional pension. A surviving child who is not eligible for a children's pension because the parent had no accrued pension rights or only had a very small pension, can receive a surviving children's allowance equal to 40 per cent of the base amount.[32]

5.2. Survivors' Benefits in Occupational Insurance

The occupational pension schemes offer three different types of protection for survivors: occupational group life insurance, repayment cover, and family protection or family pension. All three types of protection are incorporated into all intersectoral collective agreements, though the level of benefits, duration of payment and eligibility conditions differ between the agreements.

An *occupational group life insurance* is included in all occupational pension schemes. This insurance is paid as a lump sum in case of death of an employee who had been working for at least 16 hours per week or half the lump sum amount if the person had been working for at least 8 hours per week. The maximum amount paid out is EUR 26,000 in addition to a small amount in case of surviving children under the age of 21 years. After the age of 55 years, the maximum sum gradually decreases annually, unless the insured person had children.

Repayment cover is an optional insurance that pays out the accrued pension capital to survivors in case of death. The payments are typically made monthly for a specified number of years, depending on whether the person was still working or had already retired at the time of death. Repayment cover comes at a cost, namely in the form of lower payout from the occupational pension

---

[32] In 2023, around EUR 2,000.

scheme. Repayment cover can be activated or deactivated, albeit never retroactively. In the occupational pension agreements in the municipal and regional sector, repayment cover is pre-selected, meaning that the employee must actively opt out of this insurance option.[33] In all other sectors, repayment cover is an option that must be activated by the employee him- or herself.

Family protection is a life insurance policy that provides a predetermined monthly amount to survivors. It is included in the occupational pension schemes in the state, municipal and regional sector and is payable to the spouse for 5 or 6 years, with a monthly amount ranging from EUR 350 to EUR 700, and from EUR 350 – EUR 450 per month for each child. The final amount depends on the deceased person's earnings.[34] In the private sector, family protection is optional and can be selected by the employee in exchange for a reduced occupational pension. It is paid over a period of up to 30 years, with the amount determined by the insured person. Additionally, an extra *family pension* is available for high-income earners in the private sector (white collar) only, and provides exceptional survivors' protection, namely a lifelong payment of an amount equivalent to around 30 per cent of the insured person's salary.[35]

---

[33] Collective Agreement on AKAP-KR och KAP-KL. Swedish Municipalities and Regions (SKR) along with the Organisation of Employers in Municipal Companies (Sobona) and The Swedish Municipal Workers' Union (Kommunal), Public Employees' Negotiation Council (OFR) and Negotiation Council for Academics in the Municipal and County Sectors (AkademikerAlliansen), 2022-12-14.

[34] Collective Agreement on AKAP-KR och KAP-KL. Swedish Municipalities and Regions (SKR) along with the Organisation of Employers in Municipal Companies (Sobona) and The Swedish Municipal Workers' Union (Kommunal), Public Employees' Negotiation Council (OFR) and Negotiation Council for Academics in the Municipal and County Sectors (AkademikerAlliansen), 2022-12-14; Collective Agreement PA–KFS 09 for employees in Municipal Companies; Collective Agreement PA 16 on pensions for State sector employees.

[35] Collective Agreement on ITP och TGL. Confederation of Swedish Enterprise – Council for Negotiation and Cooperation for Salaried Employees in the Private Sector PTK, 2023-01-01.This benefit, which is only available for a limited group with earnings above a threshold, is included but can be opted out of, thereby increasing the occupational pension.

6. Survivors' Benefits at the Intersection of the Public and Occupational Welfare Schemes

Survivors' benefits play a limited role in the Swedish welfare system, and have not attracted much attention in public debate. It is a topic that has given rise to certain concerns, however, especially as regards the interplay between the public and occupational welfare schemes and their impact.

The public and occupational welfare schemes operate independently of each other. Whereas the public welfare scheme is regulated by public law, the occupational welfare scheme is established through private contracts in collective agreements and falls under the remit of private law. In practice, however, these two schemes largely overlap, which is obvious when examining the everyday lives of individuals who benefit from social insurance schemes. While the public welfare scheme serves as the foundation for providing a solid economic safety net, the occupational welfare scheme plays a crucial role in mitigating income loss associated with statutory benefits. but which may be difficult to accommodate in practice. This function of the occupational welfare scheme is particularly evident in relation to pensions, while the public welfare scheme only compensates approximately 65 per cent of the employee's previous earnings. It is designed with the understanding that public pension payments are typically combined with an occupational pension.[36] Consequently, occupational schemes are also a key component of the social protection available to survivors.[37]

When income compensation is provided by social partners instead of the public social security system, it can lead to a greater influence of contractual and industrial relations principles in determining the level of benefits. Consequently, certain fundamental principles of social security law may take a backseat. Contributions to the system are directly tied to the amount of the employee's earnings. The same applies to the benefits that are paid out by that

---

[36] Government Bill 1997/98:151 and Hagen J (2013) A History of the Swedish Pension System, Working Paper 2013:7. Uppsala: Department of Economics, Uppsala University, 126.

[37] Creutzer A (2015) Efterlevande – skyddad eller skyddslös. En studie av efterlevandeskyddet i dag. Allmänna änke- och pupillkassan i Sverige.

particular system, although a specified ceiling applies. Contributions must still be made, even after this ceiling is reached, yet no additional benefits are paid out. The public welfare system has a clear redistributive function, with the aim of reducing economic disparities between different groups in society. In contrast, the Swedish industrial relations system rests on the principle of autonomous collective bargaining, which may in fact contribute to reinforcing these disparities. This is most apparent between employees covered by collective agreements and those who are not. Collective bargaining primarily aims to provide employees with better working conditions than they would have without such agreements. However, there are significant differences even among the 90 per cent of the workforce covered by collective agreements. While trade unions collaborate and coordinate their bargaining to some extent, there is generally a high level of acceptance for sector-specific differences in the working conditions outlined in collective agreements. These differences arise from the bargaining process. As regards survivors' benefits, such differences are observed in the level and duration of the benefits.

The interplay between public and occupational insurance schemes can also negatively impact gender equality, undermining the fundamental principles of the social security system. While the public welfare system as a statutory regulatory instrument plays a central role in implementing national gender equality policies, this is not the case for occupational schemes. Although occupational schemes are gender-neutral and uphold the principle of equality within their scope, they are negotiated to optimise outcomes for the social partners and their members. This negotiation process may, however, inadvertently have a negative impact on gender equality overall. As regards protection for survivors, municipalities and regions include pre-selected options in their occupational pension schemes, while individuals covered by a private sector pension scheme must actively choose the type of survivors' benefits to be included.[38] This observation, though seemingly trivial, holds significant gender implica-

---

[38] The requirement of an active choice applies in the entire private sector with the very limited exception of the Family Pension for high income earners in the private white-collar sector.

tions. With over 75 per cent of public sector employees being women, compared to 37 per cent in the private sector[39], the difference between pensions schemes translates into a disparity in survivors' protection coverage. This means men are far more likely to be eligible for survivors' protection when their spouse passes away, which is paradoxical because women typically have a greater need for such protection. Due to their longer life expectancy, women tend to outlive their male spouses. Second, women still tend to earn less than men, meaning that women are more likely to have a lower pension. This disparity is further exacerbated if survivors' protection in the female employee's occupational pension scheme reduces their overall occupational pension payment.

---

[39] Swedish Occupational Register 2020, Statistics Sweden.

Bibliography

Bamber G J and Lansbury R D (1998) An Introduction to International and Comparative Employment Relations. In Bamber G J and Russell D. Lansbury R D (Eds.) International and Comparative Employment Relations: A Study of Industrialised Market Economies. London: Sage.

Biagi M and Tiraboschi M (2010) Forms of Employee Representational Participation. In Blanpain R (Ed.) Comparative Labour Law and Industrial Relations in Industrialized Market Economies. Alphen aan den Rijn: Wolters Kluwer.

Blomqvist P and Palme J (2020) Universalism in Welfare Policy: The Swedish Case Beyond 1990, Social Inclusion. 8(1), 114-123.

Creutzer A, "Efterlevande – skyddad eller skyddslös" En studie av efterlevandeskyddet i dag, Allmänna änke – och pupillkassan i Sverige, 2015.

Eriksson A (2022) Efterlevandeskydd – Finns ett behov hos pensionärer idag och ska det finnas en övre åldersgräns? The Swedish Association for Senior Citizens.

Fahlbeck R (2008) Employee Participation in Sweden: Union Paradise and Employer Hell or-? Lund: Juristförlaget.

Ferm E (2018) Skydden till efterlevande inom tjänstepensionen. Valen och valbeteendet. Swedish Pension Agency.

Greve B (2018) At the Heart of the Nordic Occupational Welfare Model: Occupational Welfare Trajectories in Sweden and Denmark. Social Policy & Administration. 52(2), 508-518.

Hagen J (2013) A History of the Swedish Pension System, Working Paper 2013:7 (Department of Economics, Uppsala University).

Jansson O et al (2018) Sweden: Supplementary Occupational Welfare with Near Universal Coverage. In Natali D and Pavolini E (Eds.) Occupational Welfare in Europe: Risks, Opportunities and Social Partner Involvement. European Trade Union Institute (ETUI) and European Social Observatory (OSE), 55-77.

Johansson C (2020) Occupational Pensions and Unemployment Benefits in Sweden. International Journal of Comparative Labour Law and Industrial Relations. 36 (3), 339-366.

Julén Votinius J (2020) Collective Bargaining for Working Parents in Sweden and Its Interaction with the Statutory Benefit System. International Journal of Comparative Labour Law and Industrial Relations. 36 (3), 367-386.

Kirs K and Ferm E (2018) Analys av efterlevandeskyddet. Svar på regeringsuppdrag. The Pension Agency.

Meagher G and Szebehely M (2013) Marketisation in Nordic eldercare: a research report on legislation, oversight, extent and consequence. Stockholm: Stockholm University.

Numhauser Henning A (2022) Labour Law and Non-Discrimination. In: Bogdan M and Wong C (Eds.) Swedish Legal System. Stockholm: Norstedts Juridik, 295-324.

Pettersson H and Katzin M (2017) Legal approaches to private and public responsibilities for elder care. In: Numhauser Henning A (Ed.) Elder Law. Evolving European Perspectives. Cheltenham: Edward Elgar Publishing, 287-308.

Rosen E J (2009) Workplace Representation in Europe – are there any Single-Channel Systems Left? In Blanke T, Roze E, Voogsgeerd H and Zondag W (Eds.) Recasting Worker Involvement? Recent Trends in Information, Consultation and Codetermination of Worker Representatives in a Europeanized Arena. Deventer: Kluwer.

Social Insurance Inspectorate (2023) Löneväxling till tjänstepension. En redovisning av löneväxlingens omfattning och fördelning, Rapport 2022:3.

Swedish National Mediation Office (2023) Annual Report 2022.

Weiss M (2004) The Future of Workers' Participation in the EU. In Barnard C, Morris G S and Deakin S (Eds.) The Future of Labour Law: Liber Amicorum Bob Hepple QC. London: Hart, 229-252.

Åmark K (2019) De svenska tjänstepensionsavtalen 1947–2017. Tidskrift för samhällsanalys (11), 7-40.

Government Inquiry Report SOU 2017:05 Svensk social trygghet i en globaliserad värld

Government Bill Prop. 1999/2000:9 Efterlevandepensioner och efterlevandestöd till barn.

Government Bill Prop. 1997/98:151 *Inkomstgrundad ålderspension mm*

Collective Agreement on ITP och TGL. Confederation of Swedish Enterprise – Council for Negotiation and Cooperation for Salaried Employees in the Private Sector PTK, 2023-01-01.

Collective Agreement on Occupational Pension SAF–LO, 1996. Confederation of Swedish Enterprise - The Swedish Trade Union Confederation LO, 2021.

Collective Agreement on AKAP-KR och KAP-KL. Swedish Municipalities and Regions (SKR) along with the Organisation of Employers in Municipal Companies (Sobona) and The Swedish Municipal Workers' Union (Kommunal), Public Employees' Negotiation Council (OFR) and Negotiation Council for Academics in the Municipal and County Sectors (Akademiker-Alliansen), 2022-12-14.

Collective Agreement PA–KFS 09 for employees in Municipal Companies.

Collective Agreement PA 16 on pensions for State sector employees.

9 Modernising Survivors' Pension: The 2022 Reform in Finland

Suvi Ritola

1. Introduction

Survivors' pension plays a crucial role in alleviating poverty among elderly women in Finland and helps bridge the gender gap that is prevalent in pensions.[1] However, Finland's survivors' pension scheme was outdated and in need of reform. The scheme did not cover most of the working-age population, and excluded singles and persons in a cohabiting relationship. Moreover, changes in women's employment and levels of income have reduced the pension gender gap, diminishing the need for the surviving spouse's pension. The terms and conditions of the orphan's pension, on the other hand, depended previously on the family structure they lived in.[2]

The changes introduced to the survivors' pension scheme in 2022 address some of the issues raised above. As a result of this reform, the surviving spouse's pension is now paid for a fixed term of ten years, but includes a long transition period. Under certain conditions, cohabiting partners are also entitled to the surviving spouse's pension. Moreover, the reform ensures more equitable treatment of children who live in non-traditional family structures, as the cohabiting parent is now eligible for the surviving spouse's pension. If there is no eligible spouse, the surviving children are entitled to a share of the surviving spouse's pension.

---

[1] Rantala J and Riihelä M (2016) Eläkeläisnaisten ja -miesten toimeentuloerot vuosina 1995–2013. Finnish Centre for Pensions, reports 1/2016.

[2] STM (2017) Perhe-eläkeselvitys. Työeläkejärjestelmän perhe-eläketurvan kehittämisvaihtoehtoja. Sosiaali- ja terveysministeriön raportteja ja muistioita 2017:19.

The survivors' pension was introduced in Finland in 1967, five years after the Employees' Pensions Act (Finland's private sector pension act) took effect. The introduction of the earnings-related pension scheme marked the beginning of a focus on labour market-driven social insurance policy in Finnish legislation.[3] Today, the statutory earnings-related pension scheme is regulated in legislation, while the scheme's principles are largely determined through negotiations between the social partners and the government, based on a tripartite administrative model.

In 1967, the beneficiaries of earnings-related survivors' pensions were female surviving spouses and the children of the deceased, who were under the age of 18. In 1969, the national pension system introduced survivors' pensions, as well. The survivors' pension scheme underwent only one major reform prior to 2022, which took effect in 1990. The main amendments at the time included equal eligibility for men and women to the surviving spouse's pension and the separation of the surviving spouse's pension from the orphan's pension. Furthermore, the calculation of the surviving spouse's pension was adapted to include a reduction that was based on the amount of the surviving spouse's own pension.[4]

The original purpose of the survivors' pension was to compensate for the loss of income caused by the death of the family's breadwinner. The objectives of the survivors' pension were redefined in the 1990 reform to adjust the family's income to the changed circumstances and essentially to maintain its previous standard of living. The surviving spouse's livelihood was to be primarily composed of his or her own gainful employment, while the surviving spouse's pension aimed to supplement his or her means of livelihood. The key objective of the survivors' pension scheme was to ensure the livelihoods of the deceased's minors.[5]

---

[3] Kontio K (2007) History of pension provision. In: Hietaniemi M and Ritola S (Eds.) The Finnish Pension System. Finnish Centre for Pensions, Handbooks 2007:6.

[4] Hannikainen M and Vauhkonen J (2012) The History of Finnish Earnings-related Pension in the Private Sector. Summary of Ansioiden mukaan. Yksityisalojen työeläkkeiden historia; Takala M, Salonen J and Lampi J (2015) Survivors' pensions in Finland. Finnish Centre for Pensions, Working papers 02/2015.

[5] HE 173/89 (1989) Hallituksen esitys Eduskunnalle perhe-eläkejärjestelmän kokonaisuudistusta koskeviksi laeiksi.

Since the 2022 reform, the objective of the survivors' pension no longer is to maintain the surviving beneficiaries' level of accustomed income indefinitely, but instead to support them during the adjustment period following a spouse's death. The reform thus aims to provide financial support during the adjustment period only instead of providing lifelong support, to improve the fairness and inclusivity of the benefit for different types of family structures with children, and to bolster the financial sustainability of the earnings-related pension scheme.

2. The Finnish pension system and the survivors' pension scheme

2.1. The Finnish pension system

The Finnish statutory pension system comprises earnings-related pensions and residence-based national pensions (including the guarantee pension) (see Table 1). National and guarantee pensions provide beneficiaries with a basic level of income security and protection against poverty, while employment-related pensions are designed to help them maintain – at least to a reasonable extent – the level of income they earned during their working career.[6] The amount of the surviving spouse's earnings-related pension has implications for the amount of national pension he or she will receive: each euro of the beneficiary's earnings-related pension reduces his or her full national pension by 50 cents until the surviving spouse's earnings-related pension reaches a level of around EUR 1,600 (EUR 1,400 if living with another spouse), at which point the national pension is no longer provided. The pensioner is eligible for the guarantee pension if his or her total pension falls below the amount of the full guarantee pension (EUR 976 in 2024). The amount of the full national and guarantee pension is equal to around 25 per cent of wage earners' average income in Finland.

---

[6] Ritola S and Väänänen N (Eds.) (2023) Understanding Finnish Pensions, SKS Kirjat, Helsinki; Ritola S and Tuominen S (2024) Total pension in Finland 2024 – How are earnings-related pensions, national pensions and taxation determined? Finnish Centre for Pensions, Reports 4/2024.

Table 1. Main features of Finland's pension system

	Earnings-related pension	National pension (Kela)
Principle	Maintains a reasonable level of income	Guarantees a minimum income
Coverage	Employees and self-employed persons	Residents in Finland
Benefit model	Defined benefit, accrual rate of 1.5% of gross annual earnings	Flat-rate national pension and guarantee pension, income-tested
Financing	PAYG principle, partial funding, contributions	Taxation
Survivors' pension	- Surviving spouse's pension - Orphan's pension - Amount based on pension of deceased person	- Surviving spouse's pension for those under the age of 65 years - Orphan's pension - Fixed amount, means-tested

Employer-specific pensions, pensions based on labour market agreements and personal insurance policies are not widespread in Finland because the statutory earnings-related pension scheme covers the entire workforce with no upper limits on contributions or pensions.

The purpose of the national non-contributory pension scheme is the provision of basic security to beneficiaries. At the end of 2022, the total number of retirees in Finland (including those who received a survivors' pension) was 1,648,000. With a total population of 5.6 million, this means that over one quarter of the population received some form of pension. The number of pensioners receiving a national pension has decreased due to the legal amendments introduced by various reforms, while the amount of earnings-related pensions has gradually increased. At the end of 2022, a total of 66 per cent of all retirees received an earnings-related pension only, whereas the pensions of 29 per cent of retirees were drawn from both the earnings-related and the national pension schemes, and roughly 5 per cent received a national pension only.[7]

2.2. The concept of family in social security

The Nordic concept of social security is grounded in individual rights. This principle has been further reinforced in Finland over the years, with the revised Constitution of 2000 enshrining fundamental rights as individual rights. The taxation unit has been the individual since 1976, and not the household. However, according to the Marriage Act, married spouses are obligated to contribute to each other's maintenance, which includes meeting both their joint and individual needs. The surviving spouse's pension can be seen as a continuation of this maintenance obligation once the spouse passes away.[8]

Many families' structure differs from the traditional concept of the nuclear family consisting of two parents and children. Many principles derived from this notion continue to influence the concept of family, both in everyday debate and in legislation. Since the 1970s the Nordic countries have implemented legislation that aims to treat different forms of living arrangements impartially. Policy aims to secure children's rights through legislation that does not distinguish between different family structures, for example whether the parents live together or not. Defining a family based exclusively on marriage is problematic. Considering only certain types of family structures as 'proper' families is a moral viewpoint that should not be reflected in legislation.[9]

From a legal perspective, only marriage or a registered partnership bears any significance for family relationships and the division of property. Cohabitation gained more legal weight in 2011, when the Act on the Dissolution of the

---

[7] Finnish Centre for Pensions (2023a) Statistical yearbook of pensioners in Finland 2022. Statistics from the Finnish Centre for Pensions 11/2023. Helsinki 2023.

[8] Hietaniemi M (2014a) Perhe-eläkkeeseen vaikuttavat muutossuuntaukset. In Hietaniemi M and Ritola S (Eds.) Näkökulmia perhe-eläkkeen kehittämistarpeisiin. Finnish centre for Pensions, reports 4/2014.

[9] Faurie M and Kalliomaa-Puha L (2010) Jääkaappi, osoite vai sukuside? Perheen määritelmät sosiaalilainsäädännössä. In Hämäläinen U and Kangas O (Eds.) Perhepiirissä. Kelan tutkimusosasto, Helsinki.

Household of Cohabiting Partners entered into force. Accordingly, if cohabiting partners have lived together for at least five years or have a child together, they are also entitled to compensation for their contribution to the joint household.[10]

The Finnish survivors' pension, particularly the surviving spouse's pension, was initially grounded in the notion of the traditional family. The principle of indefinitely maintaining the surviving spouse's standard of living reflects the idea of lifelong marriage and the single earner family model. Despite changes in the concept of family, including shifts in the division of labour, the purpose of the survivors' pension remained largely unchanged.

2.3. Surviving spouse's pension

The reform of 2022 did not modify the eligibility rules of the surviving spouse's pension for married spouses. If the surviving spouse has or had a child (biological or adopted) with the deceased, and if they got married before the deceased reached the age of 65, the surviving spouse is entitled to the surviving spouse's pension without meeting any other eligibility criteria. If the spouses did not have a child together, the surviving spouse is only entitled to the surviving spouse's pension if the following conditions are met:

- the surviving spouse had already reached the age of 50 at the time of the principal beneficiary's death or had been receiving a disability pension for at least three years;
- the spouses married before the surviving spouse reached the age of 50 and before the deceased had reached the age of 65, and
- the spouses had been married for at least five years.

Payment of the surviving spouse's pension ends if the surviving spouse remarries before reaching the age of 50. Registered partners are treated equally to married spouses. Same-sex marriages have been legally recognised in Finland since March 2017. New registered partnerships can now no longer be established, but existing ones remain valid and can be converted into a marriage by notification.

---

[10] Act 26/2011. Act on the Dissolution of the Household of Cohabiting Partners. Unofficial translation, Ministry of Justice, Finland.

Since 2022, cohabiting partners have also been entitled to the surviving spouse's pension if the following criteria are met:

- the spouse died in 2022 or later;
- the surviving common-law spouse has a dependent child under the age of 18 together with the deceased;
- the surviving common-law spouse and the deceased shared a household for at least five years before his or her spouse passed away;
- the surviving common-law spouse and the deceased spouse began sharing a household before the deceased spouse turned 65, and
- that neither of the common-law spouses was married to another person.[11]

Since 2022, the surviving spouse's pension is provided to surviving spouses born in 1975 or later for a total of ten years. The surviving spouse's pension is in any case paid until the youngest recipient of an orphan's pension turns 18 years. A surviving spouse's pension granted on the basis of a common-law marriage is also provided until the youngest child turns 18 years.

Survivors' pensions are calculated based on the deceased person's pension entitlement and his or her number of beneficiaries. The reform did not change the rules for determining the amount of survivors' pension. The basis for calculating this amount is the amount of the deceased person's old-age or disability pension. If the deceased was not yet retired when he or she passed away, the basis for calculating the amount of survivors' pension is the disability pension the deceased would have been entitled to at the time of his or her death. The surviving spouse's pension may be reduced depending on the amount of the surviving spouse's own pension.

The total amount of the surviving spouse's pension (before any reduction) and the orphan's pension as a share of the deceased person's pension is presented in Table 2. If the surviving spouse is the sole beneficiary, then the surviving spouse's pension amounts to half of the deceased spouse's pension. The combined amount of the surviving spouse's pension and the orphan's pension may, at most, total the full amount of the deceased person's pension.

---

[11] Työntekijän eläkelaki [Employees Pensions Act] 19.5.2006/395. Finlex.

Table 2. The surviving spouse and children's share of the survivors' pension

Number of children	0	1	2	3	4+
Surviving spouse's pension	6/12	6/12	5/12	3/12	2/12
Orphan's pension	-	4/12	7/12	9/12	10/12
Total	6/12	10/12	12/12	12/12	12/12

The surviving spouse's pension based on an earnings-related pension is reduced once the youngest child reaches the age of 18 years. If there are no children as beneficiaries, the surviving spouse's pension is reduced after an initial period of six months, provided the surviving spouse is under the age of 65. The surviving spouse's pension is reduced immediately if he or she is retired at the time of the spouse's death.

The purpose of reducing the surviving spouse's pension is to adjust his or her total income to a level that is comparable to that he or she had prior to the spouse's death. The surviving spouse's pension is reduced if the surviving spouse's own pension – or the computational disability pension, in case he or she has not yet retired – amounts to more than EUR 818.50 (in 2024). The full surviving spouse's pension is reduced by half of the difference between the surviving spouse's own pension and this specific threshold. Consequently, the amount of the surviving spouse's pension depends on the difference between the two spouses' incomes and he or she will continue to receive it, even if his or her own pension is high, provided the deceased spouse's pension was equal to or higher than the surviving spouse's pension.

The reduction typically affects the amount of the surviving spouse's pension paid to widowers, as men's pensions are usually higher than women's. As a result of this reduction rule, about 36 per cent of widowers do not receive the surviving spouse's pension. The corresponding share for widows is around 6 per cent. In 2022, the average surviving spouse's pension based on an earnings-related pension (excluding zero-euro pensions) amounted to EUR 673 per month. The monthly surviving spouse's pension for women was EUR 713, on average, and EUR 378 for men.

Entitlement to the surviving spouse's pension normally ceases upon divorce. A former spouse may, however, be entitled to the surviving spouse's pension based on his or her spouse's earnings-related pension if the deceased was required to pay alimony to his or her former spouse under a legally binding decision. The amount of this pension benefit is based on the amount of alimony the former spouse received and intends to ensure a minimum income for him or her rather than to maintain his or her previous level of income. It is rare for a former spouse to be granted the surviving spouse's pension; fewer than 10 surviving spouse's pensions have been granted annually to former spouses over the past decade.

Within the scope of the national pension system, Kela provides the surviving spouse's pension to the surviving spouse who is under the age of 65, that is, to an individual who has not yet reached statutory retirement age. Former spouses are not eligible for a surviving spouse's pension provided by the national pension system. In all other cases, the benefit provided by the national pension system is granted under the same conditions as in the earnings-related pension scheme. All surviving spouses are entitled to an initial surviving spouse's pension for a six-month period following their spouse's death. The fixed amount of this initial pension – regardless of the surviving spouse's own earnings or wealth – is EUR 383 per month in 2024. Following this 6-month period, the surviving spouse may be entitled to continued payment of the surviving spouse's pension consisting of a basic amount and a means-tested supplement.[12]

If the spouse's death was caused by a workplace accident or a traffic incident, family members might be eligible for a survivors' pension through either mandatory workers' compensation insurance or motor vehicle liability insurance. These benefits take precedence over the earnings-related pension, which is only paid for the part that exceeds the primary benefit.[13]

---

[12] Kansaneläkelaki [National Pensions Act] 11.5.2007/568.
[13] See, for example Ritola S and Tuominen S (2024) Total pension in Finland 2024 – How are earnings-related pensions, national pensions and taxation determined? Finnish Centre for Pensions, Reports 3/2024.

2.4. Orphan's pension

The orphan's pension is provided to the biological or adopted child of the deceased parent. The surviving spouse's child or adopted child may also qualify for an orphan's pension, if the child resided in the same household and if his or her parent was married to the deceased. This pension is provided to children under the age of 20 years. Prior to the 2022 reform, the age limit was 18 years. The total amount of orphan's pension (Table 2) is distributed among all eligible children. Since 2022, the surviving spouse's share of the pension is paid to the children in the form of an orphan's pension if there is no surviving spouse who is entitled to the surviving spouse's pension.

Within the national pension system, Kela provides the orphan's pension to the deceased person's biological or adopted children, or to children who were under his or her care, provided they are under the age of 18 years. If the child is a full-time student, the orphan's pension is provided until the child reaches the age of 21 years. A student's pension benefit only includes the basic amount of the orphan's pension. If both of the child's parents or guardians are deceased, he or she receives the orphan's pension for both of them. The orphan's pension consists of a basic amount (EUR 60/month) – regardless of the child's own earnings – and the additional amount (capped at EUR 90/month). The additional amount is offset against any other orphan's pension the child receives and is not paid if that pension amount exceeds EUR 236.

3. Changes in society as the driver of the reform

The functioning and relevance of the survivors' pension are influenced by changes in family structures and the way men's and women's pensions are accumulated. The share of people in Finland who live alone or are in cohabiting relationships has increased, resulting in a decrease in the payment of surviving spouse's pensions. Moreover, women's participation in the labour market has increased since the 1960s, reducing the need to supplement women's income in old age with the surviving spouse's pension. However, it is expected that the gender gap will persist in the future.

3.1. Changing family structures

Marriage continues to be the prevailing form of cohabitation, but significant changes in family structures have been observed in recent decades. The number of married couples with children has decreased since the 1990s, while other types of family structures have become more prevalent (see Figure 1). The most common family structure in 1992 was a married couple with children. By 2022, however, the most common family structure was a married couple without children. The number of families consisting of a married couple and children has been steadily decreasing. At the same time, the number of families consisting of a cohabiting couple without children and a cohabiting couple with children has been on the rise.[14]

Figure 1. Population by family status in 1992–2022, %*

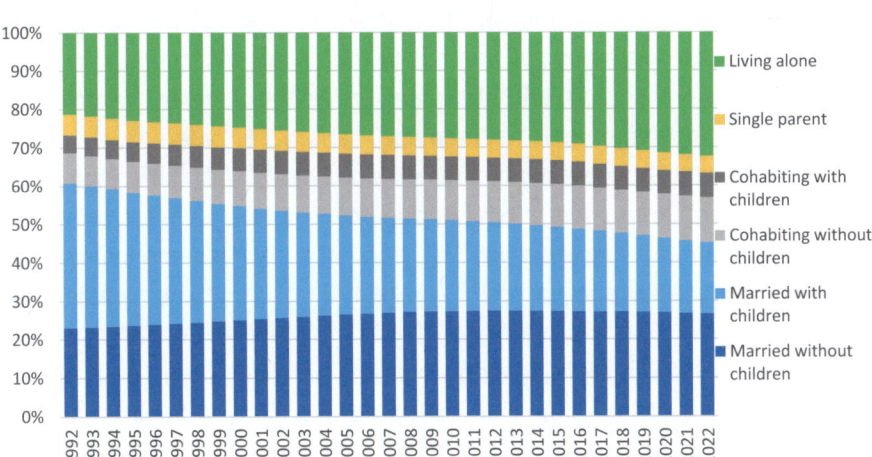

*Excluding children, people not belonging to the family but who are not living alone, institutionalised persons and an unclassified population.

---

[14] Statistics Finland (2023a) Families. Reference period: 2022. Helsinki: Statistics Finland [Referenced: 24 January 2024].

The share of reconstituted families has slightly increased since the 1990s, but has remained relatively stable over the last decade. A reconstituted family refers to a family with at least one child under the age of 18 years, which belongs to only one of the parents. As of the end of 2021, around 9 per cent of families with children were classified as reconstituted families compared to 7 per cent in 1990. Roughly half of the parents of reconstituted families are cohabiting, while half are married.[15] According to the survivors' pension rules, if the parents of a reconstituted family are not married, the children are only eligible for the earnings-related orphan's pension after the death of their own parent.

The number of new marriages declined between 1970 and 1990, increased in the first decade of the 21st century and then returned to the level of the late 1990s. The marriage rate, i.e. the ratio of those who are married to those who are eligible to marry, has been decreasing almost continuously since 2008. The divorce rate has remained stable since the 1990s. The average age at first marriage has been rising continuously. The average age of women entering their first marriage was around 27 years at the beginning of the 1990s, increasing to 32.5 years of age in 2022. Men are two years older than women, on average, when they enter their first marriage, namely 34.3 years.[16]

Cohabitation has become more common since the 1970s. Cohabitation has gradually evolved from being a brief arrangement before marriage to a long-term commitment to living together. This trend has also become increasingly common among older age groups.[17] The number of cohabiting couples has grown from around 200,000 in the early 1990s to currently 360,000.[18]

The share of individuals living alone has also increased from 14 per cent in 1992 to 23 per cent in 2022, while that of people living in families has decreased. Living alone is a significant contributor to poverty, especially among

---

[15] Pietiläinen M and Toivola J (2023) Valtaosa lapsista kasvaa edelleen aviopariperheessä – avopareja aiempaa enemmän, uusperheitä vähemmän. Tieto and Trendit 11 January 2023.

[16] Statistics Finland (2023b) Changes in marital status [Referenced: 5 February 2024]. Accessed: https://www.stat.fi/en/statistics/ssaaty

[17] Kontula O (2016) Lemmen paula. Seksuaalinen hyvinvointi parisuhdeonnen avaimena. Perhebarometri 2016. Katsauksia/Väestöliitto, Väestöntutkimuslaitos. E50/2016.

[18] Statistics Finland (2023a) Families. Reference period: 2022. Helsinki: Statistics Finland [Referenced: 24 January 2024].

older women.[19] If the gender gap in life expectancy continues to narrow, it is expected that women will spend more years living together with a spouse in the future, while living alone will become more common among men. Despite this trend, the share of women living alone in the future is still expected to exceed that of men who live alone.[20]

Prior to the survivors' pension reform, the fact that singles paid the statutory survivors' pension contribution as part of their total earnings-related pension contributions without ever benefitting from it was criticised.[21] It was argued that the surviving spouse's pension could be considered an income transfer from singles to married couples. Statistics indicate that married men earn a higher pension on average, and also live longer than single men.[22] The survivors' pension scheme could therefore be considered an income transfer from a population group that is at a disadvantage and has a lower life expectancy to a group that enjoys both a higher income and a higher life expectancy.[23] From a different perspective, however, supporting families through a collective survivors' pension is considered justifiable, as the pension system is an intergenerational link. It is argued that the pension system, as well as society at large, should support families and help boost birth rates.[24]

---

[19] Rantala J and Riihelä M (2016) Eläkeläisnaisten ja -miesten toimeentuloerot vuosina 1995–2013. Finnish Centre for Pensions, Reports 1/2016.

[20] Martikainen P, Murphy M, Moustgaard H and Mikkonen J (2016) Changes in the household structure of the Finnish elderly by age, sex and educational attainment in 1987–2035. Kela working papers 88.

[21] Lilja R (2014) Suomalainen perhe-eläkejärjestelmä tulee uudistaa. Talous & yhteiskunta 3/2014.

[22] STM (2017) Perhe-eläkeselvitys. Työeläkejärjestelmän perhe-eläketurvan kehittämisvaihtoehtoja. Sosiaali- ja terveysministeriön raportteja ja muistioita 2017:19.

[23] See e.g. Lilja R (2014) Suomalainen perhe-eläkejärjestelmä tulee uudistaa. Talous & yhteiskunta 3/2014., Määttänen N (2014) The welfare effects of the Finnish survivors' pension scheme. Nordic Journal of Political Economy. Volume 39, 2014.

[24] Kiander J (2014) Tarvitaanko enää perhe-eläkkeitä? Periaatteellista pohdintaa. In Hietaniemi M and Ritola S (Eds.) Näkökulmia perhe-eläkkeen kehittämistarpeisiin. Finnish Centre for Pensions, Reports 4/2014.

3.2. Gender pension gap

In Finland, pensions provided by the earnings-related pension scheme reflect the labour market's gender disparities. The gender gap in earnings-related pensions was 30 per cent at the end of 2022. The average monthly earnings-related pension was EUR 1,407 for women and EUR 2,007 for men. When including surviving spouse's pensions, national pensions and special provision pensions, the gender gap narrows to 21 per cent, with the average total monthly pension for men at EUR 2,112 and EUR 1,676 for women.[25]

In addition to the smoothing effect of the surviving spouse's pension, the national pension system also levels out the overall pensions of men and women. Gender disparities are particularly evident among those who receive an earnings-related pension only.[26] The national pension amount received by both female and male recipients is equal but constitutes a greater share of women's total pension. At the end of 2022, 39 per cent of female and 24 per cent of male pensioners aged 65 years or older were beneficiaries of a national pension.[27]

The comprehensive earnings-related pension scheme in Finland covers nearly all types of earnings and applies uniform conditions for eligibility. This means that part-time work and lower-wage occupations are covered by the scheme as well. The reason for lower earnings-related pensions among women and their greater reliance on national pensions is thus not associated with difficulties in meeting the pension scheme's conditions, as is the case in some occupational pension schemes in other countries, but mainly due to their level of earnings.

The gender gap in total pensions narrowed by three percentage points between 2002 and 2022. A more significant change in the structure of total pensions has been observed, however. The gender gap in earnings-related pensions decreased from 44 per cent in 2002 to 30 per cent in 2022. The change in total pensions is less pronounced due to the coordination system, where the

---

[25] Finnish Centre for Pensions (2024) Statistical database.
[26] Kuivalainen S, Nivalainen S, Järnefelt N and Kuitto K (2018) Length of working life and pension income: empirical evidence on gender and socioeconomic differences from Finland. Cambridge University Press 2018.
[27] Finnish Centre for Pensions (2024) Statistical database.

amount of national pensions decreases as the amount of earnings-related pensions rises.

While women's pension levels are expected to continue to catch up with men's, the gender gap in pensions will persist in the future. Long-term projections by the Finnish Centre for Pensions estimate that the gap in median pensions (i.e. national and earnings-related pensions) will decrease to 15 per cent by the end of the 2050s, and to 10 per cent by the mid-2080s.[28]

The gender pension gap arises from differences in the jobs and earnings of men and women. The labour market participation rate among men and women in Finland is almost equal, with women accounting for roughly half of the total workforce since at least the early 1980s. Moreover, Finnish women tend to be better educated than men.[29] In 2023, the employment rate (among individuals aged 20–64 years) was 77.9 per cent for men and 78.0 per cent for women.[30] The average working life of women who retired on an old-age pension in 2022 spanned 35.3 years compared to 36.4 years for men.[31] The working lives of the men and women who are starting their careers now are expected to be nearly equally long.

Nevertheless, women and men occupy very different positions in the labour market: women's wages are lower, they tend to work part time more often and conclude more fixed-term contracts. In international comparison, the number of Finnish women who work part time is relatively low, but this share has increased. In 2022, 24 per cent of employed women in Finland worked part time, while the EU average was 28 per cent.

The average monthly wage for men with regular working hours in 2022 was EUR 4,117, and EUR 3,476 for women. Over the last 20 years, the wage gap has narrowed from 19.0 per cent to 15.6 per cent.[32] One significant factor that

---

[28] Tikanmäki H, Reipas K, Lappo S, Merilä V, Nopola T and Sankala M (2022) Lakisääteiset eläkkeet: pitkän aikavälin laskelmat. Finnish Centre for Pensions reports 5/2022. https://urn.fi/URN:ISBN:978-951-691-351-6
[29] Statistics Finland (2023c) Educational structure of population. Reference period: 2022.
[30] Statistics Finland (2024a) Labour force survey. Helsinki: [Referenced: 6.2.2024]. Access method: https://stat.fi/en/statistics/tyti
[31] Finnish Centre for Pensions (2023b) Pension Indicators 2023. Finnish Centre for Pensions reports 6/2023.
[32] Statistics Finland (2024b) Index of wage and salary earnings. [Referenced: 9 February 2024]. Access method: https://stat.fi/en/statistics/ati

contributes to this wage difference is labour market segregation. The labour market is divided into male and female occupations, with women often holding lower positions within the same occupation. Women are also more likely to work in care and education in the public sector, while men usually work in industry in the private sector.

3.3. Pension payments for childcare periods

Another significant factor for the gender wage and pension gap is the unequal distribution of parental leave between mothers and fathers. In Finland, it is still primarily mothers who stay at home to care for the children and who bear the associated career risks. The "child penalty" is relatively high in Finland, especially considering the equal employment rates and the prevalence of full-time work among women.[33] Parental leave was reformed in 2022, with the objective of distributing parental leave more evenly between mothers and fathers. However, the effects of this reform will only become apparent in a few years.

When survivors' pensions were introduced in Finland in 1967, it was common for mothers to stay at home with the children and to be out of the labour market for extended periods. Reflecting the society of the time, only women were entitled to the surviving spouse's pension. A functioning daycare system and the possibility of combining a career with family life are essential if both parents are to participate in the labour market. Today, Finland has comprehensive policies in place to reconcile work and family life, enabling and encouraging mothers and married women to work. Spouses are taxed separately, and public daycare is widely available. In the 1970s, spots in daycare centres were first allotted based on social grounds, but such spots became an individual right in the 1990s, meaning that all children below school age have the right to access daycare.

The Finnish parental leave scheme includes an earnings-related daily allowance that can be paid flexibly for a total of 13 months and is shared between the child's mother and father (designated shares). A lower homecare allowance is provided until the child reaches the age of three. The homecare allowance

---

[33] Sieppi A and Pehkonen J (2019) Parenthood and gender inequality: Population-based evidence on the child penalty in Finland. Economics Letters 182 (2019) 5–9, Elsevier B.V.

has been criticised both in Finland and internationally for encouraging mothers to stay out of the labour market for extended periods.[34] However, the homecare allowance was retained after the 2022 reform.

From a pension accrual perspective, the duration of parental leave is crucial. Periods covered by earnings-related parental allowances do not result in pension losses compared to accruals during periods of paid employment. On the other hand, following the homecare allowance period, pension accrual is based on a fixed monthly amount (EUR 857 in 2024), often leading to significantly lower accrual compared to periods of employment. Prior to the pension reform of 2005, accrual for periods of childcare varied across different pension acts and only affected employees in certain types of employment. Although pensions compensate for childcare periods, it is likely that women's caregiving responsibilities also affect their pensions due to slower career progression and lower earnings.

3.4. Trends of surviving spouse's pensions

In 2022, roughly 211,000 surviving spouses received a surviving spouse's pension from the earnings-related pension scheme, accounting for 13 per cent of all pension recipients. As illustrated in Figure 2, the majority of recipients were women. Men have been eligible for the surviving spouse's pension since 1990, and the share of male recipients has gradually increased. At present, 16 per cent of all recipients of the surviving spouse's pension are male. The number of beneficiaries has decreased since 2007.[35]

---

[34] For example, OECD (2018) OECD Economic Surveys: Finland 2018, OECD Publishing, Paris.
[35] Finnish Centre for Pensions (2024) Statistical database.

Figure 2. Recipients of earnings-related surviving spouse's pension in 1982–2022, by sex

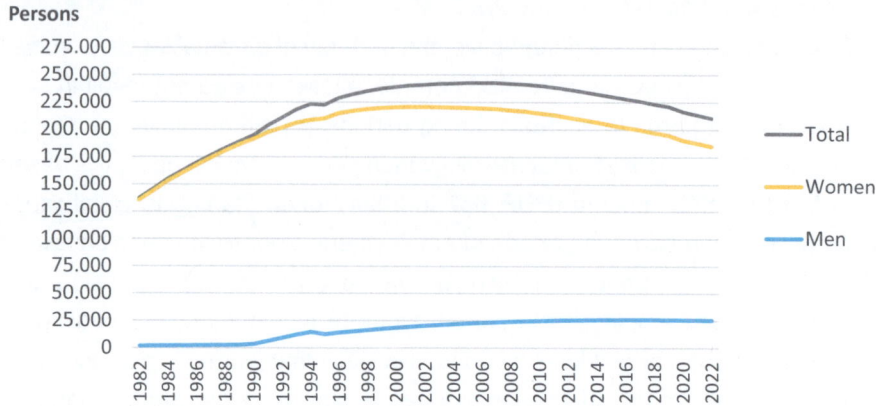

The relative significance of the survivors' pension has diminished over the last two decades. The ratio of surviving spouse's pension recipients to old-age pension recipients has decreased, while the total number of pensioners continued growing over the same period. The ratio for women fell from 43 per cent to 25 per cent between 2000 and 2021. The amount of survivor's benefits as an average share of total pensions has decreased as well.

The high share of female surviving spouses can be attributed to the longevity of women and to the fact that wives are usually younger than their husbands. The average age difference between spouses in Finland, who have been exclusively married to each other, is two years and has remained consistent for nearly 50 years.[36]

Entitlement to surviving spouse's pension has been, and continues to be, primarily tied to marriage, children and specific age limits. Consequently, shifts in societal behaviour also have an impact on the number of recipients of surviving spouse's pension. For example, the declining marriage rate and rising prevalence of cohabitation likely contribute to the declining number of recipients of surviving spouse's pension.

---

[36] Takala M, Salonen J and Lampi J (2015) Survivors' pensions in Finland. Finnish Centre for Pensions, Working papers 02/2015.

Ninety per cent of women who receive surviving spouse's pensions are aged 65 years or older, while the corresponding figure for men is 85 per cent. The age of recipients of surviving spouse's pensions is on the rise: in 1998, their average age was 71.9 years and had risen to 78.0 years by 2018. The largest demographic group among both widows and widowers consists of individuals aged 80–84 years. Among women over the age of 85 years, more than half are widows. With life expectancy projected to increase in the future, the age at which a person becomes a widow(er) is also expected to rise.

4. Objectives and impacts of the reform

The reform of survivors' pension took effect in early 2022.[37] Both the earnings-related pension scheme and the national pension system were amended. The reform was preceded by a report published in 2017 by a tripartite working group, presenting alternative models as a basis for discussion on how to improve the earnings-related survivors' pension scheme.[38] The amendments to the law were negotiated in line with the agreement reached by the social partners in June 2019.[39]

The reform's objective was to modernise the statutory survivors' pension and align it with society and families' evolving needs. Going forward, the survivors' pension scheme aims to ensure the recipients' livelihood during the adjustment period following the spouse's death. The reform also focused on survivors' pension benefits for children and families with children, and on the financial sustainability of the earnings-related pension scheme.

4.1. Surviving spouse's pension for a fixed term

The reform of the surviving spouse's pension redefined the benefit's purpose. Instead of providing lifelong support to the surviving spouse, the focus shifted

---

[37] Työntekijän eläkelaki 19 May 2006/395, Kansaneläkelaki 11 May 2007/568
[38] STM (2017) Perhe-eläkeselvitys. Työeläkejärjestelmän perhe-eläketurvan kehittämisvaihtoehtoja. Sosiaali- ja terveysministeriön raportteja ja muistioita 2017:19.
[39] Agreement (2019) Sopimus vuoden 2017 eläkeuudistuksen jatkoneuvotteluihin liittyvistä asioista. 11 June 2019, Helsinki; HE 66/2021 vp, Hallituksen esitys eduskunnalle laeiksi työeläkelakien ja kansaneläkelain muuttamisesta sekä niihin liittyviksi laeiksi.

towards helping him or her adjust to life following the spouse's death. It was therefore decided to limit the surviving spouse's pension to ten years, but at least until the youngest child reaches the age of 18. While the Ministry's report proposed to further reduce the payment period to either two or six years, the social partners were in favour of a longer fixed-term payment period.

The reform's transition period is quite long, given that the 10-year fixed-term benefit only applies to individuals born in 1975 and later. Despite the reform of the surviving spouse's pension, beneficiaries born before 1975 or whose spouse passed away before 1 January 2022 will continue to receive the benefit indefinitely. The underlying idea was to protect older generations who may not have had sufficient time to adapt their career choices like younger generations. The impact of the fixed-term surviving spouse's pension will only become apparent after several decades.

The introduction of the fixed-term benefit will reduce the number of recipients of the surviving spouse's pension and will shorten the duration of the payment of the benefit. In the long term, it is projected that the fixed-term benefit will reduce the number of recipients by more than 25 per cent, with a significant decline expected from the 2040s onwards. Even without the reform, it is expected that the duration of the surviving spouse's pension will decrease in the future: the gap in the life expectancy between men and women is narrowing, people are increasingly living longer, and the interval between the deaths of spouses is becoming shorter.

From a life-cycle perspective, the reform will have the greatest financial impact on young widows who used to receive the surviving spouse's pension indefinitely. Following the reform, the livelihood of surviving spouses is guaranteed through other social security schemes, similar to individuals who are not eligible for the surviving spouse's pension. It is consequently anticipated that the demand for other social security benefits will increase. For spouses who outlive the 10-year fixed period of the surviving spouse's pension, income-tested Kela benefits will be provided, i.e. the national and guarantee pensions as well as housing and income support.

In its report, the Ministry's working group also discussed the possibility of a joint annuity, but the proposal was not included in the reform. A joint annuity would have enabled a spouse to transfer part of his or her old-age pension to a surviving spouse's pension. This arrangement was considered one way of compensating for the reduced duration of the surviving spouse's pension while shifting the cost burden to those who actually make use of it, rather than the entire pension system bearing the costs. On the other hand, concerns were raised that this arrangement might be primarily used by those who stand to gain the most from it, while those with lower pensions might not have the opportunity to take advantage of it.

The concept of pension splitting was not included in the reform deliberations, although it had been previously raised. Splitting pension rights for the duration of the partnership or for periods of childcare aims to redistribute income within the family and potentially improve the financial situation of the spouse who earns less, for example, after a divorce. Pension splitting has also been recommended by some international evaluators of Finland's pension system.[40] This option was not pursued further in the preparations of the reform, as pension splitting was deemed an unsuitable addition to the Finnish pension system, given that both spouses' labour market participation is mostly equal. Moreover, pensions are also earned for periods of childcare. Concerns were also raised whether pension splitting might violate the constitutional protection of property.[41]

4.2. Surviving spouse's pension for common-law spouses

One key objective of the reform was to equalise the treatment of different types of families with children. Prior to the reform, children were in an unequal position depending on their parents' marital status, i.e. whether the child's parents were married or not. If the parents were married when one of them passed away, both the surviving spouse's pension and the orphan's pension were provided to the survivors. However, if the parents were not married, only the orphan's pension was provided.

---

[40] Barr N (2013), Mercer (2018), OECD (2018b).
[41] Hietaniemi M (2014b) Kehittämismallina puolisoiden työeläkeoikeuden jakaminen. In Hietaniemi M and Ritola S (Eds.) Näkökulmia perhe-eläkkeen kehittämistarpeisiin. Finnish Centre for Pensions, Reports 4/2014.

Eligibility to the surviving spouse's pension based on cohabitation only arises in case of a minor in the family. The child must have resided in the same household with the deceased and the surviving spouse. While the child's living situation may change, for example because he or she starts studying, the essential factor is whether both the deceased and the surviving spouse provided financial support for the child. For the purposes of this regulation, a child born after the parent's death is considered to have resided in the same household as the deceased.

The requirement of residing in the same household means that the spouses must have had the same address listed in the population register at the time of death and must have lived at that same address continuously for at least five years before the spouse's death. Previous periods of cohabitation that were subsequently interrupted do not meet the condition of joint household. Brief or temporary separations, for example due to a work assignment or temporary institutional care that lasted a few months, are not considered a break in continuity. If the common-law spouses lived abroad, the pension claimant must provide sufficient evidence of their cohabitation.

Another precondition is that the surviving common-law spouse and the deceased must have moved into the same household before the deceased turned 65. The age limit corresponds to that applicable to married spouses, preventing situations in which an individual over the age of 65 is discouraged from marrying someone simply to secure that spouse's future eligibility for the surviving spouse's pension. Marriage after the age of 65 does not, however, disqualify the surviving spouse from entitlement to the surviving spouse's pension if all other conditions are met. Moreover, it must be verified that neither the deceased nor the surviving spouse was married to someone else at the time of death. During their cohabitation, the deceased and the surviving spouse may have been married to someone else.

The surviving spouse's pension is only provided to common-law spouses who have children and ceases when the youngest child reaches the age of 18. In practice, given the usual age an individual becomes a widow or widower, the surviving spouse's pension primarily benefits married spouses.

The changes for common-law spouses took effect immediately in 2022. Within one year of the reform, only 44 surviving spouse's pensions were granted to common-law spouses. It is estimated that fewer than 200 such benefits are granted annually, with the number expected to decline further in the future. This trend is attributed to the decreasing mortality rate among people in the typical age range for having underage children.

4.3. Changes to the orphan's pension

The primary aim of the common-law spouse's pension is to improve the surviving children's financial situation. Changes have also been introduced to improve the orphan's pension. The age at which the orphan's pension ceases has been raised from 18 to 20 years, considering that most children are not yet self-sufficient at the age of 18. While parents' legal obligation to provide for their children ends when the child reaches the age of 18, current legislation requires parents to continue paying for their children's education under certain conditions beyond this age. Unlike in national pension legislation, there is no requirement for the child to be studying to continue receiving the orphan's pension after the age of 18. This requirement would prevent the most disadvantaged groups from benefitting from this change.

Since early 2022, the surviving spouse's share of the earnings-related pension can be transferred to the deceased's children in the form of an orphan's pension if there is no eligible spouse. In such cases, the children receive the full survivor's pension amount, ensuring the children's financial security in families without married or cohabiting parents. An imputed share of the survivor's pension is added to the orphan's pension under certain conditions: if there is no eligible recipient for the surviving spouse's pension; if the surviving spouse who was eligible for the survivor's pension also dies, or if the surviving spouse's pension ceases because he or she remarried before the age of 50. If the surviving spouse's pension ceases because the child has reached the age of 18, the child cannot receive an imputed share of the survivor's pension until the age of 20.

During the preparations of the reform, it was anticipated that the changes to the orphan's pension within the earnings-related pension scheme would not increase the total number of persons entitled to it, but would instead raise the number of recipients on an annual level because it would be paid for two additional years. In the long term, however, the number of orphan's pension recipients is expected to decrease due to the declining mortality rate among people of working age, resulting in fewer deaths of parents of minors.

The benefit amount increases when the surviving spouse's imputed pension is paid to the deceased's surviving children. Previously, around 40 per cent of orphans' pensions were paid in situations where there was no eligible recipient for the surviving spouse's pension. This was the case, for example, when parents lived together but were not married, when they were divorced, or if the deceased or the surviving parent was a single parent. Since the reform, the surviving spouse's pension can be provided in cases of cohabitation or, if there is no eligible recipient, the imputed share can be transferred to the deceased's children. The impact on the average amount of the orphan's pension in 2022 is presented in Figure 3.

Figure 3. Orphan's pension recipients and the average pension amount 1990–2022

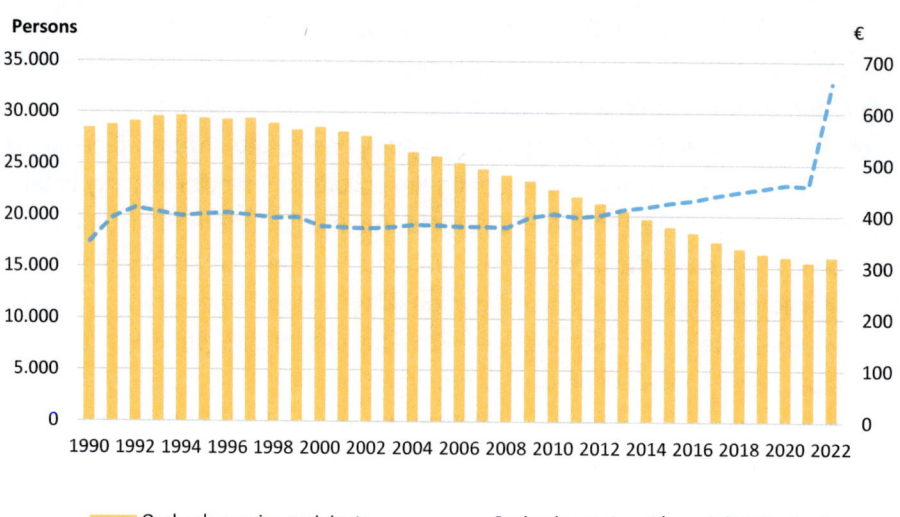

4.4. Financial impacts of the reform

One of the reform's goals was to secure the financial sustainability of the earnings-related pension scheme. In 2022, survivors' pensions accounted for 5.5 per cent of the expenditure of both the earnings-related pension scheme and the national pension system, down from 8.7 per cent in 2002. The expenditure primarily consists of the surviving spouse's pension, accounting for 93 per cent of total expenditure, while the orphan's pension accounts for only 7 per cent.[42] In 2022, a total of EUR 34.9 billion in pensions was paid in Finland, with earnings-related pensions constituting EUR 31.4 billion, or 90 per cent of total pension expenditure.

Figure 4. Earnings-related and national pension systems' expenditure in 2002–2022, by pension benefit

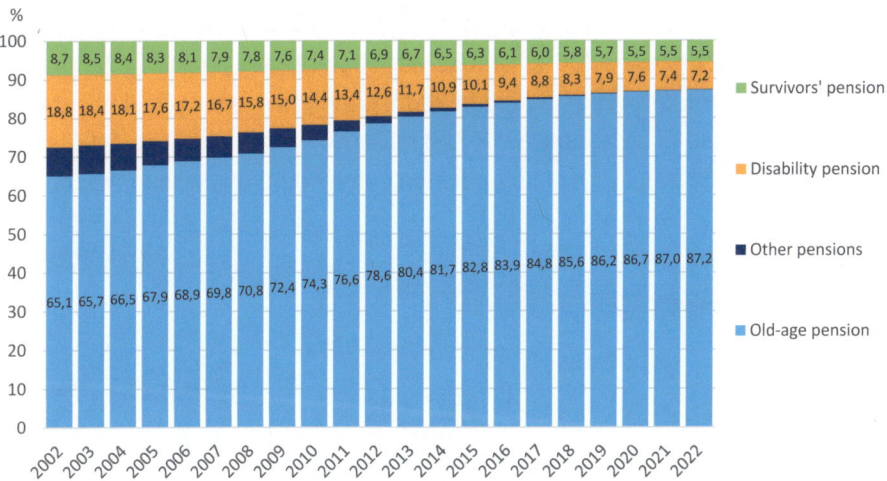

In the private and local government sectors, earnings-related pensions are mainly financed through contributions by both the employer and employee. National pension expenditure is financed fully by the State through tax revenues. In the partially funded system for private sector employees, funds are allocated

---

[42] Finnish Centre for Pensions (2024) Statistical database.

for future retirement and disability pensions, while survivors' pensions are financed through pay-as-you-go contributions.

Survivors' pension expenditure in relation to wages is projected to fall from currently 1.8 per cent to around 0.9 per cent between 2022 and 2070. Population ageing will contribute to this drop as the number of survivors' pensions decreases. The introduction of a fixed term for the surviving spouse's pension reduces the average duration of the benefit, even though it will only enter into force in the second half of this century. Moreover, in line with the projected mortality rates, people will live to increasingly older ages. This will reduce the duration of widowhood and, consequently, the annual number of surviving spouse's pensions. The amount of the average surviving spouse's pension relative to the average wage is expected to fall as well.[43]

The survivors' pension reform is anticipated to increase earnings-related pension expenditure by 2048. At its peak annual level, the impact is estimated to be approximately EUR 51 million in 2030 (at 2018 prices). Thereafter, the reform's impact is expected to reduce earnings-related pension expenditure. By the end of the projection period in 2085, earnings-related pension expenditure is estimated to be around EUR 680 million lower annually (at 2018 prices) compared to the earnings-related pension expenditure under the previous legislation.

---

[43] Tikanmäki H, Reipas K, Lappo S, Merilä V, Nopola T and Sankala M (2022) Statutory pensions in Finland – Long-term projections 2022. Finnish Centre for Pensions, Reports 3/2023. https://urn.fi/URN:ISBN:978-951-691-361-5.

Table 3. Impact of changes in survivors' pension legislation on earnings-related pension expenditure in 2020–2085

Earnings-related pension expenditure (in million €)	2020	2022	2025	2030	2045	2065	2085
Without reform	29308	30471	32172	34915	39764	55273	75660
With reform	29308	30478	32206	34966	39781	54975	74981
Effect	0	7	34	51	17	-299	-680

In the initial decades following the reform, changes in earnings-related pension expenditure will mainly arise from adjustments to the pension entitlements of cohabiting spouses and to orphan's pensions, which will increase the annual number of survivors' pension recipients, and the total amount of pensions paid. Over the longer term, however, the projected decrease in earnings-related pension expenditure will predominantly be attributed to the fixed term introduced for the surviving spouse's pension.

Furthermore, turning the surviving spouse's pension provided by the earnings-related pension scheme into a fixed-term pension will also have implications for public expenditure. Expenditure for national pensions, guarantee pensions, pensioners' housing allowance and social assistance would increase if these state-funded benefits remained unchanged. The estimated rise in expenditure will follow a linear trajectory, with projections indicating an increase by EUR 3 million in 2045, by EUR 18 million in 2055, and by EUR 72 million in 2065. Beyond 2075, expenditure is expected to stabilise at an annual level of around EUR 150 million.

5. Concluding remarks

Survivors' pensions are an integral part of the collectively funded social security system. The system must therefore be justifiable from the perspective of both the recipients and the sponsors of benefit schemes. The reform represents a step towards a survivors' pension scheme that is better aligned with contemporary society's family structures and the widespread participation of persons of all genders in working life.

The reform also improves the conditions for different types of families and their children. It reduces the amount of pensions for married spouses. Yet the reform can only be considered a partial solution. The long transition period means that the previous regulations will remain in place for many more decades, and that the reform's impacts will only take effect in the distant future. The fixed-term period of ten years implies a relatively long adjustment period. In addition, the entitlement of cohabiting spouses to the surviving spouse's pension is only limited to parents of minors and does not provide cohabiting spouses with the same security in old age as married spouses.

Surviving spouse's pensions predominantly benefit women, which means that the reform and its changes has implications primarily for women. The surviving spouse's pension currently still provides essential income support to elderly women. Because of the changes in working life, people born in 1975 and later who become widowed will likely have more opportunities than earlier generations to secure their income during retirement through their own earnings-related pension.

Bibliography

Act 26/2011. Act on the Dissolution of the Household of Cohabiting Partners. Unofficial translation, Ministry of Justice, Finland.

Agreement (2019) Sopimus vuoden 2017 eläkeuudistuksen jatkoneuvotteluihin liittyvistä asioista. 11 June 2019, Helsinki.

Barr N (2013) The pension system in Finland: Adequacy, sustainability and system design. Evaluation of the Finnish pension system / part I. Finnish Centre for Pensions.

Faurie M and Kalliomaa-Puha L (2010) Jääkaappi, osoite vai sukuside? Perheen määritelmät sosiaalilainsäädännössä. In Hämäläinen U and Kangas O (Eds.) Perhepiirissä. Kelan tutkimusosasto, Helsinki.

Finnish Centre for Pensions (2024) Statistical database. https://tilastot.etk.fi/pxweb/en/ETK/?rxid=837f44f0-5197-48ab-973e-f9e7649e6fb6

Finnish Centre for Pensions (2023a) Statistical yearbook of pensioners in Finland 2022. Statistics from the Finnish Centre for Pensions 11/2023. Helsinki 2023. https://urn.fi/URN:NBN:fi-fe20231023141051

Finnish Centre for Pensions (2023b) Pension Indicators 2023. Finnish Centre for Pensions, Reports 6/2023. https://urn.fi/URN:NBN:fi-fe20231030141868

Hannikainen M and Vauhkonen J (2012) The History of Finnish Earnings-related Pension in the Private Sector. Summary of Ansioiden mukaan. Yksityisalojen työeläkkeiden historia.

HE 66/2021 vp, Hallituksen esitys eduskunnalle laeiksi työeläkelakien ja kansaneläkelain muuttamisesta sekä niihin liittyviksi laeiksi. https://www.eduskunta.fi/FI/vaski/HallituksenEsitys/Sivut/HE_66+2021.aspx

HE 173/89 (1989) Hallituksen esitys Eduskunnalle perhe-eläkejärjestelmän kokonaisuudistusta koskeviksi laeiksi.

Hietaniemi M (2014a) Perhe-eläkkeeseen vaikuttavat muutossuuntaukset. In Hietaniemi M and Ritola S (Eds.) Näkökulmia perhe-eläkkeen kehittämistarpeisiin. Finnish Centre for Pensions, Reports 4/2014.

Hietaniemi M (2014b) Kehittämismallina puolisoiden työeläkeoikeuden jakaminen. In Hietaniemi M and Ritola S (Eds.) Näkökulmia perhe-eläkkeen kehittämistarpeisiin. Finnish Centre for Pensions, Reports 4/2014.

Kansaneläkelaki 11.5.2007/568. [National Pensions Act] https://www.finlex.fi/fi/laki/ajantasa/2007/20070568#O3

Kontio K (2007) History of pension provision. In: Hietaniemi M and Ritola S (Eds.) The Finnish Pension System. Finnish Centre for Pensions, Handbooks 2007:6.

Kontula O (2016) Lemmen paula. Seksuaalinen hyvinvointi parisuhdeonnen avaimena. Perhebarometri 2016. Katsauksia/Väestöliitto, Väestöntutkimuslaitos. E50/2016

Kiander, J. (2014) Tarvitaanko enää perhe-eläkkeitä? Periaatteellista pohdintaa. In Hietaniemi M. and Ritola S. (Eds.) Näkökulmia perheeläkkeen kehittämistarpeisiin. Finnish Centre for Pensions, Reports 4/2014.

Kuivalainen S, Nivalainen S, Järnefelt N and Kuitto K (2018) Length of working life and pension income: empirical evidence on gender and socioeconomic differences from Finland. Cambridge University Press.

Lilja R (2014) Suomalainen perhe-eläkejärjestelmä tulee uudistaa. Talous & yhteiskunta 3/2014.

Martikainen P, Murphy M, Moustgaard H and Mikkonen J (2016) Changes in the household structure of the Finnish elderly by age, sex and educational attainment in 1987–2035. Kela working papers 88.

Mercer (2018) Melbourne Mercer Global Pension Index 2018. https://info.mercer.com/rs/521-DEV-513/images/Mercer%20-%20MMGPI%20Report%202018.pdf

Määttänen N (2014) The welfare effects of the Finnish survivors' pension scheme. Nordic Journal of Political Economy. Volume 39, 2014.

OECD (2018) OECD Economic Surveys: Finland 2018, OECD Publishing, Paris.

OECD (2018b) "Are survivor pensions still needed?", in OECD Pensions Outlook 2018, OECD Publishing, Paris.

Pietiläinen M and Toivola J (2023) Valtaosa lapsista kasvaa edelleen avioPariperheessä – avopareja aiempaa enemmän, uusperheitä vähemmän. Tieto&Trendit 11 January 2023. https://www.stat.fi/tietotrendit/artikkelit/2023/valtaosa-lapsista-kasvaa-edelleen-aviopariperheessa-avopareja-enemman-uusperheita-vahemman-kuin-ennen/

Rantala J and Riihelä M (2016) Eläkeläisnaisten ja -miesten toimeentuloerot vuosina 1995–2013. Finnish Centre for Pensions, Reports 1/2016.

Ritola S and Tuominen S (2024) Total pension in Finland 2024 – How are earnings-related pensions, national pensions and taxation determined? Finnish Centre for Pensions, Reports 3/2024.

Ritola S and Väänänen N (Eds.) (2023) Understanding Finnish Pensions, SKS Kirjat, Helsinki. https://urn.fi/URN:NBN:fi-fe202401051525

Sieppi A and Pehkonen J (2019) Parenthood and gender inequality: Population-based evidence on the child penalty in Finland. Economics Letters 182 (2019) 5–9, Elsevier B.V.

Statistics Finland (2024a) Labour force survey. Helsinki: [Referenced: 6 February 2024]. Access method: https://stat.fi/en/statistics/tyti

Statistics Finland (2024b) Index of wage and salary earnings. [Referenced: 9 February 2024]. Access method: https://stat.fi/en/statistics/ati

Statistics Finland (2023) Families. Reference period: 2022. Helsinki. [Referenced: 5 February 2024]. Access method: https://www.stat.fi/en/publication/cl8jxlulw9u9a0cvz1lafhjk0

Statistics Finland (2023b) Changes in marital status [Referenced: 5 February 2024]. Access method: https://www.stat.fi/en/statistics/ssaaty

Statistics Finland (2023c) Educational structure of population. Reference period: 2022. [Referenced: 6 February 2024]. https://stat.fi/en/publication/cl8mz3a272d130cvzwa7nz195

STM (2017) Perhe-eläkeselvitys. Työeläkejärjestelmän perhe-eläketurvan kehittämisvaihtoehtoja. Sosiaali- ja terveysministeriön raportteja ja muistioita 2017:19.

Takala M, Salonen J and Lampi J (2015) Survivors' pensions in Finland. Finnish Centre for Pensions, Working papers 02/2015. https://www.etk.fi/en/julkaisu/survivors-pensions-in-finland-3

Tikanmäki H, Reipas K, Lappo S, Merilä V, Nopola T and Sankala M (2022) Statutory pensions in Finland – Long-term projections 2022. Finnish Centre for Pensions, Reports 3/2023. https://urn.fi/URN:ISBN:978-951-691-361-5

Työntekijän eläkelaki 19.5.2006/395. Finlex. [Employees Pensions Act] https://www.finlex.fi/fi/laki/ajantasa/2006/20060395

10 Survivors' Benefits and the New Concept of Family: Challenges for the Spanish Social Security System

María Salas Porras

1. Introduction

The concept of family deliberately remains loosely defined in the Spanish legal system, which allows for adaptations to new social realities. Examples of modern family structures include single parenthood, same-sex relationships, registered partnerships and divorce. While such structures have become more common in civil society, they must also be reflected in social protection policies.

In this context, collective studies such as this one on survivors' benefits present an opportunity to compare different approaches to these new concepts. This paper is structured around three sections to present the Spanish perspective. The first section provides a general introduction to contextualise Spain's approach to the death grant and survivors' benefits. Current survivor benefit schemes in the context of modern family structures are explored in the second section, while the final section offers concluding remarks.

2. Survivors' benefits in Spain: an overview

The Spanish pension system combines elements of both the Bismarckian and Beveridge models,[1] with the objectives of the two models reflected in Spain's survivors' benefits.

---

[1] Monereo Pérez J-L (2015) William Henry Beveridge (1879-1963): La construcción de los modernos sistemas de seguridad social, *Revista de Derecho de la Seguridad Social*, n. 4, 286.

As is the case in many other Member States, the death grant and survivors' benefits in Spain aim to mitigate the financial hardship surviving family members, who are financially dependent on the breadwinner, face in the event of his or her death. While it is generally true that survivors may experience financial insecurity following the breadwinner's death, further clarification is necessary, as some of the specific benefits extend beyond the aforementioned scope of providing support to survivors. Accordingly, one of the benefits aims to help survivors cover the deceased's funeral costs, while others such as the widowhood and orphan's benefit are intended to supplement or compensate for the beneficiaries' loss of income caused by the breadwinner's death[2] instead of adequately addressing survivors' genuine needs.

Therefore, although the causative event is the breadwinner's death, Spain's legislation only stipulates three specific situations that give rise to the right to protection in the form of survivors' benefits.

The first situation arises when the breadwinner's death results directly from a work-related incident, such as a workplace accident or an occupational disease. However, other specific situations have been included, for example if the deceased suffered from a recognised absolute permanent disability or was considered severely disabled. In those cases, if the disability was caused by a work-related incident, the death is *iuris et de iure* presumed to have resulted directly from the individual's occupation (Art. 217.2 LGSS[3]).

The second situation relates to disappearances following an accident (work- or non-work-related), leading to the presumption of death. In this case, the right to social security protection is established when the individual has not been heard from within 90 days from the accident.

However, if the disappearance is not caused by an accident, the declaration of death is subject to the following conditions. On one hand, 10 years must have elapsed since he or she was last heard from, i.e. since his or her disappearance. On the other hand, a declaration of death can be issued if 5 years have lapsed from the last time he or she was heard from, or failing that, from

---

[2] Spanish Constitutional Court, Sentence No. 184/1990, 15 November (ECLI:ES:TC:1990:184).

[3] These acronyms correspond to Royal Legislative Decree 8/2015, 30 October, which approves the consolidated text of the General Law of Social Security.

his or her disappearance, if at the expiration of said period, the missing person has reached 75 years of age. Finally, a declaration of death can be issued after only one year if the individual has not been heard from within that year from the date of his or her disappearance, which is the result of an imminent risk of death due to violence.

Moreover, children are entitled to survivors' benefits if the death of their mother was the result of gender violence (Art. 216.3 LGSS).

On the other hand, entitlement to survivors' benefits arise if the deceased was employed or had been contributing to a social security scheme. This requirement does not apply if the breadwinner's death resulted from gender violence (Art. 216.3 LGSS). In other cases, it is crucial to determine when this contribution period was fulfilled, and to distinguish between the contingencies that led to the breadwinner's death (Arts. 217 and 219 LGSS).

First, if the breadwinner's death resulted from a common illness, he or she must have been affiliated with, i.e. registered in a social security scheme or be in a so-called "assimilated situation". Such situations include one of the following categories: forced leave, total and subsidised involuntary unemployment, involuntary unemployment after exhaustion of all unemployment benefits, job seekers, recipients of social security assistance benefits, periods of inactivity of seasonal workers, prisoners in penitentiary institutions, non-contributory disability pensioners, workers on strike or lockout, and recipients of a minimum income. Individuals in this group must have contributed at least 500 days to the social security scheme over the five years immediately preceding the date of the causative event.

When the death results from an occupational disease or accident (work-related or non-work-related) and the deceased was affiliated with a social security scheme or in an assimilated situation, no prior contribution period is required.

If the breadwinner, on the date of his or her death, was neither affiliated with a social security scheme nor in an assimilated situation, a minimum contribution period of 15 years is required (Art. 219 LGSS).

Any individual convicted in a final judgment of intentional homicide in any of its forms against the deceased breadwinner is excluded from eligibility for survivors' benefits (Art. 231.1 LGSS).

After outlining the main criteria defining survivors' benefits, the next section provides a general overview of the specific measures included in this benefit but also focuses on the main legal problems that have arisen from the emergence of new types of relationships.

3. A general overview of Spanish survivors' benefits

The Spanish framework for survivors' benefits consists of five key measures. As will be discussed, each of these benefits presents challenges in application, as evidenced by case law and leading studies on the subject.[4]

3.1. Death grant ("auxilio por defunción")

The death grant is an immediate payment of EUR 46.50 to cover funeral expenses. The beneficiary is the person who has incurred these expenses, presumed to be, unless proven otherwise, in the following order: the widowed spouse, the surviving partner of the unmarried couple, the deceased's children or other relatives who had lived in the same household with the deceased.

The right to claim this benefit expires five years from the day after the date of the breadwinner's death.

Currently, the minimum cost of a funeral in Spain is between EUR 3,000 and EUR 6,000[5] which highlights the benefit's complete inadequacy. Alternative measures could be adopted to ensure that this allowance provides genuine support to individuals with particularly low incomes. For example, funeral expenses could be capped or zero-interest loans offered to cover these costs. Such measures would also align with the provision in Art. 39 of the Spanish Constitution, which guarantees social protection for families and individuals as part of the country's economic and social principles.

---

[4] Taléns Visconti E E (2022) Las prestaciones por muerte y supervivencia y su compatibilidad con el trabajo y otra serie de pensiones. *Revista Internacional y Comparada de Relaciones Laborales y Derecho del Empleo*, vol. 10, No. 4, 60-82.

[5] According to the Spanish Consumers and Users Office, this is the average cost of a funeral in 2023 https://www.ocu.org/dinero/seguros/informe/servicios-funerarios-morir-sale-caro, last visited 06/02/2024.

3.2. The widowhood benefit: lifetime or temporary ("pensión vitalicia o temporal de viudedad")

In the introductory paragraph, we highlighted that according to the Spanish Constitutional Court, the primary aim of survivors' benefits in cases of widowhood is to compensate for the financial loss caused by the reduction in income following the spouse's death. The benefit not only intends to address the survivor's financial needs resulting from the breadwinner's death. This may explain the specific requirements and conditions attached to eligibility for this benefit and set it apart from a traditional benefit.

3.2.1. Existence and legal nature of the relational bond

To be eligible for the widowhood benefit, a recognised relational bond to the deceased must have existed, regardless of gender (Arts. 219 to 223 LGSS).[6] However, important distinctions apply depending on the nature of this bond.

As a rule, entitlement to a widowhood benefit presupposes the existence of a previous marriage as defined in the Civil Code. However, specific assumptions must be taken into consideration.

On one hand, if the partner's death resulted from a common illness that existed before the marriage, the surviving spouse must meet one of the following requirements: he or she must either have common children with the deceased or the marriage must have lasted for at least one year prior to the spouse's death. If neither of these requirements is met, the surviving partner will only be entitled to a temporary widowhood benefit (Art. 222 LGSS) equivalent to the amount of widowhood benefit they would have otherwise been entitled to, but is limited to two years. We will discuss the calculation of these amounts later.

On the other hand, in the case of *de facto* couples, access to the widowhood benefit presents challenges related to the union's legal security. To resolve these challenges, Art. 221 LGSS restricts the concept of *de facto* couples to unions that meet a series of requirements. First, neither partner in the couple should be legally prohibited from getting married or may not be part of another

---

[6] Law 13/2005, 1 July, which amends the Civil Code regarding the right to marry, clarifies that same-sex couples are only entitled to the survivors' pension if the death occurred after the law came into effect. Consequently, this law does not apply retroactively.

de facto couple. And secondly, they must demonstrate that they were in a stable cohabiting relationship for an uninterrupted period of at least five years at the time of the partner's death, supported by a registration certificate. If the couple has common children, it suffices to prove the existence of having been part of a de facto couple by providing certification from the relevant registries in the Autonomous Communities or the City Council of the place of residence.

3.2.2. Breakdown of the relational bond and its consequences

One of the most problematic aspects[7] of the widowhood benefit is the breakdown of the marital bond and the existence of a new partner.

Since divorce is legally recognised in Spain, the widowhood benefit has been extended to cases of separation, divorce and annulment of the marriage, provided that the individual has not remarried or is part of a de facto couple. Extramarital cohabitation does not entitle an individual to the widowhood benefit. In cases where a separated couple subsequently reconcile without legally formalising it, the period of this renewed cohabitation does not count towards increasing the amount of the benefit. Furthermore, the separated or divorced spouse must be eligible for a so-called compensatory pension in line with Art. 97 of the Civil Code. The loss of income following the ex-partner's death is consequently offset by the widowhood benefit (Art. 220 LGSS). In any case, women who, while not eligible for a compensatory pension, can prove that they were victims of gender-based violence at the time of their legal separation or divorce are also entitled to survivors' benefits (Art. 220.1 LGSS).

In case of multiple beneficiaries after divorce, each former spouse is entitled to a share of the deceased's pension, allocated in proportion to the time each beneficiary cohabited with the deceased. A minimum of 40 per cent is guaranteed for the surviving spouse. However, if the ex-spouse passes away, his or her current spouse at the time of death is entitled to receive the full benefit. This measure, inaccurately referred to as "accretion",[8] restores the benefit to its original scope, given that there is no new causative event and the pension

---

[7] Sempere Navarro A V (2021) Notas de jurisprudencia sobre pensión de viudedad. *Revista Española de Derecho del Trabajo (REDT)*, 247/2021, 13-35.
[8] Sentence of the Spanish Supreme Court No. 613/2021, 09 June. ECLI:ES:TS:2021:2313.

is not recalculated. These same requirements and provisions apply to de facto couples.

Exceptions are made in case of multiple beneficiaries due to polygamy. In such cases, the case law of the Spanish Supreme Court[9] stipulates that the benefit is to be distributed in equal shares between the two widows. Although polygamy is contrary to Spanish law, if an international agreement has been concluded with a country where it is legal, Spain must comply with its provisions, including the allocation of survivors' benefits.

3.2.3. Content of protective measures

The amount of widowhood benefit is determined by applying a percentage to the regulatory base as outlined below.

a) The regulatory base

The regulatory base for the widowhood benefit varies depending on whether the deceased was actively employed or not. If she or he was actively employed or was in an "assimilated" or "affiliated" situation, a further distinction must be made according to whether the cause of death was due to a work-related incident or not.

In case of the death of an actively employed worker due to a non-work-related incident or a common contingency, the regulatory base is calculated by dividing the sum of the individual's contribution base over an uninterrupted period of 24 months by 28, chosen by the beneficiaries. This period must fall within the 15 years immediately preceding the causative event.

However, in the event of an actively employed person's death due to a work-related incident or of a person who is in an assimilated or affiliated situation, the regulatory base is calculated based on his or her annual salary, including overtime.

Finally, if the deceased was a recipient of a retirement or permanent disability pension, that same regulatory base will be used to determine the amount of the widowhood benefit. In these cases, the amount of the widowhood benefit includes any increases or adjustments that have been introduced since the

---

[9] Sentence of the Spanish Supreme Court No. 4150/2019, 17 December. ECLI:ES:TS: 2019:4150.

date of the causative event leading to the deceased's retirement or disability pension.

b) The applicable percentage

The standard percentage applied to the regulatory base to determine the amount of the widowhood benefit is generally 52 per cent. However, this rate may increase to 60 per cent or even 70 per cent if any or all of the following requirements are met.

First, the rate increases to 60 per cent when one or more of the following conditions apply: the individual must have reached the age of 65 years; is not entitled to another Spanish or foreign public pension; does not receive income from employment or self-employment and does not earn income from capital or economic activities exceeding the annual income limit established in the national budget. When any of these requirements are no longer met, the higher rate is suspended and the standard rate of 52 per cent is restored.

The rate of 70 per cent applies if the widowhood benefit constitutes the surviving pensioner's primary or exclusive source of income. This occurs when the annual amount of the pension represents at least 50 per cent of the pensioner's total annual income. Any applicable minimum supplement is also included in this calculation.

Secondly, the 70 per cent rate applies if the surviving pensioner's total income does not exceed a certain threshold. Specifically, the pensioner's annual income across all sources may not exceed the limit set each year to qualify for the minimum supplement, added to the annual amount of the widowhood benefit.

Finally, the surviving pensioner's family responsibilities must be taken into consideration, i.e. whether he or she lives in the same household with children under 26 years of age or older if they have a disability or if he or she is a foster parent to minors. In these cases, the total family income divided among all members of the family household, including the pensioner, may not exceed 75 per cent of the national minimum wage.

In practical terms, these percentages mean that for the year 2023, the widowhood benefit in Spain varied between EUR 590 per month when its amount is set at 52 per cent of the regulatory base; EUR 730 when the rate is increased to 60 per cent, and around EUR 900 when the maximum rate applies. The maximum amount of all benefits combined is EUR 3,000 per month,[10] which falls significantly short of the annual national minimum wage, which amounts to EUR 15,120,[11] and even further below the average national annual income of EUR 30,320.[12]

We compare this information with the requirements outlined in Art. 50 CE and Art. 4 of the Additional Protocol to the European Social Charter. Accordingly, public authorities must ensure "adequate and up-to-date pensions" which, however, as demonstrated in the Spanish case, often fall short in addressing survivors' needs, and merely satisfy the legal obligation of providing the minimum benefit and non-contributory pension amounts, without independently considering their impact on society. These low rates are justified by two compelling reasons. On one hand, as previously mentioned, the widowhood benefit is not intended to address the survivor's financial needs but to compensate for the eventual loss of income caused by the partner's death. And, on the other hand, the low rates aim to incentivise survivors to enter the labour market or to continue working. In a country like Spain, unemployment is high at currently 11.7 per cent,[13] and is even higher among women at nearly 16 per cent. Achieving lower unemployment rates likely requires more targeted measures than providing minimum widowhood benefits.

3.2.4. Evolution of social protection

a) Commencement of social protection

The right to claim a widowhood benefit – as is the case for other benefits related to death and survival, with the exception of the death grant – is imprescriptible.

---

[10] Information available at https://www.seg-social.es/wps/portal/wss/internet/Pensionistas/Revalorizacion/30431, last accessed in February 2024.
[11] Information available at https://www.sepe.es/HomeSepe/que-es-el-sepe/comunicacion-institucional/noticias/detalle-noticia.html?folder=/2023/Febrero/&detail=El-salario-minimo-interprofesional-publicado-para-2023-se-establece-en-1080-euros, last accessed in February 2024.
[12] Information available at https://datosmacro.expansion.com/pib/espana, last accessed in February 2024.
[13] Information available at https://datosmacro.expansion.com/paro/espana, last accessed in February 2024.

However, in case of delays in applying for the benefit, it will only apply retroactively up to three months before the date on which the application was submitted (Art. 230 LGSS). In the event of the individual's disappearance due to an accident, compensation of the benefit will apply retroactively to the date of the accident in case of delayed application (Art. 217.3 LGSS).

As with the death grant and other survivors' benefits, the recognition and management of entitlement to the widowhood benefit fall under the jurisdiction of the National Social Security Institute if the death resulted from a common illness or non-work-related accident. If it was caused by a work-related accident or occupational illness, responsibility for the benefit lies either with the aforementioned Institute or the Mutual Collaborator with social security which has an agreement with the employer of the deceased for coverage of occupational risks.

The General Treasury of Social Security is responsible for payment of the benefit, though in case the death resulted from a work-related accident or occupational disease, responsibility for payment may shift to the Mutual Collaborator.

b) Duration and termination

The widowhood benefit, in principle, is granted for life. However, a series of circumstances may lead to its termination. Under Spanish law, the benefit ceases upon the beneficiary's death; if a final court judgment determines that the death of the breadwinner was caused by the beneficiary; and if the beneficiary remarries or registers as a de facto couple. However, even in these cases, certain exceptions are provided.

Thus, the surviving pensioner may continue to be eligible for the widowhood benefit if he or she is over 61 years old or younger but has a recognised absolute or severe permanent disability or a disability level equal to or greater than 65 per cent.

Secondly, he or she may continue to receive the widowhood benefit if it constitutes his or her primary or exclusive source of income. This condition is met when the annual amount of this benefit represents at least 75 per cent of his or her total annual income, including any applicable minimum supplement.

Finally, the beneficiary continues to be eligible for the widowhood benefit when the de facto or married couple has a combined annual income – including the widowhood benefit – that does not exceed twice the amount of the annual minimum wage in effect at the time of the former partner's death. In cases involving multiple widowhood benefits, the death of the new spouse entitles the beneficiary to an additional widowhood benefit which, however, is incompatible with any previously received widowhood benefit.

c) Compatibility regime

The widowhood benefit is compatible with any employment income the beneficiary earns, as well as with a retirement or permanent disability pension (Art. 223.1 LGSS). Moreover, the widowhood benefit is compatible with receipt another widowhood benefit from any social security scheme, provided that the contributions credited in each of the schemes overlapped for at least 15 years (Art. 223.1 LGSS). However, this compatibility is subject to an annual cap set by the State's general budget.

3.2.5. Temporary widowhood benefit

The surviving spouse or de facto partner may be entitled to a temporary widowhood benefit if he or she does not meet the requirements for eligibility for survivors' benefits. This applies in situations when they cannot demonstrate that their marriage lasted for at least one year, do not have common children or if the registration as a de facto couple occurred less than two years prior to the partner's death.

In these cases, the amount of the temporary benefit is equivalent to that of a permanent benefit. However, it is limited to two years (Art. 222 LGSS), and the same rules concerning the benefit's commencement, compatibility and termination apply (Art. 223.3 LGSS).

3.3. Orphan's benefit ("pensión de orfandad")

3.3.1. Requirements related to the deceased

Except for children whose mother has died as a result of gender-based violence and who are therefore exempt from the following requirements, entitlement to an orphan's benefit arises when the breadwinner dies. The breadwinner must have been in an affiliated or assimilated situation, must have held a contributory retirement pension or a permanent disability pension. An orphan is also eligible for a benefit even if the deceased was not affiliated or in a situation similar to affiliation at the time of his or her death, provided that the breadwinner had accrued a minimum contribution period of 15 years (Art. 224.1 LGSS).

3.3.2. Beneficiary eligibility requirements

a) Age

As a rule, for an orphan to qualify for protection, he or she must be under 21 years old at the time of the breadwinner's death (Art. 224.1. LGSS). However, this requirement is more flexible if the beneficiary is incapacitated for work due to an absolute permanent or severe disability, with eligibility determined on a case-by-case basis.

Additionally, Art. 224.3 LGSS states that the orphan may continue receiving the orphan's benefit until reaching the age of 25 if he or she is not engaged in paid work as an employee or is self-employed; or if he or she is employed, but his or her annual income is lower than the current amount of annual minimum wage. If the beneficiary is a student and turns 25 during the school year, the orphan's benefit will continue to be paid until the first day of the month following the start of the next academic year.

Finally, more flexible requirements have been introduced for orphans whose mother – whether biological, adoptive or foster – died as a result of gender-based violence, regardless whether the violence occurred within a marriage or a de facto couple. In such cases, provided that the children are left in circumstances comparable to 'absolute orphanhood' and that they do not meet the standard requirements for eligibility for an orphan's benefit, the law provides for a non-contributory pension payment. The age limit of beneficiaries has been extended to 25 years if they are not engaged in paid work or if their income from work does not exceed the annual minimum wage (SMI). The amount of the orphan's benefit is set at 70 per cent of the minimum contribution base among those in effect at the time of the causative event, provided that the total income of the family household – including the orphan(s) and divided by the number of members that compose the household – does not exceed 75 per cent of the annual SMI. The same rules apply when the orphan has been adopted, meaning that the orphan's benefit is not terminated as a result of the adoption itself, but that the quantitative rule of poverty must be observed. If this 75 per cent threshold is exceeded, the orphan's benefit is terminated, though it can be restored if the household income falls below that threshold again.

b) The nature of affiliation

Art. 224.1 LGSS explicitly states that the pension shall be distributed equally among all children of the deceased, regardless of the nature of their affiliation. Denying the pension on this basis would violate the principle of equality of children, as established in Art. 39.2 CE.

Therefore, the existence or absence of a marital bond between the deceased and the surviving parent should be of no relevance. However, exceptions apply to children that the surviving spouse brought into the new marriage, regardless of whether the other biological parent has passed away or not. In such situations, entitlement to the benefit arises if the marriage took place at least two years prior to the date of the partner's death; if financial dependence can be demonstrated; if the orphans are not eligible for any other social security benefits; and finally if there are no family members who have the obligation or possibility to support them in line with civil law. Therefore, it can be concluded that the requirements for these orphans are stricter, which complicates efforts to protect them from poverty and financial need.

3.3.3. Scope of protective measures

a) The regulatory base

The amount of the orphan's pension is calculated by applying a 20 per cent rate to the deceased's regulatory base, in line with the rules established for the widowhood benefit. This general rule, however, may be adjusted under two specific circumstances: in case of multiple beneficiaries and when an increase in the amount of orphan's benefit is allowed.

When there are multiple beneficiaries, the total amount of the death grant and of survivors' benefits cannot exceed 100 per cent of the regulatory base.

However, this limit may be exceeded in case several orphan benefits are combined with a widowhood benefit. This is possible when the rate that is applied to the regulatory base is greater than 52 per cent. Nonetheless, the combined total of the orphan's benefit may not exceed 48 per cent of the corresponding regulatory base (Art. 229.3 LGSS).

An increase in the orphan's benefit is permissible by adding the percentage of the widowhood benefit in cases of absolute orphanhood or similar situations, such as when the orphan has only one known parent or where there is evidence of a state of heightened need. In such cases, the orphan's benefit may be increased under the following terms and conditions:

First, if there is no eligible beneficiary for the widowhood benefit at the time of the breadwinner's death, the amount of the orphan's benefit will be increased by applying 52 per cent to the regulatory base.

Secondly, if there is an eligible beneficiary for the widowhood benefit at the time of the breadwinner's death, the orphan's benefit may be increased by applying the percentage of the widowhood benefit that has not been assigned to another beneficiary, to the regulatory base.

Third, if the surviving parent, who was the eligible beneficiary for the widowhood benefit, passes away, the orphan's benefit will be increased by adding the percentage that would have been applied to determine the amount of the terminated widowhood benefit.

Fourth, if multiple orphans are entitled to the benefit, the corresponding percentage increase will be divided equally among all of them.

Fifth and finally, when the orphan's benefit is increased by the widowhood benefit, the minimum supplement limit only applies to the share of the widowhood benefit generated by the increase in the orphan's benefit (Art. 59.2 LGSS).

To conclude this section, it is important to note that the minimum amount of the orphan's benefit for 2023 in Spain was set at EUR 240 per month per beneficiary, and up to EUR 830 in case of absolute orphanhood. The youth unemployment rate stands at 28 per cent,[14] amounting to around 3 million unemployed young people, 500,000 of whom are under the age of 25. Given that eligibility for an orphan's benefit typically ends when the child turns 21, this poses a significant challenge: rather than motivating young people to enter the workforce, the current socioeconomic environment makes it extremely difficult to prevent orphans from falling into the poverty trap.

3.3.4. Evolution of protective measures

a) Commencement of protection

Entitlement to an orphan's benefit takes effect from the date of the breadwinner's death, provided that the request for the benefit was submitted within three months from that date. If the request for the benefit was submitted after this deadline, it applies retroactively up to a maximum of three months from the request's date of submission.

However, in the event of the breadwinner's disappearance due to an accident or in the case of birth of a posthumous child, the financial benefits are applied retroactively to the date of the accident or the child's birth, respectively (Art. 217.3 LGSS).

The benefit is paid to the individual responsible for the beneficiaries if they are minors or if they are legally incapacitated adults, unless that individual has been convicted of intentional homicide of the deceased. If the beneficiaries are of legal age, the benefit is paid directly to them, unless they have been convicted of homicide of the deceased.

b) Duration and termination

The orphan's benefit terminates when the beneficiary reaches the established age limit, unless his or her capacity for work is reduced due to permanent, absolute or severe disability; if the orphan marries (unless he or she suffers from an absolute permanent or severe disability); if the orphan dies or if he or she is adopted. If the beneficiary's orphanhood is the result of gender-based violence, the benefit is maintained if the household's total income, divided by

---

[14] According to data from December 2023, this information is available at https://datosmacro.expansion.com/paro/espana?sc=LAB-25-, last accessed in February 2024.

all household members – including the adopted orphan – does not exceed 75 per cent of the currently applicable annual minimum wage (Arts. 224 and 228 LGSS). Finally, according to recent case law, absolute orphan's benefits may be granted even if the beneficiary's biological parent has not died,[15] provided that the minor has experienced parental neglect due to the surviving parent's failure to fulfil his or her obligations even prior to the death of the other biological parent.

c) Compatibility regime

The orphan's benefit is compatible with any income earned from employment, except if he or she marries or exceeds the established age limit. For orphans who have been declared incapacitated for work,[16] the orphan's benefit is not compatible with the widowhood benefit to which he or she may subsequently be entitled, i.e. the orphan must choose between the two benefits.

3.4. Benefits for family members: pension and allowance ("prestaciones en favor de familiares: pensión y subsidio")

3.4.1. Requirements related to the deceased

As already outlined, both actively employed workers and recipients of allowances for temporary disability, for childbirth and for the care of a minor, pregnancy or breastfeeding entitlements, as well as of contributory permanent or retirement disability pensions are eligible for survivors' benefits (Art. 217 LGSS). To qualify, the deceased must have been affiliated with a social security scheme or in a comparable situation and must have accrued a contribution period of 500 days within the five years preceding the date of death, unless the death resulted from a work accident or occupational disease, in which case this contribution requirement is waived.

---

[15] Sentence of the Spanish Supreme Court No. 3490/2022, 07 of September. ECLI: ES:TS:2022:3490.

[16] In this regard, see Ortíz González-Conde F M (2020) La pensión de orfandad de personas incapacitadas para el trabajo y su compatibilidad con la pensión de jubilación. *Revista Española de Derecho del Trabajo (REDT)*, 233/2020, 205-242, and Rodríguez Iniesta G (2023) Prestaciones por muerte y supervivencia modalizadas en caso de discapacidad. *Revista Crítica de Relaciones de Trabajo*, nº extra 1, 355-379.

Similarly, survivors' benefits may be granted if, at the time of death, the deceased was neither affiliated with a social security scheme nor in a comparable situation but had accrued a minimum contribution period of 15 years (Art. 226 LGSS).

3.4.2. Beneficiaries

These benefits serve as a "residual or subsidiary" form of protection provided to certain blood relatives of the deceased who can demonstrate economic dependence on him or her and meet the relevant conditions (Art. 226 LGSS).
Economic dependence is a requirement for access to benefits intended to address the genuine financial need of certain family members following the death of the breadwinner.

To qualify as a beneficiary, the individual(s) must have lived in the same household with the deceased and been financially dependent on him or her for at least two years prior to his or her death. Moreover, the beneficiary must lack the means of subsistence and have no other family members who have the possibility or obligation to provide maintenance as stipulated by civil law; the beneficiary must also meet the specified degree of relationship with the deceased.

In this regard, beneficiaries of this benefit must be blood relatives of the deceased, for instance grandchildren and siblings under 18 years of age if the deceased was not the beneficiary of a public pension (or older but who are legally incapacitated for work); biological parents; grandparents; siblings and children over 45 years of age if the deceased was the beneficiary of a public pension.

3.4.3. Dynamics of protection

These benefits may take the form of either a pension or an allowance, depending on the degree of blood relation and age of the beneficiary. The commencement and scope of the benefit follow the same principles as those applicable to widowhood benefit and the orphan's benefit.

The reasons for termination of the benefit vary depending on who the beneficiaries are. In the case of grandchildren and siblings, the termination criteria align with those applicable to the orphan's benefit. In the case of ascendants, the benefit terminates upon marriage or death.

The amount for both the pension and allowance is set at 20 per cent of the regulatory base established for the widowhood and the orphan benefit. The difference is that the allowance is only paid for 12 months plus two additional payments, while the pension is paid for as long as the orphan benefit is provided (grandchildren and siblings) or until the beneficiary marries or dies (ascendant).

This benefit is compatible with any other pension for family members across all social security schemes, provided that the contributions have overlapped for a minimum of 15 years.

a) Pension for family members

The beneficiaries include grandchildren and siblings under 18 years of age or those with reduced work capacity due to a degree of disability or severe disability. They must either be absolute orphans or must have been abandoned by their parents, may not be entitled to a public pension and have no means of subsistence. Mothers and grandmothers – whether widowed, single or married – who are over 60 years old or suffer from absolute disability, parents and grandparents who are over 60 years old or suffer from absolute disability, as well as children and siblings of beneficiaries of contributory retirement pensions or disability pensions qualify.

b) Allowance for family members

Beneficiaries of an allowance include children and siblings who, on the date of the causative event, are over 22 years old, and are either single, widowed, legally separated or divorced.

It is paid for 12 months and includes two extraordinary payments. It terminates upon reaching the maximum duration period or upon death.

3.5. Lump-sum or flat-rate compensation if a work-related incident caused the death ("indemnizaciones a tanto alzado")

In the event of death due to a work accident or occupational disease, a flat-rate compensation is granted to widows, widowers and orphans who meet the eligibility requirements for the respective benefits (Art. 227.1 LGSS).

It is worth distinguishing between these two situations.

On one hand, supplementary compensation is added to the widowhood and orphan's benefit. It is provided to the surviving spouse and to orphans who meet the conditions to qualify as beneficiaries of widowhood and orphan's benefit. The amount equals six monthly payments of the regulatory base of the widowhood benefit (for the spouse or unmarried partner), or one monthly payment (for orphans). The compensation for absolute orphans or those with only one known parent is increased by the amount that would have been allocated to the deceased's spouse or de facto partner. If there are multiple beneficiaries, this increase is distributed equally among all of them.

On the other hand, substitute compensation is provided for the deceased's parents if they were financially dependent on him or her, are not entitled to a family pension, and if no other relatives have a right to a survivor's pension or survivors' benefits. This compensation amounts to 9 or 12 monthly payments of the regulatory base of the widowhood benefit, depending on whether one or both ascendants are still alive.

4. Concluding remarks

Over extended periods, legislators have often remained passive in response to social changes, especially those related to family structure. The increasingly demanding social and relational realities have necessitated adaptations within Spain's social security system, with significant modifications in the case of the survivors' benefits.

This study allows us to draw the following conclusions.

First, regarding the widowhood benefit, it must be highlighted that its original purpose – rooted in the antipodes of current beliefs and values – has undergone a significant change, with repercussions for its regulatory framework. Today, its primary function is not to address beneficiaries' financial need but to offset the loss of income resulting from the death of the partner. Therefore, while it remains a legal requirement for the deceased to either have been employed, be a pensioner or to have been affiliated with a social security scheme, the widow or widower is not required to undergo means testing. Furthermore, the legal concept of adequacy of the benefit amount implies modest payments designed to encourage the beneficiary to pursue employment.

The Spanish legal system's openness towards different types of couples, such as divorced, separated, same-sex, de facto unions, and even polygamous relationships, at least in terms of eligibility for the widowhood benefit, means a progressive approach is taken to survivors' benefits. This is partly reflected in legislation and in case law.

Secondly, and sometimes in direct response to these new relational realities, the orphan's benefit has also undergone changes aimed at implementing a more flexible approach. This not only allows for extending the benefit to individuals in cases where the deceased is not the beneficiary's biological parent or where the individual was abandoned as a child despite one of his or her biological parents still being alive.

Thirdly, and finally, additional survivors' benefits are provided, including the death grant, benefits for family members and lump-sum compensation for work-related incidents. In the case of death grants, the amounts are completely insufficient in supporting survivors to cover the funeral costs, but some proposals for improvement have been made. The other two benefits aim to address situations of severe vulnerability, which may to some extent help prevent situations of extreme poverty.

Bibliography

Ortíz González-Conde F M (2020) La pensión de orfandad de personas incapacitadas para el trabajo y su compatibilidad con la pensión de jubilación. *Revista Española de Derecho del Trabajo (REDT)*, 233/2020, 205-242.

Rodríguez Iniesta G (2023) Prestaciones por muerte y supervivencia modalizadas en caso de discapacidad. *Revista Crítica de Relaciones de Trabajo*, n° extra 1, 355-379.

Sempere Navarro A V (2021) Notas de jurisprudencia sobre pensión de viudedad. *Revista Española de Derecho del Trabajo (REDT)*, 247/2021, 13-35.

Taléns Visconti E E (2022) Las prestaciones por muerte y supervivencia y su compatibilidad con el trabajo y otra serie de pensiones. *Revista Internacional y Comparada de Relaciones Laborales y Derecho del Empleo*, vol. 10, n° 4, 60-82.

List of contributors

Martina Axmin serves as the Swedish Public Representative for Social Security (allmänna ombudet). It is an independent office, appointed by the Government. It´s main task is to appeal decisions made by the Swedish Social Insurance Agency and the Swedish Pensions Agency to the administrative courts, where there is a lack of uniform application of the law or a need for further guidance. She is appointed for six years and is on the absence of leave from the Faculty of Law at Lund University.

Ulrich Becker has been Scientific Member of the Max Planck Society and Director at the Max Planck Institute for Social Law and Social Policy since 2002, as well as honorary professor at the Faculty of Law at Ludwig Maximilian University in Munich. He was a DAAD fellow at the European University Institute in Florence and an Emile Noël Fellow at Harvard Law School, and he held a Chair of Public Law at the University of Regensburg from 1996 to 2002. His research focuses on the development of, and challenges to the welfare state and social protection systems from a legal and comparative perspective.

Stamatia Devetzi is Professor of Social Security Law at the University of Applied Sciences in Fulda, Germany. She studied law in Athens, Rome and Osnabrück. After working as a legal expert with the German Pensions Insurance Institution (1998-2003), in 2003 she became professor in Fulda. From 2011-2016 she was delegated as professor for Public Law and European Social Security Law at Osnabrück University, Faculty of Law. She has been active in teaching and research in the fields of Social Security, European Law and Law Comparison for over 20 years. She is director of CINTEUS (Center for Intercultural and European Studies) in Fulda and a member of the advisory board of FNA (Research Institute of the German Pensions Insurance).

Eberhard Eichenhofer is a retired professor for civil law and social security law at the universities of Osnabrück (1989-1997) and Jena (1997-2016). His recent books include *Werner Maihofer, Vordenker des Sozialliberalismus* (Grimma, 2022); *Sozialrecht*, 2021(12. edition), translated in Mandarin 2019 and Korean 2021; *Sozialrecht der Europäischen Union*, 2022 (8 th edition); *The*

Law of the Activating Welfare State, 2015; *Soziale Menschenrechte im Völker-, Europa- und deutschen Recht* (Social human rights in international public, European and German Law), 2012.

Christoph Freudenberg serves as a senior economist at the research department of the German Federal Pension Insurance. His work focuses on pension and social policy issues. He has been working for the Technical Commission on Pensions of the International Social Security Association (ISSA) and as a consultant for various national and international organizations, such as the World Bank, European Comission and the IMF. He holds a PhD in Economics from the University of Freiburg.

Thomas Gächter holds the chair of constitutional law, administrative law, and social security law at the Faculty of Law of the University of Zurich (since 2006). From 2004 to 2006 he was associate professor at the University of Lucerne (social security law) and Research Professor of the Swiss National Fund. He became the dean of the faculty in 2020.

Guido Van Limberghen has been since 1992 a full time professor at the Vrije Universiteit Brussel where he teaches social security law. His main fields of research are old age and survivors' pension schemes on the one hand and fundamental social security rights (of the self-employed, migrant workers, refugees, asylum seekers, undocumented migrants and prisoners) on the other hand.

María Salas Porras is a Doctor in Law and senior lecturer at the Department of Labour Law and Social Security, University of Malaga, Spain, where she teaches at levels of Degree, Master and PhD. Her research activity has made her travel to Bulgaria, Brasil, Germany, Italy, Malta, Portugal, Romania and Switzerland. Her main lines of research are migration, public employment policies, social economy, European Labor Law and Comparative Labor Law, and Social Professional Provision. She is currently the director of the University of Malaga's Master of Law and Prosecution program and the Academic Secretary of the Department of Labor Law and Social Security.

Hans-Joachim Reinhard is a Doctor in Law. In 1984 he joined at the Max-Planck-Institute for Foreign and International Social Law in Munich. Since 2003 he was also Professor for Social Law and Private Law at the University of Applied Sciences, Fulda. He was appointed Administrative Director of the BA degree course on Social Law and since 2009 he was nominated as Administrative Co-Director of the MA degree course on Social Law and Social Economy at the University of Kassel. From 2016-2023 he was elected as Dean of the Department of Social and Cultural Sciences at the University of Applied Sciences Fulda. He has participated in various international projects in and outside Europe and gave lectures in Spain, France, Poland, Croatia, Hungary, Japan, China and Latin America. In 2011, he was invited by the Government of the Mexican State of Morelos for a research stay at the Autonomous University of Morelos at Cuernavaca. His scientific work comprises plenty of publications in various languages on social law, European law and family law with focus on the situation of women in case of divorce and bereavement.

Suvi Ritola works as a Special Adviser at the Finnish Centre for Pensions (ETK). She holds a Master of Economic Sciences and a Licentiate in Political Sciences. Her expertise is in pension determination and benefit development. She has participated in the preparation and impact assessment of the survivors' pensions reform in Finland.

Jenny Julén Votinius is a professor of private law at the Faculty of Law, Lund University. She has wide experience of interdisciplinary and international research collaboration and of labour law research in comparative, EU and international settings. Her research is characterized by an interdisciplinary approach, integrating perspectives from social science and political philosophy in the legal analysis of Swedish and EU labour law and collective bargaining. She has been a visiting researcher at University of California Berkeley, and Université Lumière Lyon 2, and she serves in the European Commission Network of Legal Experts in Gender Equality. Julén Votinius' main research areas are non-discrimination and the implication of labour law for vulnerable groups in the labour market, with a particular focus on work-family balance, young workers, digital work, and the ageing workforce.

Verena Zwinger works for the Austrian Pension Insurance Institution, at the business division law and science. In doing so, she reflects on legal issues in the broader sense of pensions and rehabilitation on a national and international level, including old-age, invalidity and survivor pensions. She participates in the Technical Commission on Pensions of the International Social Security Association for Austria. Verena has completed her doctorate in law at the chair of Prof. Franz Marhold at the University of Economics and Business Vienna.

AN INTERDISCIPLINARY SERIES
OF THE CENTRE FOR INTERCULTURAL AND EUROPEAN STUDIES

INTERDISZIPLINÄRE SCHRIFTENREIHE
DES CENTRUMS FÜR INTERKULTURELLE UND EUROPÄISCHE STUDIEN

CINTEUS • Fulda University of Applied Sciences • Hochschule Fulda
ISSN 1865-2255

1   Julia Neumeyer
    Malta and the European Union
    A small island state and its way into a powerful community
    ISBN 978-3-89821-814-6

2   Beste İşleyen
    The European Union in the Middle East Peace Process
    A Civilian Power?
    ISBN 978-3-89821-896-2

3   Pia Tamke
    Die Europäisierung des deutschen Apothekenrechts
    Europarechtliche Notwendigkeit und nationalrechtliche Vertretbarkeit einer Liberalisierung
    ISBN 978-3-89821-964-8

4   Stamatia Devetzi und Hans-Wolfgang Platzer (Hrsg.)
    Offene Methode der Koordinierung und Europäisches Sozialmodell
    Interdisziplinäre Perspektiven
    ISBN 978-3-89821-994-5

5   Andrea Rudolf
    Biokraftstoffpolitik und Ernährungssicherheit
    Die Auswirkungen der EU-Politik auf die Nahrungsmittelproduktion am Beispiel Brasilien
    ISBN 978-3-8382-0099-6

6   Gudrun Hentges / Justyna Staszczak
    Geduldet, nicht erwünscht
    Auswirkungen der Bleiberechtsregelung auf die Lebenssituation geduldeter Flüchtlinge in Deutschland
    ISBN 978-3-8382-0080-4

7   Barbara Lewandowska-Tomaszczyk / Hanna Pułaczewska (ed. / Hrsg.)
    Intercultural Europe
    Arenas of Difference, Communication and Mediation
    ISBN 978-3-8382-0198-6

8   Janina Henning
    In Dubio Pro Europa?
    An Analysis of the European External Action Structures after the Treaty of Lisbon
    ISBN 978-3-8382-0298-1

9   Claas Oehlmann
    Europa auf dem Weg zur Recycling-Gesellschaft?
    Die EU-Rohstoffinitiative im Kontext der Strategie Europa 2020
    ISBN 978-3-8382-0401-7

10 Volker Hinnenkamp / Hans-Wolfgang Platzer (ed. / Hrsg.)
    Interkulturalität und Europäische Integration
    ISBN 978-3-8382-0573-1

11 Vera Axyonova
    The European Union's Democratization Policy for Central Asia
    Failed in Success or Succeeded in Failure?
    ISBN 978-3-8382-0614-1

12 Lisa Moessing
    Lobbying Uncovered?
    Lobbying Registration in the European Union and the United States
    ISBN 978-3-8382-0616-5

13 Andreas Herberg-Rothe (ed.)
    Lessons from World War I for the Rise of Asia
    ISBN 978-3-8382-0791-9

14 *Agnieszka Satola*
Migration und irreguläre
Pflegearbeit in Deutschland
Eine biographische Studie
ISBN 978-3-8382-0692-9

15 *Vera Axyonova (ed.)*
European Engagement under
Review
Exporting Values, Rules, and Practices
to the Post-Soviet Space
ISBN 978-3-8382-0860-2

16 *Işıl Erduyan*
Multilingual Construction of
Identity
German-Turkish Adolescents at School
ISBN 978-3-8382-1201-2

17 *Hans-Wolfgang Platzer*
Bronislaw Huberman und das
Vaterland Europa
Ein Violinvirtuose als Vordenker der
europäischen Einigungsbewegung in
den 1920er und 1930er Jahren
ISBN 978-3-8382-1354-5

18 *Aileen Heid*
Erinnerungspolitik
Nordirlands langer Weg zum Frieden
ISBN 978-3-8382-1351-4

19 *Juliana Damm, Maren Mlynek*
Die AfD und Geflüchtete
Was rechte Ideologie gesellschaftlich
bewirkt
ISBN 978-3-8382-1448-1

20 *Julian Wessendorf*
Euroskeptizismus auf dem
Vormarsch
Positionen der politischen Rechten im
Europaparlament
ISBN 978-3-8382-1557-0

21 *Kirsten Nazarkiewicz,*
Norbert Schröer (Hrsg.)
Verständigung
in pluralen Welten
ISBN 978-3-8382-1345-3

22 *Stamatia Devetzi (Ed.)*
Practical issues of European
Social Security Law: A Dialogue
between Academia and
Practitioners
ISBN 978-3-8382-1706-2

23 *Jasmin Berger, Geronimo Groh,*
Simone Lettner (Hrsg.)
Sprache(n) und Grenze(n) –
Sprachgrenzen
Übersetzen, Dialekt und Literatur,
Literarische Mehrsprachigkeit
Frontières linguistiques –
langue(s) et frontière(s) :
L'art de la traduction, dialecte et
littérature, plurilinguisme littéraire
ISBN 978-3-8382-1918-9

24 *Stamatia Devetzi, Hans-Joachim*
Reinhard (Eds.)
Provision for Surviving
Dependants in Social Security
A New Architecture for the 21st
Century?
ISBN 978-3-8382-2036-9

ibidem.eu